DATE

OTHER BOOKS BY NORMAN E. ZINBERG

Psychiatry and Medical Practice in a General Hospital (ed.)
The Normal Psychology of the Aging Process
(edited with Irving Kaufman)

DRUGS
AND THE
PUBLIC

Norman E. Zinberg
AND
John A. Robertson

SIMON AND SCHUSTER
NEW YORK

The authors wish to thank the following for permission to reprint selections from their publications in this book. Any inadvertent omissions will be corrected in future printings on notification to Simon and Schuster.

Her Majesty's Stationery Office for extracts from *Reports by the Advisory Committee on Drug Dependence on the Powers of Arrest and Search in Relation to Drug Offenses and Cannabis* (Chairman of the Advisory Committee: Sir Edward Wayne, M.D., D.S.C.).

The *Houston Law Review* for extracts from Rotenberg & Sayer, "Marijuana in the Houston High Schools—A First Report," 6 *Houston Law Review* (1969).

Prentice-Hall, Inc., for an extract from "An Analysis of Marijuana Toxicity," by David E. Smith and Carter Mehl, which appeared in *The New Social Drug: Cultural, Medical, and Legal Perspectives on Marijuana,* Ed. David Smith, © 1970, Prentice-Hall, Inc.

Random House, Inc., for two stanzas from "Law Like Love," by W. H. Auden. Copyright 1940 and renewed 1968 by W. H. Auden. Reprinted from *Collected Shorter Poems 1927–1957,* by W. H. Auden.

Stanford University Press for an extract from *The Limits of the Criminal Sanction* by Herbert L. Packer, © 1968 by Herbert L. Packer.

John Wiley & Sons, Inc., for an extract from *Justice Without Trial* by Jerome Skolnik, © 1966 by Jerome Skolnik.

The World Publishing Company for two extracts from *Marijuana—the New Prohibition* by John Kaplan, copyright © 1970 by John Kaplan.

DEDICATION

The private foundation is a remarkable social institution which has flourished particularly in the United States and consistently supported work and workers interested in social change. Without the generous support of the Guggenheim Foundation, the Ford Foundation, the Walter F. Meyer Research Institute of Law, and the Field Foundation, this work could not have been done. Nevertheless this book is dedicated to the willingness of all the private organizations to take a chance on research and researchers who want to ask questions about the status quo, and not just those four foundations whose help is so appreciated.

ACKNOWLEDGMENTS

Writing a book on a subject as complex as drug use requires extraordinary cooperation from a vast number of persons. It is a subject that people like to expound upon but not talk about personally. Hence, the research for this book could not have been done without the kindness, compassion, and patience of almost 1,500 people.

All the contributors cannot be mentioned by name, but there are a few people whose particular devotion of time, energy, and intelligence should be noted, among them David Cavers and Maurice Rosenberg of the Walter F. Meyer Research Institute, Leslie Dunbar of the Field Foundation, and Mitchel Svirdoff of the Ford Foundation. Andrew Weil's assistance was invaluable, and the research chapter in particular rests heavily on his work. Beryl Geber of the Social Psychology Department of the London School of Economics provided valuable assistance in procuring data from British students, apprentices, doctors, and police. Abram Chayes, Baroness Wootton, Hilda Himmelweit, Morag Rennie, Peter Beedle, E. H. Spear, Edward Kass, Matthew Siefert, C. R. B. Joyce, R. S. P. Weiner, Carolyn Coon, Simon Albury, Michael Scofield, John Kaplan, Mary Frances Robertson, and Dorothy Zinberg are among those whose special commitments to our efforts in England and in the United States enabled us to begin, continue, and finally publish this analysis of the drug issue.

Jo Anne Austad and Miriam Winkeller, with remarkable skill, translated illegible scribbles into legible manuscript. But most particularly we want to acknowledge the assistance of Gemma Fenton, whose editorial skill enabled us to achieve whatever semblance of organization has been managed in this book.

CONTENTS

Law is the wisdom of the old,
The impotent grandfathers feebly scold;
The grandchildren put out a treble tongue,
Law is the senses of the young.

. . . .

And always the loud angry crowd,
Very angry and very loud,
Law is We,
And always the soft idiot softly Me.

—W. H. AUDEN

One Law for the Lion and Ox is Oppression.

—WILLIAM BLAKE

1

WHAT IS THE DRUG ISSUE?
AN OVERVIEW

Drug use is now commonplace in the United States and other Western countries and will undoubtedly increase. Numerous myths and fallacies have gathered around the subject, with the result that an issue which, contrary to the general impresson, is a comparatively small matter as far as public health is concerned has taken on a critical social importance.

The social importance of drugs does not lie in their capacity to injure and reduce the capabilities of drug users, though when misused drugs can inflict psychological and physical harm. These casualties are a small minority, and in most cases they could be treated if a less punitive legal policy were operating. Indeed, the worst effects of drugs, such as the crimes committed by addicts and their deaths from overdoses, are a direct result of the law. Certainly casualties occur often enough among drug users to warrant some form of control: Individuals are hurt by the drugs themselves and by the law, or they suffer from a damaged sense of usefulness. But the loss to society of such members may be of less importance than the loss of the quality of wholeness that comes from broad agreement on critical issues.

Most of the controversy arises because at present we have only two categories for all the ways of altering by chemical means inner and outer reality. The first category is socially approved: one can be dependent on a drug, suffer its physical and psychological ill effects or enjoy its aftermath, and escape all condemnation so long as the drug has been prescribed by a doctor. (There is a niche in this category for alcohol, caffeine, nicotine, and similar palliatives.) All other drug-taking falls into the second category—the pursuit of self-destruction, pleasure, insight, or relaxation by means of a drug that has not been prescribed, is not socially acceptable, and is usually illegal.

There is obviously some loose thinking here (and it is not merely on a semantic level) in defining exactly what a drug problem is and working out whether substances in common use like alcohol and nicotine should be classified with drugs. It arises out of our hazy ideas about individual and social goals, how to attain them, and who has the right to decide the means. In a socialistic society the goal is obvious: the individual exists to serve society, and personal satisfaction takes second place. But in a democratic society, especially one officially dedicated to life, liberty, and the pursuit of happiness, there is endless room for conflict between an individual's desires and society's right to control.

Drug users may be grouped into three categories. The first consists of dependency-prone persons who, because of psychological and personality problems, have become heavily immersed in drug use and drug subcultures. The heroin and barbiturate addict, the speed freak, and some chronic marijuana users are in this group. Their drug use is merely incidental; personal and social maladjustments, not drugs, have set them on a course of self-destruction. In a different age they might have chosen another avenue of destruction (alcohol, delinquency, violence), but the powerful drugs, so much in public consciousness, were a natural choice. The ghetto dweller, suffering the shock of cultural displacement and the hopelessness of a filthy slum, is in this category. So are the twenty-four youngsters who died in 1968 from inhaling the fumes of aerosol containers.[1] So are those street people of 1970, who will smoke, eat, or inject any substance for a kick. They present society with the tasks of preventive medicine, rehabilitation, and comprehensive medical care—tasks that society so far has been reluctant to perform.

The second group, although continually identified by the public with the first, differs markedly in number, motivation, and drug choice. A decade ago this group did not exist. The psychedelic and marijuana explosion of the past eight years, however, has thrust them into the center of the drug controversy. This group uses marijuana, and many of its members have tried LSD, amphetamines, and, to a lesser extent, heroin and cocaine. Though officially labeled drug abusers, they are strictly speaking drug experimenters. This group consists mostly of young people—who from time immemorial have indulged in some mild form of deviant activity to the horror of their outraged parents. In the present social setting, when drugs are readily available, the young are most likely to turn to marijuana or another drug.

Since the marijuana explosion of the mid-1960s, every young person growing up in America has had to make a conscious decision on whether or not to smoke "grass." He knows that the option to drop mescaline (currently somewhat more popular than LSD) or even to sniff "smack" (heroin) is open. At present our official policy, backed by all possible social pressure, insists that he reject this option. This policy fails entirely to take into account what the general public's black-and-white view of the situation suggests to him, and what he makes of our hostile and self-righteous rejection on his behalf of practices that seem to him reasonable, or at least worth investigating.

The third group of drug users consists of people who at first seem to blend with the drug-experimenting group. They are disturbed youngsters who express their difficulties in drug use and find the support they need in the drug subculture. They can be pushed into the first, dependency-prone group by exaggerated public reaction to their dabbling in drugs or may be helped back into ordinary life by rational support. This group is significant not because of its size—it is very small—but because it highlights the social factors that may push it over the boundary line.

Perhaps the greatest influence on each category of drug user is the public. We hope to make clear in this book that the public wields fearsome power; by condemning drug use so violently, it has made it a much more serious matter than it would otherwise have been. For instance, the first group, as a result of the public's definition of its dependency as criminal and immoral, is often led into more destructive activities. The second group may decide to try new drugs, may develop new attitudes and values, or may slide into more deviant activities simply because the public reacts with condemnation and horror at what the user sees as a natural choice. Again, the nondependent types of the third group may be pushed by their social definitions into crossing the line into harmful use.

Part of the difficulty besetting drugs is the tendency of the public, particularly as represented by the laws articulating its attitudes, to treat the three groups as if they were one: all drugs are held to be equally dangerous and all drug users equally at risk. To this public we address our efforts to disentangle and evaluate the issues of drug use which have been distorted and sensationalized.

We have chosen to stress the large group who have to make a decision about whether or not to try an illegal drug rather than the other groups who can be shown to be harmed by drug use. In terms of damage to health, the first is more important. Thousands of people, perhaps as many as 200,000, of whom a growing percentage are under 25, are hooked on heroin and lead a ghastly existence.[2] Some users of psychedelic drugs become psychotic; a few commit suicide. Anyone caught in the "ups" and "downs" cycle—taking amphetamines for stimulation and barbiturates for sedation, and alternating them for kicks—exhibits one of the most horrifying syndromes known to man. (These two drugs are often medically prescribed, which paradoxically puts them on the socially acceptable side of the dichotomy. Thus despite the severe damage they cause they receive less publicity than many other abused drugs whose withdrawal syndromes are less severe and whose use is less destructive.) Even marijuana, the mildest of the heavily used drugs, results in a miserably debilitated condition when it is used incessantly. All who risk destruction by drugs require far greater medical and social attention than they have yet received. Yet as long as society condemns and punishes them as immoral and criminal, it is unlikely that treatment and rehabilitation will be forthcoming.

The second group, vastly greater in number and yet presenting few of the health problems of the first group, is the one that has made the subject of drug use a social crisis. The real drug problem arises out of the almost hysterical public reaction to common news items like the following: in the past five years each class entering American colleges has contained a higher percentage of drug users than the one before.[3] Such youngsters, as we shall show, are not neurotic, antisocial, or destructive. When they are perceived and treated by a society alarmed at new patterns of drug use as criminals and a health problem of major proportions, a conflict of far-reaching implications unfolds. This conflict is at the heart of the drug controversy and makes drug use a critical social issue.

Drug use is a complex matter, and when faced with complex problems society frequently opts for a simple, if possible familiar, solution, rather than dealing with doubts and ambiguities. Recent reactions to the nonmedical use of psychoactive drugs illustrate this tendency. The label "drug user" or "drug sympathizer" evokes for most people an entire system of behavior and mores of which they disapprove. Thus they conveniently package a number of contradictory and confusing facts and include types of people and kinds of behavior that they would otherwise have to tackle individually and laboriously. So much ambiguity is disposed of in this neat package that it is no surprise to find these same members of the public reacting with powerful and irrational condemnation. Perhaps they package it in order to respond in a particular way.

The unquestioning alacrity with which people have continued to accept the old categories in the face of all that has happened in the past ten years is a dramatic example of the difficulty most people have in tolerating ambiguity—the discomfort of mixed feelings on an emotive subject. This tendency has led individuals, groups, and institutions to attempt facile blanket solutions to the problem of drug use and abuse, and these solutions may in fact have exacerbated the situation.

Some states have reacted to the drug "menace" by starting vast educational programs in which the young are taught the risks of cannabis, the terrors of LSD, and the destructiveness of heroin, in order to dissuade them from trying these drugs. But how well informed are those who are in the most influential educational positions? To take one example: A questionnaire survey* with a 73 percent response from the faculty of one of the most prominent law schools in the United States showed that while 80 percent believed possession of marijuana should be legalized, 86 percent called for more federally financed research into its use in order to determine if it was more dangerous than the now legal barbiturates and amphetamines. There were similar contradictions about methadone. One hundred percent of those responding felt that "methadone treatment for all addicts should be made available in all states," while the same respondents equally unanimously agreed that "methadone substitutes one addictive drug for another when used for heroin addiction."

Perhaps of greater significance is the number of questions left unanswered. Fewer than 27 percent were willing to comment on whether more than half the graduating law school class had tried pot, and the percentage dropped to 15 and 8 percent, respectively, when questioned as to whether users were more apt to be at the top or bottom of the class and whether marijuana use was more damaging than amphetamine use.

Why, in this atmosphere, do young people try drugs? We will try for a rough answer to that question in Chapter 3; here we will simply observe that they do, and "they" are not just that small group of the population who are ready for any socially disruptive enterprise, but a far larger group who are impatient with social barriers of all sorts. We cannot understand either the educators or the users in isolation; all the elements in the drug issue are constantly responding to each other.

* The law school faculty respondents answered the questionnaire only on the condition that they remain anonymous.

Why has drug use become a burning issue at this juncture? Some commentators[4] see it as a simple question of time lag. It is often years before a new behavioral pattern engenders a corresponding change in social attitudes, and even longer before these changes are reflected in our institutions. With marijuana use we have the classic evolutionary situation. A small group's ritualized use of a drug has gradually spread and become part of a larger social ethos, but has not yet become acceptable in the eyes of the general public. The public is acutely alarmed not only at the spread of an abhorrent practice, but also at the challenge to respected institutions such as the Bureau of Narcotics and Dangerous Drugs and the various state agencies for drug control, whose role in combating evil has hitherto gone unquestioned. The new state of affairs naturally creates social ferment.

According to another view,[5] the controversy over drug use originates in the anxiety generated by pervasive technological innovation. All technologies increase man's ability to alter, and thus control, his environment. Drugs, natural or synthetic, may be seen as a technology that alters the relation to the environment by controlling mood, feeling, ideation, and pain. Perhaps it is not surprising that, already overburdened with choices and responsibilities flowing from his technical knowledge, there is a strain of stubborn resistance in modern man to the extensive use of a chemical technology. And this resistance is further complicated by mixed feelings on the subject of drug use: we look to medically prescribed drugs to free us from pain and unhappiness.

A third reason why drugs are a burning social issue is that they are at the vortex of conflict among individuals, groups, and social institutions. Drugs and laws dealing with them serve as symbols that attract strong condemnation from different sides of the argument. The nonuser citizen feels that society is undergoing disruptive social change beyond his control. One element in the change is the nonmedical use of drugs, and here he sees a clear threat to his well-being that he can make some attempt to control. His condemnation of drug use is a proxy for other fears and dislikes. On the other hand, the drug user perceives in the drug laws a confirmation of the hypocrisy and corruption of government which he has observed in other areas. Thus for both sides drugs become the vehicle by which conflicts and dissatisfaction on many extraneous subjects are vented.

Finally, there is the ambiguity of the drugs themselves. On the one hand, the general public believes that drugs are destructive; on the other, drug users believe that they may be the source of great benefits. Like beauty, the qualities of drugs are usually in the eye of the beholder. The psychic changes that drugs produce vary widely, as does the interpretation of those changes, so that each side can adduce evidence for its point of view.

In our examination of the drug controversy and the public response to it, we intend no apologia for drug use, though we do deflate some of the traditional notions about the harmfulness of drugs and suggest some new ways of viewing their use. Our aim is to unravel the more emotional responses to nonmedical drug use, see why they have heated up the drug issue, and find a way to put drugs back into a social framework where their harm can be minimized and their benefits enjoyed.

A NEW DRUG POLICY

In any discussion of the drug laws, the question immediately arises whether enough information exists to formulate a more rational drug policy. The answer is both yes and no. We need to know more about basic pharmacological mechanisms, dose-response curves, and the long-term social consequences of drug use. It is astonishing, given the chronic public alarm, that so many fundamental questions remain unanswered. (Basic clinical data about marijuana, for instance, were not gathered until 1968.[6]) In many cases the legal and bureaucratic obstructions to research have suggested that "we don't want to know" is the prevailing attitude. Equally remarkable are the irrational responses and blockage of knowledge that have so muddied drug and similar issues. For example, why have the United States, the United Kingdom, and

Sweden, three nations traditionally committed to freedom, tolerated for the sake of drug control repressive law-enforcement practices that undermine the rule of law and provoke serious social conflict?

Yet in many respects our knowledge is more than adequate. Enough information has certainly been gathered to enable us to state that not all drug use is harmful. We also know that existing policies have not halted drug use and have instead imposed excessive social costs. The next step is to encourage objective discussion which will lead to a rational drug policy, and then to formulate a flexible policy with a built-in response to experiment and change.

Present policy is to prohibit drugs, the theory being that drug use is harmful to the individual and society, and the fewer available drugs the fewer users there will be. The law, it must be noted, represents a social standard—in this case, a standard according to which drug use is bad. When the social standard is accepted by most of the public, the law works: it deters at the cost of punishing as few as possible. Should a significant segment of the public decide that the standard no longer applies, then the symbolic nature of the law changes. Its traditional function as a deterrent yields; maintenance of the law becomes a symbol of control for the minority of its supporters. The supporters wish to punish those who oppose them, and usually demand that the punishing strictures be made more and more harsh, as though this will somehow restore the social standard to its former place.

For those who oppose the standard and its legal expression (which now supports the standard instead of the reverse), the law symbolizes a club designed to beat them into submission. Both sides lose sight of law as a device to help society organize, regulate, and promulgate standards acceptable to most (though never to all) of its members. It is society's job to reassess and formulate the standards to be translated into an acceptable law; the law is then restored to its traditional function. The symbolic use of a law for control and punishment leads to disrespect not only of those who serve it but, as in the case of Prohibition, of the law itself as a social institution. We discuss in Chapter 6 how drug laws function to enforce morality, and thus act not to deter harmful conduct but to symbolize conflicts that go far beyond the question of the harm drugs do to individuals or to society. The social costs of such a situation must guide us in the formulation of new policy. Hitherto, all the costs have been thought to flow from drug use; the social costs of a devalued law have seldom been considered.

A successful drug policy—one that minimizes harmful drug use without generating unpleasant side effects—will require a systems or a cost-benefit approach. Just as transportation systems must adapt to new technology, patterns of employment, urban blight, and air pollution, similarly a workable drug policy must be sensitive to the factors throughout the social system influencing its operation. A new drug policy must be flexible, responsive to change, quick to innovate, abreast of new fads, and willing to evaluate and monitor its results. We have at our disposal only the most meager resources and the crudest measurement techniques, and there is little attempt to evaluate existing programs. The results of imposing mandatory minimum penalties for drug offenders, and of the myriad other laws passed in the past twenty years, have never been collected and examined. New institutions, sheltered from political squalls, must be set up to collect and process information on drug policy, and old institutions, such as the law, adapted.

A FUNCTIONAL APPROACH

In our study of drug use we chose a functional approach. The central orientation of functionalism is to interpret data by establishing the consequences of an action or a situation for the larger structures with which it interacts.[7] We call an item of human experience functional if it defines a mode of response that is governed by a given social unit—whether an individual, a group, or a culture. For example, the general public's insistence that there is a drug progression—that the drug user inevitably desires more and more and stronger and stronger drugs—justifies their support of punitive laws concerning marijuana use. This item functions as a source of justification to the public for their fear of drugs, as a spur to the police, as a deterrent to doctors prescribing psychoactive medications, and as a threat to the young man contemplating drug use. Its multiple functions serve both the individual, who feels comfortable in his support of current drug laws, and society, as an aid in maintaining the status quo. There is a very real fear of social chaos if drug use becomes widespread.

Every item has both manifest and latent functions. A manifest function of the argument against drug use is to establish that it is a public health hazard that must be eradicated; a latent function is to exert control over the threateningly ebullient younger generation. A manifest function of the argument in favor of drug use is that since most of the authorities' pronouncements on marijuana are factually wrong, the authorities are completely discredited; a latent function is to support the young drug user's tendency to reject the values of the older generation.

Robert Merton[8] has warned that while all societies have achieved some degree of integration, none is so tightly integrated that every standardized activity or belief functions positively for the whole of society or for everyone in it. An antidrug law, for example, may very well be functional for some social units and dysfunctional for others: it may be a source of reassurance to the Rotary Clubs of America, but if it is an ineffective law difficult to enforce, it may serve as an irritant to policemen and thus undermine their self-confidence.

A functional approach assumes a certain skepticism; it requires one to look behind what is stated explicitly to discover what is less conscious. This skepticism has had a special purpose in the context of drug use and has determined the precise brand of functionalism we have employed. The heavy emotional burden carried by drugs, the reluctance to base opinions on empirical information, the inability to tolerate ambiguity, and the sacrifice of other social values to maintain present controls, strongly suggest that the salient elements in the drug issue operate at a subterranean level. If we are to come to terms with drugs we must dig for this level of functioning.

One of the major advantages of the functional approach for us is that we are not confined to the terminology of a single discipline. Issues as diverse as the ambivalence of the young drug user toward his family can be treated alongside the question of the law's effectiveness as a deterrent. Perhaps most important, a functional approach gives coherence to a problem that cannot usefully be studied in isolation. As an example of the functional approach, let us take the medical-police model on which treatment of the drug problem has always been based in Great Britain and the United States. The medical-police model reduces the question to a single axis of sickness and deviance versus health and normality, and certain consequences flow from this in both countries, despite differences in the law. For instance, in Britain registered heroin addicts are regarded as sick, while in the United States they are regarded as criminals (with the important side effect that Britain suffers little from the massive criminal element in the American drug scene). Nevertheless there are great similarities in the public attitudes to addicts in both countries. In both Britain and the United States nonmedical drug use is considered bad and wrong, and the heroin user is made to feel like a pariah. A doctor at a drug-control clinic who sees his job as getting the user off the drug, or at very least forcing him to reduce his dose and thereby show that his intentions are "good" and that he is "trying," represents a social judgment just as surely, if not as punitively, as a policeman.

The manifest function of both doctors and police is to correct: doctors cure the sick, policemen catch criminals. Both also have a preventive function, which is still manifest but slightly more obscure: the policeman acts as a deterrent to overt crime, but does not his presence have a symbolic reassuring function, not dissimilar to the magical value attached to the regular medical checkup? The hopes people place in policemen and doctors have a basis in reality when it comes to a crime like a holdup or a disease like cancer. But when we come to a crime whose victim is thought to be society, and a medical problem which consists in otherwise normal, law-abiding people ingesting a substance thought harmful, are we not moving into the realms of latent function, and asking policemen and doctors to do things that fall outside their professional role?

We do not underestimate the importance of the first, dependency-prone group of drug users. We do suggest that it would be more to the point to separate the drug problem into a drug illness problem and a social problem, treating the first on the medical-police model and the second on a social model.

SOURCES OF INFORMATION

Much of the data and information on which we base our analysis of the drug situation was obtained from observing and interviewing in depth drug users in Britain and America. In addition, in both countries we held extensive discussions and formal interviews with a wide variety of informed persons, including officials and professionals concerned with drugs. We also drew on our own considerable experience—one author is a psychiatric consultant on drug problems, the other a lawyer concerned with the impact of the drug laws. The sampling techniques were methodologically crude, but the number and types of respondents, as well as our opportunity to probe deeply into matters, may compensate for the lack of true random sampling.

We interviewed 525 drug users, almost all of whom had tried marijuana. Seventy had had at least one LSD experience; 10 had mainlined methadrine, and 105 had taken opiates. We also interviewed 420 nonusers. These ranged from adolescents to adult members of the informed public aged between 21 and 70 and came from a wide variety of social classes including professionals (90 physicians) and public officials. The interviews of both users and nonusers were conducted over a period of six years.

For an idea of the range and variety of interviewees, the main groups of respondents were as follows:

In the United States:

1. Naive subjects for a study of acute marijuana intoxication (provided 76)
2. Black adolescents (34)
3. Students (graduate and undergraduate) (207)
4. Physicians prescribing to patients regarded as opiate problems (31)
5. The patients of the above (70)
6. Additional physicians (interview as part of a study concerning use of psychology in medical practice) (59)
7. University faculty (27)
8. Nurses (20)
9. Police officers (31)
10. Lawyers (71)
11. Skilled and unskilled workers (42)
12. Business individuals (162)
13. Public officials (49)
14. High school students (60)

In Britain, as part of research specifically investigating drug use, 68 doctors, 39 students, 41 working-class youths, 37 members of the drug squad, and 31 public officials were interviewed or filled out questionnaires. The British subjects for the most part also did not know that either the interviews or the questionnaires concerned a drug study. The addition of the 216 British subjects brought the total of our sample to 1,161.

The interviews varied in depth and focus, as they were undertaken for a variety of purposes. This has made neat presentation difficult, but far outweighing this, we feel, is the fact that our analysis of the issues and our view of the multiple functions of drugs grew out of the interviews rather than vice versa. Most research consists in having a number of hypotheses and arranging interviews to prove them.

However, in general, our interview format ran like this: The interviewer began by asking about the general educational, geographical, and social background of the subject and his family. The subject's emotional relationships with family and friends were discussed, along with medical history, including any psychiatric contact, actual or considered. There were general questions about use of cigarettes, alcohol, and other drugs during a discussion of social habits, but detailed questions were held until near the end of the interview. The interviewer tried to determine the subject's economic, political, and aesthetic attitudes and values, pausing for more specific questions in any area that interested the subject, caused him to become more reticent, or seemed important in other ways for the further delineation of character structure.

The interviewer then questioned the subject thoroughly about drugs. If he admitted having tried any drug, he was asked exactly what he had taken, who had given it to him, whether he had given it to anyone else, what it had felt like, and what he saw as the long-term effects of the drug use on his personality, attitudes, and behavior. If he had not taken any drug, he was asked whether he had had the opportunity to do so. He was also asked to discuss any knowledge of drug use he had obtained from friends or from the mass media, and to give his own overall attitudes toward drugs. Until the end of the interview, none of the subjects guessed that drug use was a principal focus. In the opinion of the interviewer, all the material presented was offered freely and seemed reliable.

Numerous interviews revealed not only the unsuspected consistency of peoples' attitudes toward drugs, but also a marked emotionalism and inhibition of knowledge on the subject. Next we directed our attention to the influence of the law, the police, and social policy and interviewed lawyers, judges, police officers and officials, MPs, congressmen, and members of government organizations. Still finding great consistency in the arguments and their functions, we pushed into many different groups, always looking for the extent of repetitious attitudes, particularly if we felt that the attitudes were clearly based on myth or misconception.

Our approach to our interview material was somewhat unrefined. For example, when a generally well-informed person who acknowledged reading newspapers, magazines, or books containing sufficient information on drugs to enable him to differentiate between "hard" and "soft" drugs said, "I never get them straight, is it heroin which is stronger than cannabis?" we would assume that he suffered not from cognitive ignorance but from an emotional inhibition against such information. We tried to remain objective and, in some interviews, after a comment like that, found that our assumption of inhibition was shaky, and accepted the possibility that the man simply hadn't been presented with information. However, further probing would usually indicate that the facts had been available to him and he had simply psychically mislaid them.

Given this blunt approach to the interview material, our diverse sources, our interest in showing how these attitudes were used, and the effect of them in a qualitative sense, we decided not to attempt a statistical analysis. That approach was hard to resist, particularly when we were dealing with public attitudes, where we found an astonishing repetition of what we considered to be mythic positions. (These will be dealt with more fully in Chapter 3.) But, reluctantly, we bowed to the fact that in the last analysis our statistical classification of the information would be based, inevitably, on our own interpretation of the interviews; and to attempt to qualify in statistical terms such human judgments, no matter how objective we tried to be, appeared to be simply another way of insisting that we were right.

And this, above all, we wanted to avoid, for we do not want to convince, but rather to stimulate new thinking. We found during our interviews that people desire very strongly to be convinced about the drug issue and be rescued from the painful doubt this particularly menacing problem evokes. We hope to make the ambiguity tolerable, presenting a method of considering the question that cuts through emotionalism and provides lines of thought which can be followed fruitfully on this and similar social issues.

At present there is no basic agreement on what a successful

outcome for this issue would be, let alone how to achieve it. But waiting for more information, more education, more understanding, for a better climate of opinion, could subtly defeat any chance of righting the situation. If concessions on marijuana are wrung from an unwilling majority, we predict more social unrest and a repeat of the bitter controversy between generations, most likely over another drug or about whether we are becoming a "permissive society"—a phrase that has come to mean a society where there is little or no respect for authority, order, or regularity in human affairs. But if adherents of both sides of the question could agree that innovation and experiment are necessary to prevent a bad situation from getting impossible, then there is hope that a bold new plan could be worked out and put into practice. In the final chapter we suggest the lines along which such a plan could run. The drug policy and social controls we will suggest will take full account of the radical changes that have taken place in the past eight years and of the distinction, never officially recognized, between drug dependents and drug users. Certainly, creditable studies of particular drugs and of drug use in general must be carried out, and if it is found that they are destructive, then we might well wish to curtail freedom to use them. No one quarrels with the restrictions on arsenic or cortisone, because they are known for certain to be very dangerous, and restrictions on their use have nothing to do with any supposed immorality. In our proposals for drug control in Chapter 8, we insist on a regular reassessment of the situation so that newly collected evidence can be incorporated into the program. Of course, it must be possible to use this evidence to decrease restrictions as well as to increase them.

Other factors too must be recognized in our policy if we are to achieve clarity about the issues and a valid consensus. In Chapter 3 we discuss some of the social conditions and technological changes that set the scene for the cannabis explosion of the 1960s and show that the conditions influencing drug use are basic to our society. Thus the all-pervasive influence of television must be taken into account, for it may have wrought changes in the generation who grew up under its baleful eye as vast as the more obvious cataclysms of World War II and the Great Depression.

Throughout history men have thought that their own era was one of crucial importance in the history of mankind. We are no exception, and skeptics may detect an inflated self-importance. But we think it is quite safe to say that the crucial moment for re-examining drug policies is indeed now, especially since the drug issue is linked with so many other matters of social importance.

2

PUBLIC ATTITUDES TOWARD
ILLEGAL DRUG USE

The public controls and supports social institutions and thus creates the social setting in which the illegal user operates. This setting is the predominant influence on drug use, and in order to understand its impact we must understand the public that shapes it.

Here we discuss the common attitudes toward illegal drug use, showing how they are based to a large extent on inadequate information, poor arguments, and extraordinary examples—the chronic heroin user with his destroyed veins, the suicidal barbiturate addict with gangrened limbs. We go on to explain the social and psychological functions of these attitudes and show that they maintain themselves in the face of a mass of contradictory evidence.

The public response to nonmedical drug use is overwhelmingly one of moral disgust, condemnation, and fear at the threat of social and personal chaos that drug use seems to portend. During the years 1965–69 we questioned 430 people about this subject, and their answers confirmed the findings of the national polls. In *Time* magazine's poll,[1] conducted by Lou Harris in 1969, over 90 percent of those questioned associated drug use with moral corruption and decay. Forty-two percent of the parents questioned were willing to turn their own children over to the police if they used drugs; and 73 percent of parents said they would report a son to the police if they knew that he was selling marijuana to his friends for a profit. In a Massachusetts poll[2] conducted by the *Boston Globe* in 1969, 83 percent regarded nonmedical drug use as their greatest concern for the future of the country in general and for youth in particular. Even among the young (18 to 25), 63 percent expressed deep concern about "drug use as a very serious problem." "It's a problem that hits the very young and shatters their minds. The government should crack down," was the feeling of typical interviewees. In our interviews there was almost unanimous agreement among nonusers on this point, despite the interviewees' varying class, educational, and professional background.

Public attitudes both reflect and inspire the treatment of drug use by the mass media. Newspapers are full of stories about drugs. On August 14, 1970, a day chosen at random, when there was no sensational item of drug news, the *Boston Globe* devoted 11 columns, the *Washington Post* 16, and *The New York Times* 19 to it, and discussed the problem in terms more suitable to a major cholera epidemic than to a practice that in fact does serious harm to a very small number of people. As often happens in an emotionally charged atmosphere, the opinion-forming groups in society—the politicians, journalists, teachers, doctors—use the increasing number of newspaper reports of young people damaged or killed by drug use as irrefutable evidence of a drug epidemic. In fact, the drug problem is exaggerated by the newspapers and we suggest that it is worsened by this overreaction.

Nevertheless, the shock and fear are very understandable. Not only has the whole issue changed in a remarkably short time, but the drug users themselves are deliberately provocative.

The underground press,[3] an acknowledged spokesman for the drug scene, makes extravagant claims for drugs and strikes at the very foundation of the average man's view of Western society:

> How can they [the square world] believe they have the truth about life? Those bastards building their atomic bombs, computers, foul motor cars and dehuman space ships have a monopoly on nothing. They have produced a culture with an unbalanced rational consciousness which has given rise to the precarious state

of modern civilization. Anything that differs is immediately denounced as a crime against nature.

This artificial society manifests hysteria when [phantastica] drugs [hallucinogens, psychedelics including marijuana, THC and lots more] are suggested for purposes of self exploration and the enhancement of sensory experience. The psychotropic drugs which are socially acceptable, including alcohol, barbiturates and tranquilizers, are far more likely than phantastica to rob man of his initiative and individuality. The phantastica allow man greater freedom of choice to act for himself free of blind conditioning and cultural imperatives—they have more to offer than abstract ideologies. If nothing else they may free man from the crap that normal consciousness is a unitary state of man and not a value judgment. Phantastica drugs will deepen man's understanding of nature, leisure, comfort, and his goals in life. They enhance and diversify experience. It is impossible to predict what the future will bring, but it can be said with absolute confidence that alternative consciousness, once the prejudice and cowardice about them are overcome, will help man to evolve so that he can change his own structure as well as his environment. We hope to God his life will never be the same again.

The paper contends that marijuana use (with a touch of the psychedelic ideology) enables us to alter our perceptions of reality. It also condemns the Western scientific technological view that reality is measurable and objectively verifiable as a constricting repressive force. Some well-publicized psychiatrists, R. D. Laing,[4] for example, support the idea that society's view of objective reality is simply a method of imposing conformity on its members.

This call to perceive new realities can provoke envy if the fresh vision is presented as poetic, idyllic, or sensual. But it can also frighten those who find one reality more than enough to cope with, especially if they are challenged to face this unfamiliar world when they are well past the age when it might have been an adventure. For ordinary members of the general public, Laing, Leary, and the newspaper *IT* stir up primitive fears of social chaos. They are terrified by the prospect of a society where anyone can drop out:

our present interdependent society could not continue to function; our social institutions would break down; traditions and values would no longer be upheld or even, perhaps, tolerated.

By reacting in this way, most members of the public reveal that they have accepted the drug users' wildest imaginings and see illegal drugs as fantastically powerful. This is hardly surprising when we reflect that the general public already believes in the power of medically prescribed drugs. Our rapidly increasing dependence on medically prescribed drugs for survival, freedom from pain, and longevity was given shocking but short-lived publicity at the Kefauver hearings in 1951, at the time of the thalidomide scandal in 1965, and again at the 1966 American Medical Association convention.*

Expenditure on drugs is rising faster than either general consumer spending or population growth. Measured in doctor visits and hospital days, adverse drug reaction has become one of our largest disease entities.

We believe this increasing devotion to medical drugs bears witness to a deep-seated fantasy, shared by both doctors and the public, of the possibility that drugs can enable us to lead lives unmarred by physical or mental distress. Although the overall efficacy of many of the drugs (e.g., the tranquilizers and energizers) is still unproved, doctors argue that they must prescribe them because their patients demand and need them. Or they will contend with some validity that an inexpensive course of tranquilizers can sometimes help a patient as much as extended and costly psychiatric treatment and, more important, can do so very much more quickly.

England and the United States share a remarkably similar set of emotional attitudes on drug use, especially the fear of an epidemic and the value of police action in averting one. When the number of known heroin addicts in the United Kingdom grew

---

* In 1963, American consumers spent $2.3 billion on drugs, and $8.1 billion in 1969. This figure does not include the drugs charged to hospital or clinic bills, or money spent on drugs by public or private agencies.

from 172 in 1962 to 2,340 in 1968, discussion emphasized the percentage of increase, not the extremely small numbers involved. This disproportionate emphasis was clear in our interviews with British police. In an interview in April, 1968, Inspector S. pointed out that the number of addicts in Britain had doubled in a five-year period, and estimated that if the present rate of increase continued, by 1980 the figure would quadruple. He agreed that there were only about 2,500 addicts in the entire United Kingdom (2,340 of whom were heroin addicts), but still stressed the percentage of increase. He also agreed that the enormous publicity surrounding drug use might have stimulated many restless and disturbed young people to try drugs, but disputed the truth of the interviewer's observation that given the extent of the publicity and the large number of susceptible youngsters, 2,500 was a remarkably low total. Inspector S., like most of the public in both the United States and Great Britain, believed that the vigilance of the police and the formation of drug squads by many small police forces were important factors in keeping down the number of users.

During the same period, however, the campaign against marijuana use was as strong as that against heroin, and a study[5] of student apprentices (a low-risk group) showed an increase from 12 percent users in 1967 to 35 percent in 1969. These figures must cast some doubt on the efficacy of police action. As for fears of an epidemic, it is now thought that the increase in heroin use in 1968 that gave substance to these fears took place only on paper; in that year England shifted from doctors prescribing to the drug-control clinic program, where for the first time addicts had to register if they were to get their drugs. In 1969 the number of heroin users decreased, and this is seen by some investigators[6] as an indication that despite poor facilities, inadequate staffing, and few efforts at rehabilitation, the clinics are succeeding in controlling heroin use. Thus the evidence of a heroin epidemic is, to say the least, conflicting, and the "drug epidemic"—and by this is meant especially the heroin epidemic—was and still is the battle cry of antidrug propaganda in both England and the United States. It was plainly one of the fears invariably voiced by the 430 people we questioned on their attitudes toward drug use.

We would like to describe a typical example of this group. We shall call him "Mr. Fry." He is not a closed-minded bigot, a depressed, gray-flannel conformist caught in a middle-aged sense of futility, nor does he feel threatened by the changing concepts of welfare. But Mr. Fry would have responded along with the majority to the *Boston Globe* and *Time* magazine polls.

A 43-year-old white, nominally Protestant college graduate, Mr. Fry has been comfortably married for 17 years, and has three children; his job is demanding, but he and his wife enjoy their leisure activities and drink and smoke moderately. He describes himself as a political liberal, and he keeps himself well informed, but he is not politically active. His national voting record is 1948—Truman; 1952—Stevenson; 1956—Eisenhower; 1960—Kennedy; 1964—Johnson; 1968—Humphrey. He thinks we should not have gotten into the war in Vietnam, but is unsure about how to get out; he is against unilateral withdrawal. He is in favor of civil rights and the "Negro cause," despite his friends' fear of riots and unrest. The death of Martin Luther King, whom he greatly admired, distressed him even more than the assassination of the Kennedys. He is worried about law and order, while disliking the phrase, and would like "younger people" (his age) in government. Mr. Fry is unsympathetic to college student unrest; he does not see their grievances as valid (apart from Vietnam), unlike those of the Negroes. The invasion of Czechoslovakia rearoused some fear of Russia, but he still regards the Cold War as exaggerated, and is convinced that but for Vietnam, we would be on better terms with Russia. China is seen as a more serious threat. He strongly supports the United Nations: "It should have more teeth."

He and his wife had sexual relations for a year before they married. He believes this strengthened the ties between them, and he approves of greater sexual freedom among the young. Since marriage he has had two "flings," but does not think such a thing will happen again, and is critical of associates who make a practice of adultery. He dislikes organized religion.

Mr. Fry describes himself as "damned worried." Not given to apocalyptic visions, he nevertheless dreads and conceives possible the breakdown of his own world. He perceives the irony of his increased personal security—good job, wife, home, friends—and decreased sense of relationship to the social context in which his children are growing up. He fears for the family as an institution in the twenty-first century.

The flurry of conflicting reports on drug use confuse him, and he is in some doubt as to what attitudes he should adopt to help maintain the social institutions he values—the law, schools, the police, the medical profession. He is also guiltily aware of a parallel between smoking and marijuana use; however, he pushes back incipient doubts and accepts the position: drugs are a threat, and nonmedical users are bad; they must be controlled and shown the error of their ways, for his sake and theirs.

During his interview, he constantly made such remarks as: "They have no sense of responsibility or they wouldn't even think of dropping out. They would want to work and contribute to society." "They will scramble their brains with that stuff so that they won't ever get anything done." He sees these not as the value statements they are, but rather as truths about what is right and good. "If so much as one sick kid is pushed out of this society by a drug," he goes on to say, "it is too much." He can justify his paternalistic position because he wants to help, though he would think it ridiculous to ban sugar, which is harmful to an impulsive diabetic. However, the diabetic doesn't offend, disturb, or frighten him.

Mr. Fry has almost ceased to question his attitudes toward drug use. He accepts that it is bad; most of the time it seems a simple, unarguable fact, though some doubts still linger in the back of his mind and he eagerly questions any "expert" he meets.

We also interviewed city employees, steelworkers, secretaries, housewives, carpenters, machinists, insurance salesmen, clerks, and police officers, and found not just unanimity of opinion that nonmedical drug use was wrong, but also a hyperemotional conviction that somehow someone should do something about it, i.e., stamp it out. Each fresh exposé in the mass media was seized on as an illustration of the extent of the evil, and served to still any remaining doubts. These interviewees saw the nonmedical drug user as one important representative of the uncontrolled social forces that were destroying all that they had worked toward.

And they saw drug users as arising on either side of them in the social framework. One group of drug users emerged from dispossessed ethnic minorities, whose demands for a just share of the economic pie many of our interviewees saw as inordinate, hasty, and threatening. The other group arose from that section of the middle class they aspired to. The breakdown in order and legitimacy in that very group who enjoyed the fruits of this society left our hardworking, less affluent interviewees feeling squeezed, and as though they had no place to go. These interviewees smoked and used alcohol and were less guiltily aware of the similarities between these practices and marijuana use than Mr. Fry's group. They resented the student drug-users' assault on the use of alcohol as a hedonistic exercise similar to arcane rituals with a joint or a sugar cube.

On the whole, the various socioeconomic groups agree on the evils of drug use, seeing in it the seeds of destruction for society and of the breakdown of normal standards of decency and self-control. We will examine the three principal attitudes that support this view.

First, and perhaps most basic, is the attitude that there is little need to differentiate among different sorts of nonmedical drugs. All drugs are equally bad and equally dangerous. Marijuana and heroin are admittedly different from each other, but, the argument goes, the first will lead to the second in an almost inevitable progression.

The second attitude is based on the belief that drugs are extremely powerful; they cause dependency which is physically destructive and turns people into criminals or indolents and generally enslaves them in a remarkably short time.

The third is that drug use is a symptom of intrinsic weakness expressed as emotional disturbance, and that the strong probability is that all drug users become mentally sick. (This argument sometimes swallows its own tail by stating further that one would have to be sick in order to use a drug.)

These three attitudes are different ways of saying that nonmedical drug use is wrong; they do not flow from informed and thoughtful opinions on the rights and wrongs of drug-taking (although they are based on strongly held values). In our experience, most people are not open to argument or even able to assimilate fresh facts on the subject of drug use. Normal standards of rational discussion are abandoned: there is no attempt to define terms, and the argument often shifts ground, or returns in circular fashion to points already shown to be false. We hope to expose the quality of public debate on the subject: in our opinion it is based on a desire to convince or control, not on a desire to find out what is true.

1. *Drugs are all alike and all equally dangerous.*

In our survey of the *Boston Globe,* the *Washington Post* and *The New York Times* on August 14, 1970, of 16 headlines about drugs, only one specified which drug was involved; 10 used the word "drugs" and 5 "narcotics." Ten of the stories never specified which drug was involved, and 3 did not specify until the last paragraph. The arrests of the Kennedy and Shriver children received the same rather cavalier treatment: UPI put out a report listing 22 other children of famous parents who had been arrested and detailing the circumstances. They had searched as far back as 1963 to garner their information, and called 9 of the items simply "drug" or "narcotic" arrests, without specifying further. Neither *Time* magazine nor the *Globe* found it necessary to differentiate among the various drugs in their polls. "Drug use" was a general concept acceptable to both the pollster and his subjects. It meant the whole range of drugs, from marijuana, the psychedelic group, the barbiturates, and amphetamines to the opiates.

Our own interviews confirmed the existence of this confusion. Some of our interviewees were able to differentiate among the drugs, particularly as to whether they were "hard" or "soft," but during the questioning and discussion they made little or no distinction.

Most U.S. federal and state laws classify all drugs under one heading. "Hard" and "soft," marijuana, cocaine, heroin—all drugs are legally branded as equally responsible for moral corruption. Chief Justice G. Joseph Tauro, of the Superior Court of Massachusetts, has by his own account devoted several months to the study of the marijuana issue. Yet in his discussion of the relationship of marijuana to crime he says: [7]

> On the national level, Director John E. Ingersoll of the Bureau of Narcotics and Dangerous Drugs has reported a 774 percent increase in drug abuse arrests for the past eight years.

He clearly implies that the 1969 statistic is relevant only to marijuana, and goes on to link marijuana to violent crime in the following case, where the defendants claimed to be acting under the influence of a nonhabit-forming drug:

> For example, two young men were recently brought before me in the First Criminal Session accused of armed robbery and attempted murder. They had approached an automobile containing a young man and his fiancee and announced their intention to rob him. At the repeated urging of his companion to kill him, the armed defendant fired at the man from point-blank range. There was no provocation and no scuffle—just a senseless attempt to kill! Only the instinctive reflex of drawing his left arm across his chest saved the victim. The bullet smashed his elbow rather than his heart.

Of course, in some important ways nonmedical drugs are alike: they are all mind-altering; they are all capable of producing dependency of one sort or another; they all induce states of intoxication; they are all potentially dangerous to the health of the user and to the safety of the community; and they are all illegal. But the differences are far greater than the superficial similarities.

These drugs vary in a number of ways, each crucial to an accurate understanding of how drugs work. Heroin and barbiturates produce tolerance and withdrawal symptoms; LSD and marijuana do not produce withdrawal but LSD produces tolerance. Some are taken orally, some smoked, others sniffed or injected. Heroin can be detected in the body a day after use; LSD metabolizes quickly. Psychic effects vary widely: some can be used without disrupting daily life; others, at least in the present setting, cannot. Finally, the effects of any single drug are not certain and definite, but depend on many psychological and physical factors.

And yet these differences among drugs have been widely aired in public. *The New York Times*[8] published a series of five long articles each by a different staff member—an unusual procedure for that paper—on a number of aspects of the drug issue including a detailed differentiation among drugs. In 1969 *Time* magazine[9] devoted a large part of a special issue to discussing drugs; *Newsweek*,[10] *Look*,[11] and *Life*[12] did the same in 1969 and 1970. All these were serious and factual reports giving ample and correct information. Local newspapers, too, such as the *Boston Globe*,[13] have provided serious reportage on the subject. Herbert Black, chief medical reporter for the *Boston Globe,* estimates that his paper has published educational information about drugs on as many as fifty occasions. Admittedly, these educational efforts are meager in comparison with the heavy output of sensational stories and articles that do not bother to differentiate. But Mr. Fry, and in fact most of our subjects, had been exposed to accurate information again and again. The fact that on the whole they noticed or remembered only what was sensational and inaccurate indicates a powerful inhibition of knowledge on this subject. The public unconsciously censors the available information and registers only what fits in with preconceived attitudes. It is an unusually comprehensive example of selective perception.

The public's unwillingness or inability to distinguish among widely varying drugs is expressed very clearly in the progression theory: that the use of a mild drug leads inevitably to the use of a strong one, and then to increasingly large doses. Marijuana and heroin are widely believed to be linked in this way, and the major differences between the two drugs are thus evaded both in public attitudes and in the law. This belief influences in some way most discussions of marijuana. Even intelligent people who have grasped the distinctions between the two drugs are seemingly irresistibly drawn back into the progression theory. In a typical interview part of the dialogue was as follows:

"I'm in favor of increasing the penalties for the bastards who start those kids off." "Start them off?" "Right. I heard of an eighteen-year-old kid in Brooklyn who got started at a party on pot. He was a weak kid, and inside three months he was injecting heroin. He went just like that."

There is no evidence of a causal connection between the two drugs, and all attempts to establish the truth of the progression theory have failed. The theory was explicitly denied in the 1937 marijuana hearings, but drug progression again became a matter of public concern in the 1940s and 1950s when an alleged increase in heroin addiction was attributed to prior marijuana use. The main support for the theory comes from studies showing a history of marijuana use in addicts. As Pet and Ball[14] show, 80.4 percent of addicts at the U.S. Public Health Service Hospital at Lexington, Kentucky, had smoked marijuana. But this *post hoc* reasoning does not stand up. By the time these people became heroin addicts they had tried everything, including liquor and milk. The real question is, what percentage of marijuana users become heroin addicts? The answer appears to be very few indeed. In his extensive study of student drug use in 1968, Blum[15] found that only 7 percent of marijuana users had tried opiates; making adjustment for the subsequent upsurge in marijuana use, this figure would now be around 3 percent. Blum, examining the population of the Oakland ghetto, found that teen-age heroin and marijuana users belonged to completely different groups who held different values. Few of the "heads" turned to heroin. These reports were confirmed by the marijuana users we interviewed, very few of whom were willing to try heroin.

Another argument used to support the drug progression theory is that heroin and marijuana arrests have been increasing at parallel rates. Bloomquist[16] in California and Paton[17] in England believe that these increases suggest a causal relationship between the use of the two drugs. Kaplan,[18] however, conclusively demonstrates the fallacy in this argument.

The tenacity of the progression argument is more remarkable because of the other factors that appear to explain heroin use. Blum found a higher correlation between use of heroin and substances like glue and gasoline than between heroin and marijuana, while tranquilizers, sedatives, and amphetamines correlated with heroin use about the same as marijuana. Many heroin users were formerly speed freaks who began to use the drug to "crash" smoothly. Indeed, it appears that the absence of marijuana, rather than the reverse, may be closely related to heroin use. When the supply of marijuana dried up after Operation Intercept (a massive search and seizure effort aimed at reducing the flow of marijuana into the United States), many young people tried heroin and other drugs that had not previously interested them. A basic pharmacological text, *The Pharmacological Basis of Therapeutics*,[19] finds evidence for progression lacking. And finally, although some writers on the subject still have not accepted their findings, every commission investigating the issue (including the President's White House Conference on Narcotic and Drug Abuse, the President's Commission on Crime, the President's Commission on the Mental Health of Children, and the Wootton Committee) has, sometimes reluctantly, come to the conclusion that the theory of drug progression is unfounded.

Perhaps the attraction of the argument for progression lies in the mechanism said to draw the user from the milder drug to the stronger—namely, the user's insatiable appetite for pleasure and passivity. Having once tasted the forbidden pleasures of marijuana, it is thought, he will soon grow accustomed to them and seek stronger drugs, particularly heroin. However, it does not by any means follow that someone who enjoys marijuana, with its experience-enhancing effects, will also enjoy heroin, which has a euphoric but deadening effect. The theory may be seen as an example of the public's desire to hold a monolithic position on drugs in order to avoid dealing with the ambiguities of conflicting information.

2. *Drugs are extremely powerful; they cause dependency which is physically destructive and leads to crime.*

Drugs are believed to be so powerful that a few doses induce a dependency that damages drug users and, by giving rise to apathy, indolence, and criminal activity, also damages society.

Let us look at some commonly held beliefs on drug dependency. Four hundred teachers attending a statewide meeting on the potential of drug education[20] were asked how many doses of a drug (the type unspecified) were necessary to produce dependency. Thirty-four thought that one dose could do it. Over 250 thought that four or five doses would be sufficient. Not one of these teachers asked the questioner to differentiate among the drugs.

When the question was rephrased and the drugs specified as marijuana, LSD, and heroin, 50 of the teachers thought that one dose of heroin could produce dependency, while only 25 thought that one dose of marijuana could. But roughly the same large majority believed that as few as four or five doses of either of those drugs could induce dependency. Our interviews tally with these results. The huge majority of our interviewees believed nonmedical drugs to be enormously powerful and capable of inducing physical dependency after only a few doses.

In fact, the ability of drugs to produce physical dependency varies widely. The opiates, barbiturates, and amphetamines induce tolerance, so that increasingly large doses are needed, and barbiturate users, especially, suffer severe withdrawal symptoms when the drug is stopped. But even with these drugs the personality of the user and the situation in which use occurs—set and setting—have to be taken into account. It is a myth that one shot of heroin makes an addict. Addiction occurs much later, often after a long period of "chipping" or a weekend habit. It has been demonstrated[21] that a number of doctors who were taking as many as four shots of morphine a day were able to stop without discomfort when they were on vacation. It appears that even the problem of severe withdrawal symptoms has been exaggerated. Withdrawal symptoms have been regarded as an inevitable and usually extremely unpleasant consequence of dependency. Yet Daytop Village on Staten Island, one of the best-known residential treatment centers for hard-core addiction, reports that it has never seen a full-blown example.* This is not to deny that withdrawal symptoms occur; but it is clear that their severity depends to a large extent on set and setting.

No physical dependency has been demonstrated as resulting from marijuana use. However, it is said to produce psychological dependency, or habituation, and this state is thought to be equally bad. It is not always clear how the words "dependency" and "habituation" are being used. Hundreds of thousands of people use marijuana regularly—say, every weekend—but are not enslaved to the drug in the sense that they seek it at all costs. When they are unable to get a supply, they can stop smoking without great discomfort. In this sense marijuana is less enslaving than tobacco. However, there are also a number of chronic users of marijuana in the United States and Great Britain, though no careful study has been made of them. Our brief study[22] of the hard-core members of the Fantasia and Paradisio clubs in Amsterdam showed that except for their overwhelming interest in music, many of them seemed exactly like the junkie stereotype. They

---

* In order to educate the public, the inhabitants of Daytop produced and acted in a play, *The Concept,* which has been widely reviewed and discussed in many feature articles. This remarkable play is in part improvised, and after the performance the actors meet the audience, discuss drugs and answer questions. Early in the play an addict has a screaming, writhing withdrawal syndrome in jail. Later, after admission to Daytop, he starts the same process. The others in his group tell him to come off it, hand him a broom, and indicate that he works or leaves. Clearly, he is still uncomfortable; but the contrast between what he experiences at Daytop and what he experienced in jail is a key point in the play. Five of our interviews had seen the play and had retained an image of the horror of withdrawal but had forgotten its minimization under different social conditions. They clung to their belief about dependency despite the vivid presentation on stage and the discussion afterward.

began to smoke as soon as they woke up in the morning, and remained stoned until they went to bed. Disturbing though these cases are, we must always keep in mind the three groups of drug users we outlined in Chapter 1. These chronic users are of the first, dependency-prone group, and must be distinguished from the second, drug-experimenting group, who form the overwhelming majority of marijuana users.

Why does dependency on drugs so frighten the general public that they inhibit knowledge about it and construct myths around it? It is believed that drugs are physically destructive and lead users into criminal activity, although evidence to the contrary has been widely published. Certainly the mass media, and even reports from professional bodies, must take part of the blame for the fear of dependency and of its results. A police journal has described the physical destruction wrought by addiction in these terms:[23]

> To be a confirmed drug addict is to be one of the walking dead. . . . The teeth have rotted out; the appetite is lost and stomach and intestines don't function properly. The gall bladder becomes inflamed; eyes and skin turn a bilious yellow. In some cases the membranes of the nose turn a flaming red; the partition separating the nostrils is eaten away—breathing is difficult. Oxygen in the blood decreases; bronchitis and TB develop. Good traits of character disappear and bad ones emerge. Sex organs become affected. Veins collapse and livid purplish scars remain. Nerves snap; vicious twitching develops. Imaginary and fantastic fears blight the mind and sometimes complete insanity results. Oftentimes too death comes—much too early in life. . . . Such is the torment of being a drug addict; such is the plague of being one of the walking dead.

However, medical authorities now widely agree that even heroin and the opiates cause no physiological damage. An addict may suffer from chronic constipation and reduced sexual potency, but assured of a drug supply he will live to a ripe old age. It is true that addicts risk collapsed or abscessed veins, and even death, but these result from unregulated doses and unsterile equipment. The addict who is a "walking death" has been brought to that condition by the present state of the law.

Marijuana also is nontoxic, unlike alcohol, which has been shown to cause destruction of brain tissue. Acute marijuana intoxication may reduce the heartbeat and produce reddened conjunctivae, but that is all. The chronic marijuana users we saw at the Paradisio and Fantasia clubs obviously suffered from malnutrition and consequently from general debilitation, resembling in this respect some addict groups; however, they showed little hypoglycemia, hypothemia, or depression of respiration—all symptoms ascribed to marijuana use by a number of professional observers. In our experience, no physical damage can be shown to result from the use of the drug itself.

Prolonged use of such drugs as the amphetamines and barbiturates may indeed have damaging physical effects, even when they are medically prescribed. We take full account of these dangers, but emphasize that the central conclusion to be drawn from this brief comparison is that only particular drugs used in certain ways are harmful. The distinctions among drugs must be carefully observed, and the monolithic attitude promulgated by the mass media must be broken down.

As we have said, it is also widely believed that the drug user becomes morally enslaved and falls very easily into criminal activity. In this view, the drug turns its user into something akin to the ordinary criminal. Here again we will distinguish between the dependency-prone and the drug-experimenting groups.

Studies[24] of the first group demonstrate that the hard-core user was criminal before he began to use drugs. There is a specific "junkie" social and psychological profile: cigarettes at the age of six or seven, liquor and sex by 13, marijuana soon after; in late adolescence, promiscuity and petty thievery merge almost automatically into prostitution and organized crime. Drug abusers of this type definitely show an ascending use of drugs, typically moving toward the one with the big kick, heroin. And, of course, it must be remembered that once they have begun to use drugs, in the United States at least, they are caught in the vicious circle in which criminal activity becomes essential to support the drug habit. The British system, whatever its demerits, prevents the development of this cycle.

The second group of drug users, the drug experimenters, over-whelmingly uses marijuana, though there is also some use of psychedelic drugs among them. There is no evidence that their use gives rise to criminal activity. In fact, a careful survey of the studies done linking marijuana to aggression or crime concludes that there is strong evidence against the link between marijuana and crime. The survey analyzes several famous cases, which have been repeatedly quoted to illustrate the criminogenic effect of the drug. Tenuousness of the evidence is revealed in each instance. Other large studies (Indian Hemp Commission,[25] La Guardia Report,[26] Blum,[27] Blumer,[28] police/arrest figures[29]) consistently find that, if anything, marijuana inhibits such antisocial activity.[30] The marijuana user is criminal only in that he uses an illegal drug. The modern marijuana user usually comes from a social class different from that of the heroin addict, and he uses the drug differently; it is as much part of his ordinary social life as a martini in the evening is for his father.

3. *Drug users are mentally ill*.

Chief Justice Tauro[31] described marijuana users as "the dis-affiliated, the neurotic and psychotic, the confused, the anxious, the alienated, the inadequate, the weak." Harris Isbell,[32] writing for the U.S. Public Health Service in 1951, described the psychological state of the addict:

> The cause of addiction is not drugs but human weakness. Addiction is usually a symptom of a personality maladjustment rather than a disease in its own right. The psychiatric conditions which underlie drug addiction are chiefly the neuroses and the character disorders. . . . They [neurotic patients] include ner-vous tense individuals with a great deal of anxiety and many somatic complaints; compulsive neurotics; persons with conver-

sion hysteria—strange paralyses, anesthesias, etc. Individuals with character disorders were formerly termed psychopaths. Usually they are irresponsible, selfish, immature, thrill-seeking individuals who are constantly in trouble—the type of person who acts first and thinks afterwards. The majority of addicts do not fall clearly into the neurotic or character disorder groups but have characteristics of both classes.

Marijuana was originally prohibited because it was thought to lead to insanity; LSD is believed to lead to certain short-term and probable long-term psychosis; and the frenzied need of the heroin addict for his fix is thought to verge on the insane. Again and again in our interviews these ideas were echoed and supported by the claim that if users were not mentally ill to start with, drugs would soon make them so. The evidence is by no means so clear-cut.

We will distinguish the three groups—the dependency-prone, the drug experimenters, and the third group who could be forced by social pressure into either camp—and then discuss some beliefs about the more common drugs.

Even among the first group, including hard-core heroin users, chronic marijuana addicts, and other "junkie" types, there is almost no evidence of mental illness. And yet it is still current thought among many doctors, and among most of the public, that addiction is a functional equivalent for psychosis. We suggest that the reason for this is that the addict's obvious disdain for social conventions, his abuse of his body, and his underlying fury at any effort, however well intentioned, to help him offend the professional observer. The doctor sees the addict as bizarre, cut off from society by his own attitudes. His use of drugs becomes a crazy action.

The long-standing belief that hard-core users are psychotic was finally disproved by Vaillant.[33] He conducted a study of heroin users (who form the bulk of this group) and found only one in the New York State mental hospitals. His work constitutes a breakthrough because it is a longitudinal study following up addicts after twenty-five years. Most of the reports about addicts from so-called experts have been impressionistic, and consist largely of generalizations from hard cases. Support for Vaillant's findings has now begun to appear from other sources. Myerson and Mayer[34] interviewed two hundred addicts in order to develop diagnostic criteria, and found no schizophrenics. They found many instances of bizarre behavior, but whatever the reasons for this, the addicts were not literally schizophrenic. However, the belief lingers tenaciously among the medical profession and the informed public that drug use is a psychotic equivalent, and this is used as one more reason for condemning drug use.

The second, drug-experimenting group differs on almost every count from the first group, but the two are confused in the public mind. There is virtually no evidence of mental illness among them.[35] A group of students who began to use marijuana after 1966 were shown to differ only in minute details of attitude and personality from their fellow students who did not use the drug. The students who used marijuana delighted in exploding officially promulgated myths about drug use; this crusading sense of "fighting for the truth" gave them a certain cohesion. They also tended to be slightly more radical than their "straight" colleagues. The more conformist students, who fully accept their country's values and are more or less typical "clean-cut" American boys, find it much harder to try marijuana.

Among college and high school students, drugs, especially marijuana, are so much in the air that it is entirely natural that experimentation should take place. Even where psychedelics and amphetamines are included in the experiments, charges of mental illness have not been proved.

Then there is the third group consisting of seriously neurotic youngsters who find the nonconformist support they need in the second, drug-experimenting group. Because everyone in adolescence seems to be in a state of turmoil, they blend with their fellows; but after two or three years, when the others have gone ahead and made the necessary life-decisions, they are left behind. Naturally, they search for another group who will accept them, and this is very likely to be a heroin-taking group.

It is far from clear that drug use itself causes mental illness in any of these three groups. With marijuana, psychedelic drugs, amphetamines, and barbiturates it is undoubtedly true that certain combinations of user and setting will precipitate psychoses, aggravate underlying conflicts, damage vulnerable personalities, and create other psychological disturbances. But it is also true that these drugs are usually used safely. Some doctors suggest that marijuana may even be used to prevent the development of psychic disturbances. David Smith[36] describes the following case which suggests that some research might possibly be carried out on the therapeutic uses of marijuana.

> A 15-year-old white male in a wealthy bay area suburb improved his performance in school after he started smoking marijuana. Prior to this time he suffered from free-floating adolescent anxiety about "who he was" and "where he was going." There was very little family communication, although his parents continually advised him about his future objectives. The boy stated that he was not needed economically or any other way in the family or the community. When he started smoking pot, however, he became a "head" . . . and entered into the "head subculture" whereby he established a new identity for himself. Temporary resolution of this adolescent crisis resolved his anxiety and he was able to perform much better in school.

LSD has inspired a number of horror statistics, and it is certainly true that there is danger of long-term damage or difficult reentry into society for prepsychotics and teen-agers who use the drug casually and without proper supervision. But when it is used carefully, and its effects are understood, the experience is temporary and, for many mature users, worthwhile. Amphetamines and barbiturates also have two faces. They are a familiar item in the doctor's armamentarium and, as such, reassuring. And yet excessive "upping" or "downing" can cause severe psychic dislocation, certainly as damaging as any of the effects of LSD. Ironically, public attention is seldom called to these drugs, presumably because they are so frequently prescribed.

THE FUNCTION OF THE PUBLIC ATTITUDE

1. *To maintain the status quo*

For seventy years drug use has been seen as symbolizing the destruction of much that ordinary people hold dear and that makes their world stable. This view serves to buttress the status quo in a number of ways. We will examine three viewpoints, briefly distinguishing between their manifest and latent functions.

First, by being greatly concerned about the potential danger of drugs, Mr. Fry is protected personally against drug-taking, alerted to the use of drugs by those close to him, and predisposed to support antidrug measures. These are the manifest functions of his concern. The latent functions are to reinforce his desire to resist the temptation to take drugs and to be a "good" person. But the depth of his desire to maintain the status quo reaches into unconscious levels, and has driven Mr. Fry, normally a reasonable man, into regarding the marijuana smoker whose only crime is his use of the drug as a dangerous criminal. By censoring material that conflicts with his views, Mr. Fry minimizes the internal conflict that would arise were he to take note of all the information available to him. We know enough about nonmedical drug use to make Mr. Fry and the others we interviewed uncomfortable if they were to acknowledge all the facts.

Second, our vision of ourselves as upright and capable of judging is reaffirmed vis-à-vis drug use, and this strengthens our resolve to maintain the status quo. Mr. Fry, for example, on the subject of drug use felt on firm ground in an insecure world. He was keenly aware that he had done little to make the world a better place for his children, and his guilt about this immobilized his wish to control the younger generation. However, when it came to drugs, he *knew* what was right. His desire to protect the kids from themselves made him certain of his position, exorcised his guilt, and permitted him to feel perfectly justified in his wish to control. These are manifest functions. Mr. Fry is unaware of the latent function, by which his very willingness and power to judge the drug user affirms the uprightness of him who judges. The myths about drug use that Mr. Fry clings to—such as that of an inevitable drug progression—permit him to retain his sense of righteousness.

We can show how this worked also with the policemen we interviewed in the United States and England.[37] Out of thirty-seven, five questioned the effectiveness of present marijuana laws, but not one doubted the need for some such law, and all asserted the social importance of a job that implemented existing laws which "supported the structure of society." In order to feel useful and beneficent when they enforced the drug laws, they felt that drug use had to be seen as bad for society. To deal with drug use directly and unequivocally, while maintaining their own self-respect, the police had to eschew all doubts on this subject. They were not so rigid on other questions: all but two of our interviewees expressed doubts about the value of the laws concerning sexual deviancy and abortion, although most of them personally condemned both practices. One difference they all noted between the sexual deviant and the marijuana smoker was that the former was generally repentant, whereas the new breed of drug users, they pointed out almost in chorus, does not accept the legitimacy of the police. Thus when the power to police and judge is accepted, doubts, too, can be accepted. But when those rights—given by law and supported as a social ethic—are questioned at their very roots, they must be affirmed in action. A convincingly single-minded performance quiets nagging doubts and reasserts the uprightness and correctness of those required to impose the law.

Third, we must remember that the very idea of following unfamiliar thought patterns can be threatening; by deterring most people from reexamining controversial and complex issues this, too, serves to maintain the status quo. A very striking example of this phenomenon occurred in the experience of a psychoanalyst of deserved international reputation, whose training should have qualified him to be especially tolerant of unfamiliarity. For several weeks a patient whom he knew well complained of vagueness, lassitude, and disorientation which caused her general difficulty in concentrating on her treatment. She had had a few puffs (literally) of hashish in Morocco two months earlier. The psychiatrist, whom we shall call Dr. Ames, told her that if she used marijuana or any other psychoaffective drugs again, he would have to cease the treatment.

A colleague whom he consulted told him that even if the patient had been psychotic (which she was not) it was unlikely that marijuana would have such prolonged aftereffects. Dr. Ames admitted that what he had told his patient had become his usual routine. He was convinced, he said, that these drugs could stimulate a profound psychic disturbance, and described a case in which a long-lasting psychosis resulted from a single dose of LSD. It was pointed out to him that he had jumped from one drug to another. Dr. Ames accepted this correction with a note of irritation, as if it were fussy of his colleague to insist on such small distinctions. Sufficient doubts had been raised, however, for him to suggest a thorough physical examination for his patient. This showed a chronic, low-grade liver infection, which fully explained the symptoms.

Dr. Ames acknowledged later that his behavior sprang from a fear that his usual methods of working were threatened by his patient's use of drugs during treatment; he felt less confident of his ability to work effectively, and the manifest function of his stern warning was to keep the treatment going successfully. He was right to stipulate certain conditions to help the psychotherapy, but he was unaware of the latent function of his attitude. The emphasis with which he forbade drug use was considerably stronger and went further than would have been the case with almost any other of his patients' activities. His acceptance of stereotyped attitudes without the sort of evidence he usually demanded meant that he had unwittingly become the purveyor of public myths whose very existence functioned to control or make scapegoats of others—the antithesis of good psychiatric treatment. He used these myths to maintain the treatment on a straightforward and familiar level, the status quo.

2. *To define evil*

Public attitudes toward drug use have a second function: that of defining evil. We need evil in order to define good, and we love evil with a truly ambivalent love.

Our interviews illustrated real and practical ways in which the drug users have served this semimystical need. Deviants have always been used to define the boundaries of the socially acceptable, and until recently few people, including users themselves, protested against drug users as the epitome of all that good people didn't want to be.

The portrait of a drug user in the pages of the 1930s Hearst magazines was an emaciated man in his twenties, usually black and probably illegitimate. He came from a squalid home with an alcoholic or criminal father and a prostitute mother. His use of heroin was the culmination of a long history of heavy smoking, drinking, use of other drugs, thievery, and various criminal activities. He was untrustworthy, fluctuating between sudden violence and whining cowardice, particularly when threatened with drug withdrawal.

But in the past few years the situation has changed. Marijuana has become the most frequently used drug, and vast numbers of relatively ordinary middle-class youngsters use it. The stereotype that offered such a clear-cut division between good and bad cannot function as directly today, when the drug user is likely to be someone who is your cousin, nephew, or child.

In a curious way the new drug user elaborates a new definition of evil and in the process creates sympathy for the heroin addict. Edward Kass, Deputy Director of the Massachusetts Division of the Federal Bureau of Narcotics and Dangerous Drugs commented, "I always thought that he [the junkie] and I understood each other pretty well. We got on, but we both knew what side we were on. I used to think that it would be a good thing if I got him and put him away for a long time. But now I see these kids throwing away their lives—these kids who have everything—I think I understand the junkies differently. They're really sick. They really can't help themselves. But these kids are just willful." To Mr. Kass, the new breed of drug users make a conscious choice of immorality, and the fact that they have so chosen gives him the right to judge them.

A number of doctors were interviewed[38] as one part of our research into drug use because theoretically they should know more about drugs than anyone. We wanted to understand how their professional knowledge affected their positions about drug use. They were unanimous in their condemnation of nonmedical drug use, although several of them seemed slightly embarrassed, one, for example, saying, "As a doctor I should be more liberal, but I really think they should all go to jail." In spite of their greater knowledge, they did not differentiate among the variety of drugs that were used nonmedically. On being asked if it was important to distinguish, one answered, "What's the difference if you do it with an axe or a hammer?" When pressed he went on: "These things are dangerous. You can't turn weapons over to children. And that's what all this self-medication that goes on amounts to. Those crazy kids only show people how necessary it is to draw the line about drugs, *all* drugs that aren't carefully prescribed. Maybe they are doing us a service."

The doctors see nonmedical drug use as a direct threat to their professional role, and therefore do not distinguish among drugs. This enables them to draw a line against people who use drugs other than under medical auspices, which then includes anyone who believes in self-medication. The drug user epitomizes the disregard of medical sanctity so thoroughly that he makes it easy to state the virtue of medical supervision.

3. *To protect psychological defenses*

Every child, to defend against early developmental conflicts when he is weaned, must give up the passive pleasure of suckling and, for the sake of his muscular and psychological development, move on to greater autonomy. At some point he not only will strongly reject the bottle but will feel revulsion at the sight of another child clutching that previously beloved object. His revulsion protects him from the pain of his longing.

This universal experience of childhood has some bearing on how the general public reacts to drug use. Drugs seem to hold out the promise of undreamed-of pleasures, and yet at the same time are considered wrong. Now especially, when drug use has increased so vastly and is constantly in the news, many people find it more than ever necessary to take a strong stand against users. Mr. Fry always disliked drug use, but until recently the users were strange and undesirable characters somewhere "out there": now they are constantly thrust under his nose, and he is forced to reaffirm his decision to forgo that sort of pleasure. To strengthen his rejection he must not only decide objectively that he prefers other forms of relaxation; he needs to feel disgust at drug-taking because he fears being overwhelmed by ancient passive longings never completely laid to rest. And, of course, being a rational man, he marshals whatever reasons he can to justify his distaste. In this crisis situation the psychic mechanisms which select what he perceives and inhibit conflicting material, striving to remove offending stimuli, automatically take over and interfere with reason and objectivity.

The violent reaction to the fear of passivity is not unfamiliar. For example, physicians have long known that patients recovering from heart attacks sometimes find bed rest threatening. Doctors have to help the patient preserve an active image of himself while following a strict medical regimen which stirs up great fears of passivity; and, indeed, they have found that some patients, once frightened into immobility after a heart attack, are difficult to reactivate.

Does the latter example lend credence to the fear that giving in to the longed-for passive experience of drug-taking will lead to total incapacity? Not at all. Mr. Fry is not an idiot; his observations and even his irrational reactions are based on valid human experience. Some experiences, however, have gotten out of perspective. To puff a marijuana cigarette or take a shot of heroin does not in reality pose the same threat as a heart attack. We think that with drug use threats of a very different order have become confused in many minds.

However, to show that people fear early passive longings throughout life and require strong defenses against them does not sufficiently explain why psychoaffective drugs have become such a focus for public fear: alcohol, for instance, also offers passive dependency, as so many psychiatrists and social scientists have pointed out. We would suggest that the reputation of marijuana— and still more, LSD—for disorganizing the minds of those who use it, buttressed by the realization that this use is out of medical control and beyond the law, makes these drugs especially terrifying.

In addition to fears of passivity and mental disorganization, another element contributes to making drug use disturbing and distasteful. The marijuana high is essentially a solitary activity. Again, in this respect it differs from alcohol; the typical alcohol user, whether suave at a cocktail party or maudlin in a cheap bar, is gregarious and loquacious. Drugs provide an intensely personal and private experience, and though marijuana users do gather and giggle a bit at each other, the amusement is more bemusement and represents little sharing of the inner experience. In this aspect, drug use resembles masturbation, the "solitary sin." A psychological interpretation of the very "private" drug experience will indicate why the moralistic society that still often thinks of masturbation as self-abuse, and as not only harmful but dirty, should also wish to suppress the drug user.

The new drug users are not divided socially from the public that abhors them. The public, therefore, must maintain a wide psychological distance, and how better than by disgust, self-righteousness and moral revulsion?

We have been comparing drugs with alcohol, and in this context one of the most telling contrasts between them is that alcohol is familiar. Its threat, as well as its capacity to stir up unconscious conflict, is dulled because we have so often watched other people take the trip and emerge unscathed. We do not have the same comforting familiarity with drugs. Howard Becker[39] suggests that when responses to marijuana and LSD are more thoroughly known, the secondary anxiety associated with them will vanish. There is evidence to bear him out: in the last six months of 1967 admission to the Massachusetts Mental Health Center or Bellevue for bad psychedelic trips ran approximately 10 percent a month; in the last six months of 1969, there were only three such admissions. There were probably many more bad trips during that period, but the sufferers knew what was happening and could wait it out. Familiarity can help one to deal with the common human fear of being overwhelmed by one's passive desires. But it will take some time for this familiarity to develop, and (if this psychoanalytic explanation holds) until the defensiveness relaxes, we can expect all the mechanisms just described to continue: the fear of passivity, of mental disorganization, and of solitary and unfamiliar activities.

In this chapter we have discussed some characteristic attitudes held by members of the public, and some of the arguments they offer in support of their attitudes. And we have indicated the underlying concerns that make it important for the public to maintain these attitudes even after they have been shown to be irrational. It has been our intention to show that this repetitious and shifting dialogue has itself become central to the drug "problem" in this country, rather than to refute the arguments point by point. Drug use lends itself to confusion because drug response is so susceptible to personality and atmosphere. Hence, a process by which many people invest emotion into attitudes and discussion, and are not open to changes in opinion, must be faced as an integral part of the issue. When members of the public ask, as they do so often, "What can we do about the drug problem?" we would ask in reply, "Who is the drug problem?" Mr. Fry would be very surprised and, unfortunately, feel very hurt to be told that he was as much a part of the problem as was any youthful drug user.

3

DRUG USE AND DRUG USERS

DRUG USE

Three factors determine how one reacts to a drug: the pharmacological action of the drug itself (what a pharmacological text says it should do); the set, which is the individual's expectation of what the drug will do to him, his personality and personality reaction; finally, the setting (the total physical and social environment in which a drug is taken).

It is possible and even likely that the combined effects of set and setting will overshadow completely the pharmacological action of a drug. For this reason it is difficult to predict how a drug will affect certain individuals when it is taken at different times and in different social situations. The vaguer and less predictable the pharmacological effects of the drug (and marijuana, the drug causing most concern today, is extremely unpredictable), the greater the influence of set and setting. For example, the barbiturates are characteristically used as sedatives, and their pharmacological action is considered to be more consistent than that of marijuana; yet they are also stimulants when taken in certain circumstances. Cocaine, usually a stimulant, can sometimes have powerful sedative effects.

Theories of pharmacological action of a drug established in

58

experiments with laboratory animals in a laboratory setting are often almost entirely irrelevant to the short-term or long-term effects of the same drug in our complex human environment. But most attempts to describe and categorize the effects of drug use began with the pharmacological effects, and experimental laboratory information was used to establish the effect of specific dosage.[1] The essence of the experimental method is the manipulation of the environment so that an observed effect may be ascribed with confidence to a known cause. Opiates can have reasonably consistent effects under laboratory conditions, so when in 1902 Charles Towne, a New York physician, described the addictive triad—increased dosage, craving for more drugs, and withdrawal syndrome when the drug is removed—he could support it with the results of laboratory experiments with animals.

The categorization of drugs was largely based on whether or not they were physiologically addictive, and this method of categorization predominated for many years, despite the severe limitations of laboratory-gained information. The result was that the physiological effect of the drug was taken to be the crucial factor in drug use, and although it was admitted that individual reactions varied, this was regarded as unimportant. Even today the common differentiation of drugs into "hard" and "soft" vaguely refers to whether the drug is physiologically addicting. This leads to confusing, contradictory situations: opiate derivatives are always considered "hard" —which in the public mind tends to mean "dangerous"—while LSD, a strong drug producing intense physiological and psychological responses, is "soft."

By 1925 observers[2] were noticing that drugs such as phenobarbital or bromides, which did not produce a consistent physiological addictive syndrome in animals, caused intense attachments in people, raising the question of "psychological habituation," so named because the problem lay less in the power of the particular drug to cause a physiological addiction than in the weakness of the user. The set—what the person brought with him to the drug experience—was recognized as a critical variable, but a basic differentiation was made, like that between hard and soft drugs, between drugs that caused addiction and those that caused habituation.

Slowly, reports[3] appeared showing that this differentiation was meaningless except in laboratory animals. Drugs such as the barbiturates, bromides, or nicotine, which were thought to be "psychologically habituating" rather than "physiologically addicting," caused pernicious and dangerous withdrawal symptoms in some individuals, while some opiate users did not develop either tolerance or withdrawal syndrome even after continued heavy use. But the question of drug use was complicated by so many political, legal, moral, psychological, and social concerns that this new understanding did not lead to research and clarification; it merely added semantic confusion.

In 1963, the World Health Organization's committee[4] on drugs capable of producing addiction attempted to clear the air by a classification according to the characteristic syndromes produced by heavy use. Thus, the sedative or stimulating capacity of a drug, and the incidence of a withdrawal syndrome after heavy use, became merely some of the properties of each drug. When one spoke of dependency of the amphetamine type, the basic characteristics of the response were clear to everybody.

This method of categorization based on dependency used the drug effect itself as a take-off point, and by laying less emphasis on the user's physiological responses made it easier to differentiate with greater subtlety among the potency, differential sensitivities, the behavior arising from the use of particular drugs, and—this only by implication—the various pleasures to be derived from them. The concept of dependency per se in the WHO categorization includes the psychological response to any extensive drug use and raises set to an equivalent position with the pharmacological effects. People who are dependency-prone, it implies, become dependent more readily than people who are not, and strong drugs spell quick trouble for the former, though weaker drugs are less dangerous. "Independent" people, by implication, can withstand a mild drug for a long time and have a fighting chance even with a strong one. The WHO position, in which strength and weakness could be considered moral properties, has puritanical overtones. Addiction is defined as a "state of periodic or chronic intoxication detrimental to the individual and to society," without any attempt to explain what "detrimental" means. The WHO classification in fact perpetuates the medical tradition of presuming that people caught up with drugs suffer, except in unusual circumstances, from personality defects.[5]

Before the drug explosion of the 1960s, much of what was written about drug use by psychiatrists, and particularly by psychoanalysts, emphasized the personality of the user. Learned articles[6] discussed unconscious motives rooted deeply in the user's character, often beginning with infancy and the earliest mother-child interaction. The typical drug user had a weak ego, a limited capacity to tolerate frustration, was unconsciously preoccupied with the oral development stages. These early concerns, it was thought, dominated later relationships with people, who were seen as objects, and led to an overwhelming preoccupation with a part-object—drugs. And, indeed, the evidence supported this view until the early 1960s. But with the increase in marijuana use the evidence no longer supports the conclusions.

The WHO categorization pays little attention to setting. Nor do the psychiatric and psychoanalytic approaches, which are concerned with demonstrating how the drug user's current choices are determined by the subtle, pervasive, unconscious influences of his past.

Sociologists categorize drug use according to the background of the user, and end up using the past in the same way: the son of immigrant parents from southern Europe, Puerto Rico, or the Deep South is shown to be more likely to use heroin than a child from "middle-class" groups.

The attitude of the WHO and the psychoanalytic and sociological approaches all emphasized susceptibility, and took heavy use for granted. Little attention was paid to the occasional user. Until the enormous change in drug use of the past few years, he scarcely mattered. But with the explosion of marijuana use and the hysterical public response things have changed. The vast majority of those who use marijuana are, in the old terms, occasional users, and it is important to distinguish them from heavy users, particularly of such drugs as heroin. But usually, the public and opinion-forming bodies make no distinctions. Some writers, such as Keniston[7] and Geber,[8] noticed this glaring mistake and tried to make the necessary distinctions. To someone who uses marijuana occasionally, and under certain social conditions, drug use is essentially peripheral; Keniston calls him a "taster": he smokes pot a few times a year at certain social events. Regular or chronic users are called heads, and cannabis smoking is central to their life-style.

The emphasis on the life-style of the user attaches importance to the social setting in which drug use occurs. The differentiating factor is how often the drug is used, and the personality of the user is examined only in order to determine what importance he attaches to drug use—whether it is central or peripheral to his life. Of course, this describes rather than explains where the individual stands in relation to his drug, and takes little account of the practical problem that neither the informed, opinion-making public nor the law makes much of the difference between peripheral and central use.

DRUG USE AND DEVIANCY

In the post-Civil War period it may well have been that those who were addicted to morphine were, on the whole, susceptible and disturbed individuals, but at that period addiction was regarded as an infirmity; drugs were readily available, and the addict could expect support and encouragement from friends and family rather than reproach and condemnation. After passage of the Harrison Narcotic Act in 1914, the changed legal position of the addict shifted public concern to the moral decay of the drug user and to the evil of the drug responsible for his downfall.

Deviance has always been defined from outside; an action

violating a particular social or legal norm is considered deviant by those who do not do it. It is our intention to show that modern drug users, though they are held to be deviants, differ little from nonusers—except in their attitude toward drug use. Their drug use is only an auxiliary trait for them, but society perceives it as a master trait. We discuss principally marijuana users, and we believe that their decision to try this drug (and even some others) is influenced more by social pressure than by personality factors. We submit that after some time attitudes toward marijuana use held by the general public, by the user's family and friends, and by the law can have a pronounced effect on his values, standards and, in the end, his personality. As we shall show, it is valid to view a young marijuana user's continuing use of drugs as a response to the social forces that have labeled him deviant.

DRUG USERS

During part of our study[9] we gathered data from a sample of English students and apprentices. About 15 percent of both groups turned out to be drug users; the vast majority had used marijuana between one and one hundred times, while a small percentage occasionally used amphetamines. The users and nonusers in this study were progressing in their careers at virtually equal rates. The groups differed little on other levels. Political opinions, for instance, varied according to class rather than drug use, and the political radicals came from the student group and not from among the apprentices. In the English apprentice group both users and nonusers tended to be more conservative than the student group; in both groups the users tended to be somewhat more liberal toward abortion, homosexuality, the abolition of capital punishment, and other controversial social issues. Nonusers and users differed greatly as to how they preferred to spend their leisure time. The users tended to be more experimental, were more interested in pop music, art movies, and so on. Nonusers drank more on social occasions, dated less, and enjoyed more conventional forms of entertainment; they also tended to be more satisfied with their jobs than the users. But the two groups did not differ obviously on how much they enjoyed their work, on the quality of imagination they brought to it, or on questions about working per se. The only basic differences the study revealed were in their attitudes toward drug use and their knowledge of the effects of drugs. The nonusers tended to see the users as untidy, antisocial, irresponsible, and potentially difficult members of the social group. The users did not share this opinion, though they were aware that this was how others saw them. They regarded themselves as socially freer and more interested in social change. They defined the nonusers just as the nonusers defined themselves—more cautious, more accepted by society at large, and more law-abiding. This indicated the capacity of the users to make accurate and reliable social observations.

In another part of our study,[10] we questioned a group of students from liberal eastern colleges in the United States who were split fifty-fifty between users and nonusers. They volunteered for testing in answer to an advertisement calling for students to participate in a psychological experiment. They were not distinguishable on any social or psychological dimension other than drug use. Both groups came from approximately the same class background and were pursuing their careers with equal rapidity. They had similar personality structures, with a low overall incidence of neurosis, and showed little difference in their political opinions. They divided in the same way as the English group in how they spent their leisure time, the users getting more involved in experimental activities and drinking less alcohol than the nonusers. The groups in this exclusively student study did not show as sharp a differentiation in the attitude of nonusers toward drug users as the earlier study had revealed, though both groups regarded the users as less cautious and controlled and more experimental than the nonusers. However, there was a significant difference in that nonusers expressed considerable fear of any drug, of the risk that it would interfere with their capacity for work, with personality organization, initiative, and responsibility. Users did not see themselves as differing from nonusers on any of these levels as a result of their drug use, but were aware of the nonusers' views.

How does this picture square with previous investigations of drug users? Probably the most comprehensive study is *The Road to H* by Isadore Chein.[11] This book is principally concerned with heroin use, but many of its conclusions are relevant to drug use in general. We found Chein's book particularly helpful because it describes three pressures influencing people in the direction of drug use: the desire for status, the desire for certain kinds of intense personal relationship, and rebellious feelings against existing social standards. Certainly these factors heavily influenced the users among our sample who had begun regular use before 1962 and used drugs other than marijuana. Even among those who had recently begun using only marijuana there was a small but significant group whom we described as "in-for-anything" types and fell into the same category as those described by Chein though they came from middle-class backgrounds, not immigrant-ghetto. They had many more affinities with the drug user of the 1930s—the more stereotyped delinquent deviant—than with the marijuana users of the 1960s. They form part of the first group that we describe in Chapter 1, and we suspect that it is from this group that the evidence for drug progression is gained. They are disturbed and will try anything—drugs, people, alcohol, or sex—and because of personality difficulty are much more likely to get into trouble with the law. Any study of arrests will show a much higher percentage of this group than of any other.

Chein's idea that the drug user desires status is certainly true for a minority-group youngster whose father has just migrated. The people who use drugs in his neighborhood are the big shots: they make money, wear flashy clothes, drive new cars. The boy wanting to break out of his background requires a model and longs for status; he will naturally emulate one who stands out from the gray faceless pattern of economic and social deprivation, and *how* his model has broken out would seem less important than that he *has*.

Few of Chein's factors hold true in the same way with the

modern marijuana user. We found little evidence in studies or in our own interviews that most of those who had begun to use marijuana in the past two or three years thought that it afforded them much status among their friends. It was so generally accepted that users did not feel they were associating themselves with big, brave people. In fact, one third of the users we interviewed had stopped, not because it was against the law but simply because they did not like it or because it was too much trouble; this did not represent loss of status.

The other two pressures influencing people in favor of drug use—a desire for intense personal relationships, and ambivalent feelings about contemporary society, particularly as represented by a number of our most prominent social institutions—do eventually become important factors to the marijuana user. According to Chein[12] these pressures are motivating forces for heroin users, but we find that initially they are not very important to the marijuana user. Their importance does grow when the latter finds himself labeled deviant, and a direct result of this is that his psychological and social position—set and setting—change markedly.

In 1972, we have a bigger illicit-drug problem than we had when the Federal Bureau of Narcotics was founded in 1930; everybody from Timothy Leary to Spiro Agnew will grant that we must be doing something wrong. We would like to suggest a new approach, one that views the drug revolution as part of a larger social process. Specifically, we suspect that the increasing switch from alcohol-based drugs, still used by the older generation, to marijuana and psychedelic drugs, preferred by youth, could be the result of our recent and still continuing advances in electronic technology.

We are experiencing a social upheaval of which the so-called drug problem is merely the part on which many older people choose to center their fears. We may even be facing a change in the nature of consciousness, induced by our technology and brought into every house by television.

Of course, there are many factors other than technology at work in the emergence of the drug culture. But none of these other influences alone, nor many of them together, could have caused the dramatic cultural revolution of the 1960s, in which pot use, for instance, skyrocketed from a few hundred thousand to somewhere between five and twenty million, and psychedelic fallout, in the form of music, light-shows, new cinematic techniques, and other by-products, inundated our country with the mystique of the electrochemical turn-on. The very phrase "turn on" itself, in fact, indicates the primarily electronic origins of the transformation that is occurring. So does the fact that most users are under 25.

This group has also been called the television generation—and not only in the United States. Marshall McLuhan suggests that electronics creates a "global village," and indeed it is conceivable that a French youth who watches television has more in common with his contemporaries in the United States than with the older generation of his own country.

No one would deny the all-encompassing, all-enveloping nature of the television medium, and most children experience its power early in life. Mothers quickly discovered television's pacifying effect on the very young. Many children, sociologists tell us, have spent more hours in front of the set by the age of 12 than they have spent in school. Finally, hard evidence, gathered from interviews with 1,000 pot smokers, has led us to believe that electronics preceded chemistry in altering their consciousness.

Alcohol was around for centuries before the problem of alcoholism became a massive social issue. The wine and beer consumed by the Greeks, Romans, Goths, and other peoples evidently produced few hard-core drunkards until two major technological breakthroughs occurred. In mid-fifteenth-century Italy, the process of distilling alcohol was discovered. Then, early in the seventeenth century, improved agricultural methods provided a surplus of grain, and alcohol in large quantities became available. Gin, rum, and whiskey appeared in a flood, and along with them came myth and misconception. It was believed that those who could drink huge quantities were stronger than those who could not, that alcoholic drinks were aphrodisiacs and possibly even love potions, and that what was thought and said under its influence was wiser and more profound than what was thought or spoken while sober. (Note that the same old claims are now made for marijuana.) Even sobriety itself acquired the appellation "stone cold," and seemed a dismal state in comparison with the warm good-fellowship of drunkenness, just as pot smokers regard non-users as "plastic" or relatively emotionless.

These myths and exaggerations had widespread and catastrophic repercussions; for instance, many artists of this period died of alcoholism. It was two centuries—some would say three, considering that there are still over five million alcoholics in this country alone—before a measure of social control began to reappear. And, of course, even this degree of adjustment did not occur until after the most stringent measure of political control—total prohibition—had conspicuously failed.

Similarly, the earliest writings of the Chinese, Egyptians, and Greeks indicates a comprehensive knowledge of drugs that fall more or less into the psychedelic category, including mandragora, belladonna, henbane—and marijuana. For millennia before the arrival of the white man, the Indians of both Mexico and the southern plains of the United States were using psychedelic drugs, including peyote (from which came mescaline, the chemical that much later turned on Aldous Huxley to the mind-expansion cult) and the "magic mushroom," *Psilocybe mexicana* (which gave Timothy Leary *his* first trip, before he ever heard of LSD). In the ancient Near East, there was another "magic mushroom" cult, which probably influenced the religious concepts of the Greeks, Jews, and early Christians, and which still lingers in Siberia. And yet there was never a mass-based psychedelic-drug *problem* until the 1960s—that is, until the first TV generation grew out of childhood.

Before centering our attention on television, however, we may avoid oversimplification by considering some of the other social factors that fed into the creation of the drug revolution.

In 1910 the Carnegie Foundation produced a vitriolic official document, the Flexner Report. This study revealed defective medi-

cal training and appalling inadequacies in basic medical research
in the United States. As a result, immediate and widespread
reforms occurred which revolutionized American medicine and the
public image of doctors. But this also propelled the profession into
a conservative and frightened position on controversial social
issues, especially abortion and drug use. When the Harrison
Narcotic Act was passed in 1914, doctors were glad to be free of
the "dope" problem and quite willing to let the government
grapple with it. The government proceeded in the only way it
knew. The addict was defined as a criminal, and scientific investigations virtually stopped as drug issues became defined as police
issues.

Then World War II and the GI Bill changed the concept of
higher education in the United States as huge numbers of students
poured into the colleges. The first wave of new students in the
forties and fifties were terrorized by the uncertainties of that war
and their childhood memories of the Great Depression; they
accepted security and life without risk as basic values. But by the
sixties students felt more removed from those catastrophes and
experienced the need for different goals and meanings.

They questioned the society that had tolerated Joseph McCarthy
and had failed to come to grips with problems of poverty and
social justice. They turned to activity—racial justice in Mississippi, international cooperation in the Peace Corps, sexual freedom in the colleges. Music, clothes, and art all opposed the past.

At the same time, the good faith of the government in general
was in question. From the U2 incident, the Bay of Pigs, and the
Gulf of Tonkin to body counts and Spiro Agnew, young people
found it hard to believe official pronouncements. Their wish for a
government they could trust led to a desire for a new politics, a
new morality, and a new intoxicant.

Thus by the 1960s a variety of social forces coalesced to create
a climate where nonmedical drug use could flourish. The emotional responses to this climate can be heard in any discussion of
drug use with young users.

One subject in our study, aged 19, said: "Sure, I use pot. It feels good. Pot slows the world down a little. I listen to myself better. Slow and hazy, but somehow clear, like a movie in slow motion or a TV show with a screen so small that it gets right into your head so you can feel what it shows on the pictures."

Another, aged 17, said: "Hell, I used grass since I was 14. This year I dropped acid and for a little while I thought it would be a bummer, but I came down and it was all right. Hell, that's enough drugs for me, although I'll try acid again. All the pictures inside my eyeballs made me think about the country and me. Music was on and I didn't really listen—it was just part of everything and I sensed everything else. I listened to people and saw they meant well but were playing games. Mostly though I thought about how I sensed them. We were all together but I watched them from here like on a TV show." Similar references to television appear again and again in our interviews.

Radio, previously one of the major influences on infants, encouraged a high degree of psychic development because the child heard people speaking on the set and this encouraged verbalization. Even musical programs, undoubtedly soothing, were interspersed with words. Probably a child learned to respond to certain words quite early in life—one could see a small child's head jerk when "Stop" came from the set. To take the next step, and to learn to understand the meaning of specific words, requires another, higher level of intellectual development, and radio made demands on the infant to attain this next level. Learning to read is also a process in which the child is rewarded for attaining higher levels of abstraction and minimizing or inhibiting feelings and sensory impressions to concentrate on a linear message.

But in the homes of the generation now reaching the age of 20, television was far more widespread than radio, and the child could participate in the experience it offered without the intellectual structures that radio demanded. The developing child's first task is to differentiate between self and the outside world. It seems possible that television permits and encourages a oneness with the screen, a sense of total participation, that does not emphasize that difference. Press the button and everything is there: turn on, tune

in—and even relax and drop out for a while. The boundaries
between inside and outside imperceptibly become diffuse. When a
field or some other outside scene is shown on the small screen, a
two-year-old tries to walk into it.

McLuhan's[13] concept of television as a low-definition medium
means that the images, particularly in contrast to print, are sufficiently indistinct to encourage "creative" participation on the part
of the watcher. This encouragement to participate, combined with
the screen's insistence that you watch it—try ignoring a turned-on
screen as you might a phonograph or a radio—gives rise to a
situation where the viewer must use his own inner processes to
complete an external situation. Rather than setting the task of
separating ourselves from external reality, television insists on
diminishing such boundaries.

Many of the current crop of drug users describe this melting
away of boundaries between their internal and external worlds as
their most important reaction to marijuana use. They insist that
organizing sensory impressions is less important than being "in"
them.

Again, many people have noted that we live in the movie
generation; modern producers, and certain young people influenced by the cinema, have indicated that the difference between
their relationship to the visual and to the printed page has been
crucial in their development. They talk about movies "washing
over" them to create sensations; they lose themselves in an experience without having to be able to describe or analyze it.

Those describing the effect of marijuana tend to stress the lack,
or rather the irrelevance, of the analytic, penetrating, active approach with its inhibition of direct sensory experience. One is *with*
the music, rather than bringing one's intellectual and emotional
powers to bear on the music. When one is experiencing a high on
marijuana, one is expected to be able to reach a state of com-
munion with one's companions that involves understanding without the medium of discrete (verbal) ideas. The wholeness of the
experience, the sensation, the understanding occur diffusely rather
than in a more logical, circumscribed step-by-step fashion.

Using an analogy from physics, one might say it partakes of the field nature of magnetic action, rather than the sequential nature of mechanical processes. But in the mechanical, preelectronic age we learned to think only in step-by-step sequences and, hence, this experience appears "mystical."

Television seems like just another gadget to adults, but to a child it is as important as the refrigerator or the toilet—and psychoanalysis has shown the importance of those facilities in the development of the young.

Contemporary drug users are formed by society, and also prepare society for future developments. They have undoubtedly already influenced certain values in modern North American society. Our institutions—schools, churches, the law—reflect a social hierarchy based on the capacity to produce or achieve. The drug users, however, have begun to promulgate a participating, contemplative, and experiencing society, which is very accurately called the counterculture.

Drugs other than marijuana are involved in this emerging pattern. The birth-control pill, for example, may be as influential as cannabis in the shift toward permissiveness; and LSD and other so-called mind-expanding drugs are taken not only to enable the individual to explore his inner self but also to break down the boundaries between people. The new value consists in being *in* oneself and others as totally as possible rather than producing and achieving *with* others.

This combination of increased individualism—doing one's own thing—together with a desire for closer bonds with a group—"Do we have to live in our own skins?"—presents a paradox that has ramifications in the larger society. Our culture now presents many of its middle-class members, at least, with a new range of decisions. Previously our choices of occupation, mate, and residence were difficult indeed and, once made, tended to preclude alternatives.

Now in the United States we have arranged for the middle class a prolonged adolescence during which a vast number of options are available. The problem is less getting what we want by overcoming obstacles and inhibitions than being able to decide what to reject out of all the possibilities open to us. We can break with our parents, get an education, shift academic field at almost any age, have a variety of sexual partners, and choose from a number of jobs. We can move to many parts of the country and think in terms of what climate as well as what social milieu we prefer. As our options proliferate, role definitions of all sorts become increasingly less clear.

Obviously this range of choice is not open to some, but enough people are presented with it for LSD users to be able to ask why dropping out should not be one of the options. When the drug user wants to have it all ways, to be at one with himself and with others, is he not reflecting a society that wishes to extend all options indefinitely, that refuses to reject anything? A society that, through the wonders of an electronic miracle, transcends all physical boundaries and offers vicarious participation in every human experience? We can literally see men killed in Vietnam before the Army knows they are dead, just as we can see an astronaut hurtling into endless space the instant it occurs. And on television the event is right there inside your house; to go outside, to do something else, makes a discrete event that is separated from the rest of your life. Almost all of us can remember the first time we *went* to the theater; and if we try hard, we can even take a pretty good guess as to which was the first movie we saw. This separation from the rest of your life permits the event to be compartmentalized into an external experience. Such external events may be moving and, by forcing you to feel or think, may enlarge your personality, but you distinctly *go* to them.

On the other hand, can you imagine anyone born since television entered the home remembering his first television show? The medium is so pervasive, so much part of our most intimate environment, that when we share a live experience on television— who can forget the murder of Lee Harvey Oswald?—we participate totally. By being insistently there, in our bedrooms and kitchens, this medium prevents us from delineating it as an unusual external event. Then, by its low definition, which forces us to fill in with fantasy and sensation what is only suggested, it further floods us with intrapsychic data. That would mean that mechanically oriented people who grew up before television's impact would hardly know what the field-oriented younger generation is talking about; and the youngsters would also be baffled by their elders. Is this not exactly what is happening?

Drug users claim that the drug experience permits a controlled descent into a realm of benign chaos. They speak of "cosmic unity" and the mystic "now" in a way that often repels those of us still print-dominated, who search for semantic clarity, rules of evidence, and a reasonable objectivity. Might they not simply be trying to explain differing patterns of sensation and thought—a way of perceiving the world separate from that demanded of us before television?

Thus we do not believe that a young man or woman who uses cannabis in today's social setting is per se neurotic. Neither do we believe that the turned-on generation found their electronic baby-sitter so gratifying that they seek to return to that early infantile experience. On the contrary, we think of the television medium as a subtle and pervasive teacher.

There is abundant evidence that the modern child learns an enormous amount—facts, ideas, values—from his watching experience. When he starts school he knows much more than his counterpart of twenty-five years ago, but most of what is learned is chaotic and disorganized, drawn from commercials, thrillers, educational programs. When an educational program such as "Sesame Street" is written to meet the learning potential of children, one realizes with awe the organized teaching capacity of the medium.

Television's ability to effect what we dub "cognitive style" can also be demonstrated in other areas than drug use. For instance, the norm for the pretelevision child, after he became a regular reader (fifth grade and beyond), was to read one book at a time. He could be diverted by other activities but would want to finish the thread of that book before starting another. Today's child seems much more at ease reading several books at a time. Somehow he can keep the different entities all going at once.

The insistence of the pretelevision generation that psychic boundaries need to be sharp and clear indicates anxiety about what happens if they are not. McLuhan's comments,[14] many of which were written before drug use became popular and the idea of a counterculture reached its present height, show his prescient awareness of what was to come:

> Television, in a highly visual culture, drives us inward in depth into a totally nonvisual universe of involvement. It is destroying our entire political, educational, social, institutional life. Television will dissolve the entire fabric of society in a short time. If you understood its dynamics, you would choose to eliminate it as soon as possible. Television changes the sensory and the psychic life. It is an Oriental form of experience, giving people a somber, profound sense of involvement.

This whole passage, especially McLuhan's unabashed use of the strong word "destroy," sounds almost as if it came from some underground newspaper advocating the drug revolution, or some government publication deploring it, yet it does not mention chemicals at all; it deals entirely with electronics. No wonder the pretelevision generation is so confused and so frightened by what is happening. They see only the drug aspect of the revolution in consciousness, and drugs are associated in their minds with narcotics and addiction; most of them believe that Oriental and tribal modes of consciousness are in all ways inferior to the mechanical Western mentality. They can literally believe that the current shift in sensibility will "destroy" their "entire political, educational, social, institutional life."

We would prefer to use McLuhan's more neutral word "change" and quiet many fears. After all, every society we know about has a way of getting high. We know too little about different cultures' acceptance and rejection of intoxicants, but we do know something of the psychology of intoxication. Alcohol generally relaxes minor inhibitions of behavior and promotes gregariousness. A society that insists on habits of linear thought, sensory detachment, uniformity of "point of view" toward cognitive material, and repeatability requires early and powerful inhibitions against spontaneous, unregulated feelings and scattered, unorganized, sensory responses. Thus a drug that gives them the opportunity to test the boundaries of such inhibitions easily attains popularity. The average, nonneurotic individual can, with two or three martinis, reassure himself that his powerful inhibitions have not become a total psychic cage. From childhood he has watched people drink and has seen the results as not too frightening. There was no hysteria in his family about the fact that he drank, no question of sending him to a psychiatrist or of regarding him as a criminal.

Could we not look at the modern nonneurotic marijuana user in the same light? Television has taught him a style of looking at the world, first as a single, global entity, then as an environment that demands a sharpened, sensory involvement. He constantly tests the extent of his capacity to absorb new perceptions and control them harmoniously. Just as with the alcohol drinker, his drug of choice contains the counterphobic anticipation of more total dissolution, here of psychic boundaries rather than inhibitions. It is not accidental that adverse reactions to marijuana sharply diminish when the effects of the drug are thoroughly familiar to potential users. Our interviews indicate that such reactions are far more frequent among the pretelevision generation when they are talked into trying it (sometimes by their children).

Of course, one must be careful to differentiate actual changes in perception or psychological response from the ideology of a movement. Changes in reading habits or shifts in capacity to tolerate sensory impressions reflect genuine changes in the way people grow up. As a result of being raised on television, these modern youngsters may have subtly changed in their responses to the world. However, this does not mean that the particular slogans, movements, and group activities that are now popular are directly related to early experience with television. There are fads and cults today, as there always have been, and the current drug craze may just be one of them. One must look deeply to find which changes are permanent and which are merely temporary adjustments.

In the present social setting, where drug use is labeled criminal and drug users deviants, subcultural responses—such as anger, exhibitionism, alienation, anxiety, the desire to be different—are stimulated. Often it is hard to tell which is part of the new consciousness and which is in response to social persecution. All we can do is to remember that such a difference exists. Then we will not dismiss new insights because they are clothed in revolutionary rhetoric or polemic; nor will we uncritically accept loose allegations and utopian visions merely because they come from alleged spokesmen for the wave of the future.

Psychologists have long known that what we allow ourselves to perceive is simply a matter of thresholds; men with game legs notice limps which the rest of us do not. The lowering of perceptual thresholds resulting from the television experience permits greater participation in sensory response which, in turn, leads to changes in behavior. Almost everything about those growing up will show change, including the chemical they use to get high on. Should not this awareness calm some of our fears?

Even if the hysteria subsides, we are left with the mighty task of transcending and mastering the changes brought about by modern technology. We cannot have the world as it was before television. Nor can we return to the concept of drug use that was current in the 1940s and 1950s. If we are to avoid whatever the marijuana equivalent of Hogarth's Gin Lane might be (and we should remember that New York's 15,000 saloons were replaced after Prohibition by 32,000 speakeasies), we must not spend our time decrying the young as deviants or neurotics.

We must not, above all, fall back on cheap moralizing or simplistic arguments based on "horrible examples." There *will* be hard cases, and people will suffer because the process of mastering this technological miracle and learning to tolerate the social disruptions accompanying it will be long and difficult. But we must make the effort. Otherwise we will have a vast, self-fulfilling prophecy: by defining a huge number of people as antisocial (criminal), we change their motives and create hatred, disruption, and true rebellion.

SOCIAL SETTING AND PERSONALITY CHANGE

Generally, when psychiatrists examine people who have used drugs regularly for some time—marijuana, psychedelics, or other drugs —they find a fair degree of personality disorganization. This disorganization permits or encourages primitive motives, so that the drug user is described as someone with powerful passive or dependent longings leading to indolence or apathy. He is said to deal with aggressive feelings by rigid, total defenses such as re-action formation ("If you don't come out for peace, I'll kill you") and is considered to be one whose cravings are direct and power-ful, with an intolerance of frustration. In such interviews psychia-trists stress the underlying personality factors that led to drug use and play down the effect of the drug and particularly the influence of social setting.

The Zinberg-Weil study[15] raised the question, concerning chronic marijuana users, about what aspect of drugs, set, and setting was responsible for the observed personality factors of vague paranoia, excessive anxiety, and dependency.

The researchers wondered whether these factors preexisted in users' personalities and led them to seek out drugs before they were popular; whether (and this was the drug users' contention) the persistent hostility of the social setting had brought about defensive reactions which resulted in personality changes; or, finally, whether the personality syndrome was a direct effect of the drug.

But this study would not necessarily differentiate between changes brought about by the drug use itself and the impact on personality of hostile interpersonal and social responses. There are among drug users many disturbed people who, influenced by the vast publicity drugs receive, unhesitatingly choose them as their vehicle of expression. There is no doubt that in some cases pre-existing personality disturbance is the crucial variable in a choice of drug use. But among other subjects of equivalent age and social status, one could not easily find personality differences between users and nonusers.

At first we were preoccupied in our interviews with what personality factors may have influenced some of them to become users. Principally we searched for expressions of dependency, antisocial aggressiveness, or personal isolation that may have determined the choice. It took a long time before we decided that most contemporary drug users drifted into the choice through mild peer-group pressure and chance.

If then we rule out preexisting personality disturbance, where do we look for the source of the personality changes that seem to accompany continued drug use?

The drug users blame the social setting. They are convinced that changes in attitudes, personality, and demeanor follow a growing and deepening awareness that a user is regarded as deviant in society.

In a theoretical approach to the problem, Erik Erikson[16] brings intrapsychic, interpersonal, and social factors together in a total developmental scheme. He characterizes each phase of the life cycle as a specific developmental task to be solved. This solution is prepared for by previous phases and is carried further in subsequent phases. He assumes an inborn coordination with a predictable environment, and this idea of mutuality specifies that crucial coordination occurs between the developing individual and his human (i.e., social) environment. The caretakers are coordinated with the developing individual by their specific responsiveness to his needs and by specific needs of their own.

Sociologist Erving Goffman, on the other hand, argues that a man's attitude toward himself is formed by the particular social situation society has placed him in, and other people's response to it. In *Asylum*,[17] his study of hospitalized mental patients, Goffman describes how friends, family, and society at large see the individual as patient, and thus he becomes what he is labeled. It is a view diametrically opposite to Freud's.

In our study of attitudes toward drug use we seek a middle way by illuminating the complex hierarchy of psychological structures within the psychic apparatus. They vary from simple automatic defense to more complex attitudes, values, ideological beliefs, and identities compatible with those accepted by society. These structures require social stimuli unique to that society, not only to maintain themselves but to develop. Though Erikson accepts instinctual vicissitudes, he insists that simple psychological structures develop into complex values through current experience, and become a complementary series of experiences. The original modes of behavior (Freud associated them with specific organs— the mouth, anus, genitalia) develop into differentiated social behavior through the impact of traditions, institutions, values, and attitudes provided by the society in which the individual develops and by the social places it makes available to him.

For an individual to grow up in any society, it is assumed that the internal structures and the codetermined socially provided rituals must fall into a lawful sequence of differentiation. And it is in precisely this area that Erikson's theoretical explorations add a dimension to our study of response to drug use. One must differentiate a complex sociopsychological response to a life situation from the rapidly changing social scene, which cannot remain static if it is to accommodate the cultural changes necessary to this cogwheeling process. Shifts in society that would formerly have been only quantitative now become, by their nature and their social potential, qualitative. The young person experimenting with marijuana or LSD knows that the general attitude of society toward the former, at least, is slowly changing. But given his kinship with his peer group, his use of the drug makes him deviant to the culture at large, and the result is a qualitatively different relationship to society. The change in attitude toward marijuana is not matched by the slow rate of change in public morality and the law—that is, there is no stable psychological regularity in the social organization's response to the individual.

How can one place the individual in this newly disruptive social context? He is part of a social system whose pressures form attitudes and values. These are part of his accepted self, and not "neurotic," even though his life may be inhibited. Compatible social rituals must be legitimized into a developmental scheme that accepts social change so that individual and social needs can be coordinated.

An example of how different levels of motivation function is the situation of a surgeon as seen psychoanalytically. If his motivation to become a surgeon is traced to its most primitive beginnings, we might find early sadistic tendencies in an aggressive youngster whose energies were directed against living things. Our psychoanalysis quickly shows us that it is not these early sadistic desires that make him a surgeon, although they may remain an underlying force. From early on he develops secondary derivative motives which allow him to grow up and perform an exacting, deeply humanitarian function instead of becoming a killer. His capacity to organize, his curiosity, his intelligence, and his manual dexterity are recognized by others in the society and rewarded. Over his life-span this mutual interaction so strengthens his secondary motives that they provide the impetus for his daily actions, the basis for a self-definition known as an identity, and an absolute defense against the breakthrough of those earliest preoccupations we call primary motives.

At a certain point in the life of this surgeon, he no longer needs social reinforcement to maintain his defenses against primary motives. His desires for an ethical standard, human dignity, rational evidence, and the like are thoroughly automatized into perceptual and discharge thresholds. But at what point does this occur? Certainly not in school or college, probably not in medical school or during the early years of surgical training. Until his identity has coalesced through experience and interaction, he is at least to some extent vulnerable. Without the consistent support of the law, his teachers, colleagues, patients, friends, and family, who not only say that he is within his rights to stick a knife into fellow humans but commend him for it, he would falter. It is unlikely that he would slip back to the pervert or killer stage, but he might easily become disorganized and apathetic, even at odds with society.

Young drug users have probably not reached the age at which

their identities coalesce. They have developed complex secondary motives which have begun a cogwheeling process in this society, leading them toward specific social tasks. Most of our contemporary drug users come from backgrounds that allow them to expect social approval from a reasonable trial-and-error effort. At no point did they expect most social institutions to be arrayed against them. Their families, discovering their drug use, become hysterical, rush them to psychiatrists, and an incredible 43 percent would turn them over to the police. Their schools and colleges threaten expulsion; the law proposes penalties that classify them with murderers; and public officials, through the mass media, suggest that they undermine the foundations of society itself.

This response of the social setting not only interferes with the development of a coherent identity but weakens the secondary motivations already prominent, thus permitting the intrusion of earlier primitive motives. The personality is too well developed for such motives to enter consciousness or behavior in any direct form. Few marijuana smokers, as one comprehensive study shows, are troubled by the more or less realistic primitive illusions/delusions that plague psychotics. But with the withdrawal of external social support, psychic energy is needed to keep the repressed early ideas unconscious. The defenses are weakened and the personality organization becomes less stable. This permits ideas about magic, transcendental experience, and visceral expression, which roughly correspond to primitive impulses, to flourish while those ego interests decrease that are dependent on social nutriments such as desire for accomplishment and organized expression of thought. We find this syndrome in drug users; and if our argument holds, it occurs because of the influence of the social setting and not because of early personality disturbance or the drug itself.

There are other straws in the wind which, though not in themselves definitive evidence, offer some support for this hypothesis. Our sample included a number of regular marijuana users who began to smoke when they were over 30. A small percentage of these subjects reported having an occasional bad experience ("I get paranoid about the people with me, I am suspicious about what they are doing." "I got sick to my stomach and then my heart began to pound and it seemed that I would never be able to pull myself together." "I have lost control and been 'taken over' by an outside force or will which is evil in intent for a while"). *None* showed the characteristic regressive syndrome. They resented being forced into a deviant role almost as much as their younger counterparts, but were less dependent on social institutions for the support of their secondary motivations and could maintain their delineated social course despite feelings of conflict around drug use. This group with a well-defined identity could usually accept their marijuana smoking as a single, deviant activity and resist seeing themselves more completely as deviants with the accompanying urge to become what you are labeled.

Twenty-two of our subjects had used psychedelic drugs frequently (25 to 250 times) and were members of communes. During the interviews we were initially struck by the extensive presentation of the sort of regressive position previously described. They characteristically expressed vague, generalized thoughts about meditation, spiritual experience, the possibility of being in touch with a higher power, perhaps by leaving their own physical bodies, along with a loss of a sense of physical boundaries. This latter sensation seemed to be connected with a change in time sense that not only resulted in the slowed perception of external events but tended to permit the idea that time flows endlessly in a stream so that past and future are somehow magically more concrete and available. While usually these sensations are presented positively, there is frequent talk of freaking out, of losing control, and particularly of becoming paranoid. Each one of this group of subjects reported periods of intense suspicion of others which they knew was unwarranted.

As these feelings were accompanied by behavior that was specifically described as attempting to reduce individualization, such as living in a commune, it was hard for the psychiatrically oriented interviewer not to respond with automatic concern about the disintegration of ego, loss of self, and other psychopathological ideation that was being expressed. While it was obvious that these people were dealing more directly with primary primitive motivations, further reflection about the material they presented showed that there were more secondary motivations and better reality testing than had appeared at first blush. For one thing the subjects recognized the difference between many of their more unusual sensations and their desire to enter another level of consciousness. They did not completely believe their feelings but would quote some text such as *The Teachings of Don Juan*[18] or *I Ching*[19] to show the interviewer that it was his blindness that prevented him from understanding the subtle combination of fantasy and reality that they expressed.

For another thing, their commune offered them the opportunity not just for the gratification of primitive merging impulses but, more important, the chance to exist in a society where they could feel useful. In the commune, they were slowly redeveloping secondary motives in a social setting that accepted and rewarded them. Their devotion to this island of people stemmed in part from their awareness that this reciprocal acceptance of themselves as human beings with secondary motives for organization, for orderly sequence of activity, for affectful interactions, for communicative discourse, albeit with different standards from the larger society, only occurred in the commune. In the larger society, they were seen as hostile deviants and had accepted the role. This interaction between them and society they understood to result in more child-like thoughts, feelings, and behavior.

Further, they knew that this effort at personal development in the commune was fragile and at the mercy of just those social institutions whose hostility had proved so disorganizing. Continued discussion of the paranoid trend evident in this group and reported by Zinberg and Weil among chronic marijuana subjects presented the question of whether this trend would exist if the attitude of social institutions toward drug use were not so hostile. Although the acid heads knew that many of their suspicious responses were personal projections, they also insisted that they existed in a society hostile to them. Their specific reactions were irrational, but they felt that their overall paranoia was a valid response to external reality. They firmly placed their personality regression at the door of the social setting.

Another important social upheaval provides an example that lends weight to this argument. In 1952 Dr. Grete L. Bibring[20] reported on a study of people, mostly Jews, who had survived Nazi persecution in Germany and had come to the United States. These people had existed for years under the most intolerable conditions, often living like animals and constantly hearing of the extermination of their friends and families. At the time of their arrival in the United States, most of them had bizarre psychosomatic symptoms and serious personality disturbances. Certainly they showed marked regression to primitive early preoccupations, and much suspicion, concern about being fed, and ill-controlled aggression.

Dr. Bibring was able to isolate two factors contributing to this condition which were far more specific than the general brutality of life under the Nazis. For one thing, they literally felt guilty about being the ones to survive. Why were they alive when so many other people were dead? But the other factor interests us more at the moment. They placed the beginning of their disturbance at the time before the real horrors began. Many described how unsettling it was when those individuals and social institutions that they had been brought up to trust turned against them. Neighbors, police, judges, the law itself were no longer there to protect them and support them. Instead they became pariahs, wore Yellow Stars, and could be beaten by a policeman or pseudo-soldier not for breaking a known law, but simply for existing.

These displaced people reported the confusion they felt about who was truly at fault. Their sense of justice and social regularity was so disrupted that they wondered if they were indeed criminal. And it was at that point that their regressive symptoms and ideation began. Like the drug users, they doubted society and questioned themselves. They felt disorganized, apathetic, often dissociated.

If the social setting is even in part responsible for personality changes, the situation is more hopeful. A change in the social climate about drugs, similar to what is taking place with abortion, should be easier to bring about than the stamping out of the wide-spread illicit use of marijuana. The first step toward such a social change is to become fully aware of the present situation and its results. As long as we think of the users in terms of being in the thrall of a powerful drug, or as a psychological weakling debilitated by mind-altering intoxicating experiences, we cannot assess collective social influence on him.

4

THE PROBLEM OF RESEARCH

One often confronts in drug discussions a plea for more and better research before any drastic change is made in existing policies. The idea persists that somehow "research"—if only we had enough of it—will convert difficult policy issues into hard certainties. Its corollary is caution: any permissiveness toward drug users is premature, for later research, as in the case of cigarettes, might show that drugs which do not now seem very harmful are indeed deleterious. Rather than risk engraining a possibly harmful practice, a hard-line approach should be kept until all the answers are in.

The prevalence of this idea is easy to document. Westerners have difficulty denying the authority of scientific findings. Also, one can agree that marijuana, LSD, etc., are not as bad as commonly thought, but still consistently resist changing existing laws. *The New York Times,* February 13, 1971, stressed the "desperate need for further research" in commending the call of a legislative commission for marijuana reform that would fall short of legalization. The editors of the *Boston Globe,*[1] after running a five-day in-depth analysis of marijuana,[2] refused to endorse the conclusion that marijuana should be legalized on the ground that all the facts were not yet in. The Secretary of HEW, in a report to Congress entitled "Marijuana and Health," cites "the many unanswered questions" about marijuana as preventing a "final verdict" on policy and concludes that "until we know more about the drug we certainly can't give it a clean bill of health."

Certainly the psychopharmacology of psychoactive drugs leaves much to be desired by way of hard knowledge in several important areas, particularly about long-term effects. The idea, however, that research will answer these questions, and then also decide the hard social and political decisions ahead, illustrates a pervasive misconception at the very heart of the drug issue. The misconception is that we must be able to give a drug a clean bill of health—a "final verdict"—before we stop criminalizing people who use it, and further that research can technically provide that answer.

The we-don't-know-enough-now argument is deficient in several respects. Perhaps the most important is its confusion between harmfulness and legality. Even if all the evidence were in, the question of whether personal use and possession of a drug should be criminal would still be open. While this subtlety has not been missed in the case of cigarette smoking, most people have great difficulty in separating the two questions where other drugs are concerned.

The more-research-before-change posture also assumes that given a little more time, modern science can come up with the desired answers. In a world where the obstacles to definitive research described later in this chapter did not exist, this argument would still be unconvincing. Usually it is lack of knowledge of long-term social, psychological, and physical effects that is used as a basis for caution. Yet it is precisely knowledge of those effects that is out of reach at the moment. Indeed, if ever we can with assurance pinpoint the long-term effects of drugs, it will be a generation too late to resolve the dilemma now confronting us.

Finally, the proponents of caution tend to overlook the vast body of knowledge concerning the effects both of drugs and of the laws regulating them that now exists. Thousand of years of opiate, cannabis, and hallucinogen use have left us with considerable, albeit rough, knowledge about their effects. A surge of research and increased knowledge in the past thirty years enables us to say some important, if not definitive, things about drugs. Even more important, over fifty years of experience with police control of drug use has demonstrated the ill effects of an unbalanced, overly moralistic approach. Although we cannot scientifically assert that marijuana smokers some thirty years from now might contract some unknown ill, we do know that the drug laws are ineffective, costly, unjust, and unnecessary in dealing with problems of drug misuse.

In a time of burning conflict over drugs, the demand for more research seems less a desire for knowledge than a ploy to maintain a particular position. In an important sense it becomes a diversionary tactic that absolves legislators and the police from rectifying past errors. The recently appointed National Commission on Marijuana and Drug Abuse demonstrates quite clearly how the call for more research is used to avoid difficult political choices. The commission is to report on the extent, type, and nature of use, give an evaluation of the efficacy of existing laws, study the immediate and long-term effects and their relationship to aggressive behavior, crime, and other drugs. From numerous reports and blue-ribbon commissions, ranging from the Indian Hemp Commission of 1893–94 to the 1969 Wootton and 1970 LeDain Report, most of these questions have been answered. Nor is a national commission needed to determine the "efficacy of the law"—most people are by now aware that it deters hardly anyone. One is justifiably skeptical when a national commission and a million dollars are needed to answer questions to which people already know the answers. Indeed, other purposes may be discerned in this enterprise. While state and national pressure for change is mounting, the existence of a commission adroitly puts off legal change until its recommendations are in. And, as experience with the Kerner, Scranton, and Obscenity commissions shows, there is no guarantee that what any commission concludes will become law. The call for research is a holding action, a desperate lunge for reassurance, in the hope that final proof that "we were right" will be forthcoming or, at least, will postpone the recognition that we were wrong.

There are other grounds for suspecting the call for more research. Given the nature of drugs and the legal and financial controls that exist over research, we doubt that research will definitively answer the currently unanswered questions. Throughout this book we argue that the base of any legal controls over drug use is general social and psychological acceptance of limits. It is not that basic research in a whole variety of areas is of little use, but the view that research will help us with the crucial issue of social control and the irrationality that pervades our feelings about drugs is fallacious.

In this chapter we will indicate three reasons why research in this field is difficult: (1) the illegality itself, (2) the moral position from which research is undertaken, and (3) that set and setting, more than the drug, determine the response to psychoaffective drugs in humans. Research, broadly considered, may comprise investigating the mechanism of the drug and the body (physiological, biochemical, or pharmacological), studying the response of the person (psychological), and determining changes in attitudes or behavior of the population as a whole (sociological).

ILLEGALITY

The illegality of drugs ensures that only researchers who are sufficiently dedicated to spend months continuously on the phone or in correspondence with more than a dozen different agencies will get under way.

One of the authors who participated in a research project[3] in which marijuana was given to human subjects experienced the difficulties firsthand. In order to do the research it was necessary to get official and explicit clearance from the FDA, NIMH, Federal Bureau of Narcotics, Massachusetts Division of Dangerous Drugs, Attorney General of Massachusetts, local police officials of the district in which the research was to be carried out, the local district attorney, the executive committee of a medical school, a research committee of a medical school, a public information committee of a medical school, a dean's office, a research committee of each university whose newspaper carried advertisements for subjects, medical departments of various universities, and several professors of departments whose specialties might be touched on by this interdisciplinary work. It was not just that these different people needed to be contacted, but in addition, each read, criticized, and requested changes in the research proposal. Several felt that their regulations concerning such research conflicted with the rules of another agency. For instance, once the Federal Bureau of Narcotics, after months of effort, licensed the investigators, agreed to refrain from prosecution of subjects, and supplied the marijuana, the NIMH questioned this permission because the research was not sponsored and funded by them.

One medical school, after months of committee meetings and numerous appearances by the investigators, declined to approve the project because it called for giving marijuana to naive subjects, and the committee on research feared that it might begin an addiction. The committee advised omitting this key part of the research and permitting only chronic users to participate. When the research was moved to another university, a professor of a related department attempted to block the project unless it was under his complete control so that he could be sure it followed the principles of his discipline.

The Attorney General of Massachusetts, after giving the project his personal approval, found that he had no legal right to exempt research subjects who had performed an illegal act from the consequences of that act. This presented a stumbling block for the local police and legal officials who did not want to interfere but who also did not want to appear to condone dangerous illicit acts.

The legal department of one medical school objected to the permission agreement signed by subjects drawn up by the legal adviser of another medical school. The latter had been hired separately because the official legal counsel of that medical school had told one investigator that he had found no legal reason why this research could not take place, but had searched his conscience and decided this work to be morally objectionable and would advise the medical school against participation. The legal department of a second medical school wanted someone to drive the subjects home after the experiments, to ask them to refrain from touching any electrical or mechanical equipment for twelve hours after smoking the drug, and to require an individual to stay with the subjects for 24 hours to be sure there were no untoward physiological or psychological reactions.

Originally the Federal Bureau of Narcotics indicated that they would give the special license to possess marijuana to a physician only if he were a qualified investigator in the field. It was the old "can't hire anyone to work without experience, and thus can't get experience if you can't get a job" bind, because without a license one could not be an investigator.

There were literally hundreds of such incidents requiring unlimited time and unending patience. The experiments finally took place only because Dr. Andrew Weil, one of the investigators, was a senior medical student at the time and had made this his senior project. His backing, together with that of Drs. Peter Knapp and Conan Kornetsky, opened several previously immovable doors and at the last possible minute, the word was go.

The experiments themselves went smoothly. The findings showed little about acute intoxication with marijuana that could be considered troublesome, but many colleagues of the investigators roundly condemned them for publishing such findings, complaining that they incited others, particularly youths, to break the law. There were comments and letters to *Science,*[4] *Nature,*[5] and *The New York Times*[6] sharply questioning the right to perform such research, the intrinsic motives of the researchers, and implied judgments. This book abounds with examples of the fact that drug use is seen as a moral issue, so it should have come as no surprise to find that this is equally true in research. It is a matter of some moment, however, because of the nature of research itself.

MORAL POSITION

Research on drug use departs from the tradition of objective study and embraces the moral position that nonmedical drug use is wrong. To many investigators it is no contradiction to attempt research on the basis that drug use is wrong. The idea has been to discover what proves nonmedical drug use wrong and to "educate" the public to these findings so that drug users will cease and desist. It is a minor scientific scandal that the researchers who found that LSD causes chromosomal damage started out with the premise that LSD was obviously worse than people thought. They decided on this research in order to find out what made it so bad and to disseminate this to the public as soon as possible in order to stop more people from using LSD.[7]

A report of November, 1969, issued by the National Institute of Mental Health[8] describes all the programs funded by them on drugs. Since this report was issued, the new director of NIMH, Dr. Bertram Brown, has sharply revised the organization's position in a 1970 report entitled, "Marihuana and Health, A Report to the Congress from the Secretary of Health, Education and Welfare" (January 31, 1971).

The later report still declines to answer the question by calling for more research before public policy changes but sharply avoids the moral tone of the special report in 1969, "Drug Abuse." It begins by delineating certain recent trends, the first of which is "the misuse of drugs is not limited to this country."[9] The beginning of the second trend is "the abuse of narcotics, sedatives and stimulants continues to increase."[10] At no point in the report is there any proof that drugs were misused specifically in other countries.

In part four of the report, "Narcotics," the researchers comment on the fact that the Bureau of Narcotics and Dangerous Drugs[11] reported the number of addicts in the United States as 64,000 as of December, 1968. The figure of approximately 60,000[12] was used in 1952, before the passage of the Boggs Act. From 1952, then, to 1968, there was no indication of any change in the essential number of addicts in the United States. Far from proving an increase in use and abuse, the report presents a figure that would indicate the opposite in light of the increase in population during that period. They write: "A most important aspect of the National Institute of Mental Health's mission is to mount needed programs to deal flexibly with the many facets of drug abuse. As the problem is complex and changing so must be the strategies designed to understand and to cope with it."[13] An official government bureau intends to proceed with an action program to cope with a problem for and against which they have no scientific evidence.

> We have consolidated all elements playing a role in the area of drug abuse into a single division, The Division of Narcotic Addiction and Drug Abuse. This consolidation permits a more rapid translation of the results of research into treatment practices, and in the opposite direction emerging problems in treatment or education can be quickly identified and researched.[14]

That this is an action-oriented program to fight or clear a present evil can be read in almost every page of this report, even though ostensibly the report is committed merely to comment on the activities of the largest organization involved in funding research on drugs in the world.

SET AND SETTING

In studying the psychoactive drugs a researcher can obtain information by actually giving a drug to subjects in a laboratory and watching what happens. He can ask users what effects they get from the drug. He can give the drug to animals; he can study the drug's action in vitro by devising a series of experiments. He can also study various body tissues and fluids to gain some understanding of the further breakdown of the drug once it is in the body. Actual follow-up of the breakdown of the chemical components of the drug in the body is obviously of great value in determining its elimination. However, none of the foregoing techniques tells us very much about the psychological affects of drugs and their effect on people's behavior and attitudes. Although a drug given to animals may tell us a great deal about toxic doses and invariant pharmacological actions, the translation of animal responses to human responses has not been so useful when connected to substances whose chief property is psychoactivity. The most important thing we have learned about drugs that affect the mind is that the pharmacological action of the drug in vitro or in animals is but one of three factors that determine how a given person will react to that drug on a given occasion. The other factors are set and setting. They are at least as important as the reaction of the drug itself unless the drug is given in toxic doses. Set is the psychologist's term for an individual's expectation of what a drug will do to him. It includes much of what we commonly call "personality." Setting is the total physical and social environment in which the drug is taken.[15]

It is quite possible for the combined effects of set and setting to completely overshadow the pharmacological action of a drug. Thus, a barbiturate that pharmacological texts tell us is a "sedative" can produce stimulation under certain set and setting conditions. Influence of set and setting is so profound that even drugs that we customarily think of as producing consistent physiological responses, such as digitalis and atropine, under certain conditions of set and setting can become stimulants or provoke anxiety reactions. These responses can be sufficiently unpredictable to make physicians careful in their initial administration of even such medically tried and true substances.

The more the drug can be considered psychoactive (in that a principal reason for ingesting the substance relates to desired changes in mood, emotion, perceptions), the more set and setting are crucial. When obtaining information about drugs it is hard to measure the importance of set and setting. Hence, the kind of information that might be obtained by questioning users may well be grossly unreliable. What each person may say will apply subjectively to him, but whether it is pharmacologically accurate and can be applied to other persons is never clear.

Nearly all the collected scientific literature on psychoactive drugs consists of this kind of information. It is a collection of rumor, anecdote and secondhand accounts. This is best exemplified by a recent comprehensive study of marijuana by Lester Grinspoon.[16] Nearly half the book is given over to culling the literature and statements of people from Le Club des Hachichins,[17] Ludlow,[18] Baudelaire,[19] DeQuincey,[20] Ellis,[21] Leary,[22] and others. When reading these charming and highly literate descriptions, many of which contradict each other, it becomes obvious not only that the statements are individualistic and idiosyncratic but that much of what is recounted has been gathered from countries where set and setting are drastically different from set and setting in an American college community or Bedford-Stuyvesant.

This is not to say that experimental, laboratory information is always "right" and information from users is always "wrong." In fact, laboratory information has equivalent problems. The essence of the experimental method is manipulation of the environment so that an observed effect may be ascribed with some confidence to a known cause (in this case, the administration of a drug). When set and setting are more influential in determining the experimental response than the drug, and those factors are unmeasurable and cannot be held constant, then the experimentalist must either guess at their effect (virtual blasphemy) or reduce his experimental field to so small a point that his results mean very little to anyone.

Consider a simple example. About nine out of any ten marijuana users we have interviewed have told us they are certain marijuana dilates the pupils of their eyes when they are high. An even higher percentage of law-enforcement agents have told us the same thing. But pupil size depends on other things besides what drug you may happen to have inside you. One obvious determinant is the surrounding illumination: dim light in a room in which one's eyes are focused will cause pupil dilation as part of the eye's accommodation for near vision.

Therefore, if a researcher wishes to measure the effect of a drug on pupil size, he is obliged to hold the other factors constant—to control them. He must measure the pupils before and after administration of the drug under constant, standard illumination with the eyes focused at a constant, standard distance.

Observations made by users or law-enforcement agents at pot parties are not likely to be this scrupulous. When Weil and Zinberg finally did an appropriate experiment in Boston,[23] they were not surprised to find that pupil size was not changed at all by marijuana. (Since the lighting at marijuana parties is often dimmer than usual, it is also not surprising the participants commonly have large pupils.)

The curious problem of the experimentalist, however, is that as he controls the laboratory environment more and more carefully in order to maximize his confidence in ascribing observed effects to known causes, his laboratory becomes less and less like the real world, which is what he set out to study. Indeed, control can proceed to the point that the experimental results are scientifically impeccable, but their relevance to anything in the real world is lost. Then, if someone comes along and says, "So what?"—as happens all too infrequently in science—the experimentalist will be stuck for an answer.

An article by A. J. Mandell and C. E. Spooner in *Science,* called "Psychochemical Research Studies in Man,"[24] attempts a definitive criticism of general research strategies. They point out that such strategies in science, despite attempts at objectivity, are often dictated by conceptual models that hold transitory sway and pass on. The attempt to understand brain function and behavior in terms of chemical events in the central nervous system may be just such a faddish "paradigm."

The authors review four leading research strategies and find them all wanting. They point out first that experiments on animals with drugs that affect human behavior look for neurochemical correlates of drug action. The problem with this approach—whenever it is tried and however carefully it is used—is that one is left with correlates of action with no obvious connection to real behavior.

When they next talk about a research strategy to give humans large doses of compounds that are thought to be precursors of behaviorally active substances in order to watch for behavioral change, the authors describe the nonspecificity of such an approach. One has no way of knowing what did cause the effect if a behavioral change should occur. Was the effect caused by the precursors' metabolism into an active compound, or did intermediates of the metabolic pathways become active? Or were the behavioral effects a consequence of a general metabolic derangement caused by an initial, large dose of the precursor?

Sleep-stage specificity, the third strategy discussed, refers to the use of sleep stages as a dependent variable to test drug effects. This approach makes it possible to have a constant across a number of species. Different chemicals produce the same electrophysiological state. However, here too, while we have a constant, sleep, which makes for neat research, we cannot obtain specific correlates between chemistry and behavior. And, finally, when one searches for metabolic errors that result simultaneously in derangements of chemistry and behavior, it is not possible to relate the chemical abnormality to specific changes in brain function or specific changes in behavior.

The authors recommend a fourth strategy: a regulatory model in which body functions are end results of complex interactions of regulatory systems that can respond in a graded fashion to external changes. Longitudinal studies on individual subjects in which chemical changes are monitored over a long time period are intended to determine correlation with behavior but would leave *correlates,* not *causes.* The data in this method become as confusing as the rest if we try to force a specific cause-and-effect relationship on them. The nonspecificity problem is inherent in any model that attempts to make physical events more determining or basic than mental events.

Very few people, scientists or users, would disagree about the extent of the influence of set and setting on the response to a psychoaffective drug. And yet many people continue to act as if this intellectual agreement had very little to do with developing social policy. They behave as if that were somehow irrelevant and look to science. The essence of science lies in our ability to describe, predict, and explain phenomena. Our chemical and pharmacological knowledge of drug use does not fit these criteria. These approaches can teach us much about the drug itself and much about the changes the drug causes in our bodies. All of this is important, and could in time influence our thinking, balanced with a number of other social and psychological considerations such as social rituals, civil liberties, and pleasure.

It is clear now that science can tell us nothing about why a morphine addict says he gets a "rush" from his shot when he takes it in a deserted pad in the South End but, when given the same shot in the antiseptic ward of a modern general hospital, feels little or no pleasure. What light does research cast on the experience of passing a joint around among friends while listening to music? Has any research method, psychological or otherwise, become sensitive enough to weigh and measure the desire to look at lights and shade and shadow when on a trip or, more mundanely but no more available to experimental rigor, the desire for good cheer and good fellowship and very often song that comes with a few beers. The form that the impulse to get high takes may vary from culture to culture and from drug to drug, but it seems to be a fairly consistent human need.

Reports of users, while more lyrical and more literate than scientific papers, are equally inconclusive as a means of formulating public policy. Certainly the survey research done by Blum[25] and others conveys by sheer numbers the knowledge that people who use a drug find it simply pleasurable. However, even here it is so hard to know what people are talking about; the margin for error is great when we consider questionnaires in rigorous research terms.

Laboratory experiments tell us a great deal about what the possibilities are but give little help in predicting an individual's specific reaction in the real world. Until we can account for set and setting in a coherent way, neither the subjective experiences nor the objective physiology will provide data sufficient to determine a rational policy in the face of increasing drug use.

The most important funding agency in the world in drug research is the National Institute of Mental Health in Washington. The research that they were supporting at the end of 1969 certainly exemplifies the leading trends in the field, and we will lean heavily on their report in order to obtain our overview of the area.[26]

1. MARIJUANA

It is worth noting that of the twenty-five marijuana research projects the NIMH reports it was supporting at the end of 1969 only one could be considered frankly psychological and directly concerned with the response of the person. This project attempts to determine the crucial decision-making points with regard to marijuana and other drugs and draws from a diverse group of subjects. The aim of that research is to determine whether a chronic user of marijuana encounters psychological problems. Decision-making points determine whether he uses marijuana to escape life or stress, and are an attempt at finding whether his mental growth may be impaired by not knowing how to deal with frustration and other problems. The study further tries to decide whether a user may drop out of active involvement in school or work. The moral bias of this research seems unquestioned. It begins with the premise that the use of marijuana is a crisis decision and indicates by the way that the proposal is stated that marijuana use is seen as an escape. The research questions this social pathway to determine not whether but how it interferes with the user's following a "better" way of life.

Six listed projects fall under the general heading of sociological. These are surveys of the extent of drug use and questionnaires to determine the characteristics of users. Most deal with the use of drugs other than marijuana.

Other funded sociological research is intended to determine something about the marijuana user, and it does look at the relationship of marijuana use and other drugs, the question of how much people smoke, the correlation of their political principles with marijuana use, the relationship of their sexual practices to marijuana use, and their views of patriotism. Generally speaking, these studies point to where the marijuana user can be placed on the conservative-liberal-radical dimension in a number of areas of psycho-socio-political life. However, none of the studies funded by NIMH pays any attention to the relationship of setting to the development of these attitudes and views on the part of the user. One expensive study puts marijuana users and alcohol users together in a group and has the rather impressive finding that observers could distinguish subjects who were high on marijuana from subjects who were high on alcohol.

The remainder of the studies but one were interested in experimenting with the ways of separating tetrahydrocannabinol (THC) by liquid chromatography or through an extract by a red oil method which will separate as much of the noncannabinol types of material as possible without destroying the THC content. There is a metabolic study of cannabinol compounds in marijuana, as well as a variety of biosynthetic methods to detect the remnants of marijuana in body fluids as well as in biological tissues.

Two of the studies are intended to try to find the remnants of isolated THC in body molecules. The more explicitly described of these two concludes sadly that the degree of metabolic change may depend more on the amount and purity of the material subjected to the smoking procedure than on the measurement of THC itself.

There is at least one study that will indicate the effect of marijuana on blood levels and urinary excretion and will correlate some of the results (with human subjects) with motor skills and conventional psychometric testing. The larger studies seem to be on animals and investigate the effect of ingestion in rats and guinea pigs. Particular attention is paid to the effect on fertility with rats, hamsters, mice, and rabbits.

One research project attempts to separate two principles considered active in marijuana. The investigators plan to subject as many animals as possible to the two compounds. Tetrahydrocannabinol will be run through a general central nervous system screening procedure using psychological test procedures and electrophysiological techniques. These will measure things such as motor activity, interaction with alcohol, barbiturates, and amphetaminelike properties. Procedures will be conducted such as self-stimulation reciprocal conditioning and the effect of THC on visual and auditory thresholds in these animals.

Some of the studies have ingeniously worked out ways in which a respirator can be hooked up to a cigarette so that a dog will get some marijuana content through smoking. Electroencephalographic changes are being studied with great care in a variety of animals. None of these studies can take into account set or setting or give any clear indication as to the relationship between what is learned from animals and the real-life situation. There is no reason that this form of research cannot provide highly specific knowledge on drugs which would otherwise be gained through clinical trials on humans. On the other hand, given the moral bias of the research, as indicated earlier, along with this lack of real-world practicality, it is hard to imagine what information will help to make the difficult social-policy decisions.

One other marijuana project funded by the NIMH is a strictly applied project. The grant permitted publication of an empirical study of the marijuana law-enforcement administration policies in Los Angeles County. Law students randomly selected cases from the 1966 file of the Los Angeles District Attorney's office and the Juvenile Court and interviewed representative members of the police force, the DA's office, and so on. They found that an officer may spend up to eight hours arresting and booking a suspect and then appearing in court to testify: time, the researchers point out, diverted away from discovering and preventing crimes against persons and property. They also found that 72 to 80 percent of the marijuana in Los Angeles County is shipped to Los Angeles by a group of separate, loosely knit syndicates. They found that the use of informants and undercover agents is effective in discovering violators but makes little headway in halting the spreading use of marijuana. When faced with the alternative of a felony conviction or acquittal, a significant number of judges have chosen to acquit the educated, middle-class user without prior record who, except for his marijuana activities, appears to be law-abiding.

NIMH is doing one other thing that will be of value for researchers. They are funding the growing of marijuana in Mississippi so that the plants used and even the THC separated will be fairly standardized. Thus, researchers in the future will have a clearer idea of what they are working with.

With the range of research just listed, one might assume the field was being well covered by this agency. However, a review of recent marijuana research published by Dr. Charles Gordetzky,[27] director of the Section on Drug Metabolism and Kinetics at the NIMH Addiction Research Center in Lexington, Kentucky, takes a different view. There are probably few people in a better position to assess research than Dr. Gordetzky, not only because of his official position in NIMH research, but because he has collaborated with Isbell[28] on basic THC work. Gordetzky questions how difficult it will be to standardize a sample of marijuana that will help with information about other strains because "the amount of resin found in different plants varies so widely with such factors as the climatic conditions under which the plant is grown, and the variation in the geographical area in which it is grown."[29] His assessment of THC studies: "For example, we are still not sure if delta-9-THC is the only active principle. The relationships between oral ingestion of THC or smoked tobacco cigarette injected with known amounts of THC and a smoked marijuana cigarette which has been assayed for THC has still not been fully defined."[30] He goes on to say:

> There are discrepancies between effects observed from smoking marijuana cigarettes which are assayed for THC and those which we would expect from experiments with similar amounts of THC being injected into a tobacco cigarette. With regard to smoking versus oral potency, it may be that the passage of THC initially through the liver after ingestion may produce metabolic changes in the drug which are not seen when THC is smoked and some can get to the brain without passing through the liver. It is also possible that during combustion new products are formed and there also may be some interaction between the components of marijuana not seen between THC and tobacco or vice versa.
>
> . . . You may notice that I have continually said marijuana assayed for THC rather than marijuana of known THC content. This is purposeful since some question has recently been raised

regarding the accuracy of the assaying done on marijuana used in some reported studies.[31, 32]

He goes over studies that try to relate THC content to extremely unpleasant toxic or even psychotic reactions. He concludes that it is likely that this represents idiosyncratic reaction and not a dose-related toxicity of the drug.

Many of the sociological studies backed by NIMH are geared to indicate whether marijuana leads to other drug use, and the relationship between frequency of marijuana use and other drugs. Dr. Gordetzky,[33] in his discussion of this form of research, goes on to say this:

> Opponents of marijuana frequently argue that its use inevitably leads to other drugs, for example, heroin. This argument probably begins with a perversion of the appropriately determined statistics that most heroin users began on marijuana. Reversal of this statistic is certainly not logically justified and is in fact probably far from the true situation.

He concludes his comments on marijuana:

> You can see that our present state of knowledge is still incomplete and a great deal of work needs to be done before any definitive statements regarding such areas as absolute and relative safety can be determined.

Would the result of such careful work as that of Dr. Gordetzky lead us to believe that we should put off any decisions regarding changes of the law until such information as research has to offer will be available? Dr. Gordetzky clearly takes a dim view of much of the research work that has been done so far, and many of his statements indicate that we can expect little from any of the projects now backed by the NIMH. Another indication of this view is some work done under the supervision of Dr. John C. Krantz at the Maryland Psychiatric Research Center.[34]

We do not know what the positive aspect of the new work will be; however, the negative implications are of importance. The findings of Krantz *et al.* indicate that it is impossible to treat THC as if it were the only active ingredient of marijuana. It becomes clear that the cannabinols which were previously considered inactive can be active in either potentiating or blocking the effects of other ingredients. This throws great question on the work of any investigators dealing with a fraction of marijuana which they consider the principal active ingredients, not just because there may be other active ingredients, but because it may be the interaction among ingredients that determines activity. Berger's work lends credence to the view that there are a number of factors in the marijuana preparation which not only act to potentiate each other but may act to inhibit each other and may be of different intensities in different samples.

This work also has important implications for the difference between smoking and the oral ingestion of marijuana. Isbell's work with Gordetzky maintains that THC injected into a tobacco cigarette and smoked is about three times as potent as THC taken orally on a milligram-for-milligram basis.[35] This finding has been unscientifically disputed by a number of users. The indication that even the most careful investigators fall into the error of accepting a scientific premise simply because there is "experimental" evidence can be shown by Grinspoon's interest[36] in this. He quotes Walton,[37] who says that cannabis taken orally is more "abrupt" in the onset of its effects than cannabis smoked. Grinspoon goes on to say, "He [Walton] does not mean that the oral route increases the potency or if he does he is mistaken as Isbell *et al.* have shown."[38]

Many users indicate that at times oral ingestion is more potent than the smoked route and also say that the effects are qualitatively different. These again are matters about which we know little or nothing.

One could go on detailing the contradiction that comes from supposedly scientific reports on marijuana. The American Medical Association[39] noted that after the administration of cannabis the "sensation of pain is distinctly lessened or entirely absent and the sense of touch is less acute than normal." However, Allentuck and Bowman[40] report that there is "increased sensitivity to touch, pressure, and pain stimuli."

What one is left with, when a survey is taken of attempts to treat marijuana experimentally solely as a research problem and to remove it in any way from the human situation, is that one finds that the data are contradictory and that, unless one becomes comprehensively involved in concepts of set and setting, then very little sense can be made out of the data. It is not that researchers have not attempted to go into the more subjective aspects. There has been research on the contention that marijuana use increases one's sensitivity to music. One result reported in *Life* magazine[41] relates, ". . . the swinging musician ascends to new heights of virtuosity," when high on marijuana. Walton[42] came to exactly the opposite conviction. He says, "There is very little probability that a musician's performance is in any degree improved over that of his best capabilities. As judged by objectively critical means, the standards of performance are no doubt lowered." But Winick,[43] who has been one of the leading observers of the drug scene for a number of years, has his doubts. He points out that Walton's study failed to demonstrate enhanced musical ability:

> . . . a test in which non-musicians are given objective questions on matters like the consonance of pitch between two sounds, can hardly be compared to the musical creativity and expertise required of the jazz musician playing in a group situation which is based on mutual reinforcement and in which improvisation may be extremely important.

He concluded that the jury was still very much out on that highly subjective question.

2. HALLUCINOGENS

One of the seventeen projects funded by the NIMH[44] on hallucinogens is a large survey report that indicates a decreased use of LSD. This finding is directly contradicted by Gallup polls,[45] the most recent of which indicates that 14 percent of all those under age 25 now have joined the "have used" category. At the time of the NIMH report they contended that the "have used" category had dropped from a high of 10 percent down to a low of 6 percent. Our interviews indicate a gradual increase of use of LSD with the implication that one might not notice it so much because use has become more private and less connected with total change in life-style. Our subjects have reported that LSD is one of the things that people of this generation simply plan to do, and it is not considered necessarily an aberration or a desire to join a commune or a hippie way of life. There have been consistent reports of decreased use ever since the original chromosome papers were published in 1967. These reports probably represent wishful thinking rather than accuracy of the samples.

Most projects funded by NIMH[46] are biological and biochemical. They study peyote fractions by going back to the direct biochemistry of mescalines and related alkaloids to determine the prototype of the hallucinogens. There is an attempt to study the chemical components of the cactus seed to determine peyote's major biosynthetic pathway. In one project, the synthesis in the central nervous system is studied through drug-treated animals. The Texas Research Institute of Mental Science is studying the effects of twenty substituted phenylethylamines in disrupting animal behavior. Identification of the hallucinogenic activity of unknown chemical compounds is the aim of another project.

The preoccupation with chromosomes continues. Four projects study chromosomal changes in rats and mice, another in schizophrenic children who had been treated with LSD between 1961 and 1966 before "the damaging effects of LSD to chromosomes had been reported."

One psychosocial research project attempts to distinguish those research subjects who were exposed to LSD during the 1959–65 research (before the drug was taken up for pleasure) and sought out the drug later from those who did not. A little more than 25 percent of the group of experimental subjects in those original studies took LSD illicitly after their legitimate exposure. An attempt is made to divide, on a personality basis, the continuers from the noncontinuers. Other studies are intended to show the changes in value systems and career patterns of psychedelic-drug users. Another is concerned with the legal significance of hallucinogenic-drug research, and yet another attempts to show the relationship of hallucinogens to the development of a poly-drug scene. The data from this last study are directly contradicted by data reported from yet another study that indicates that the speed freak and the LSD user have quite a different set of motivations for drug use and in fact get on very poorly together. One project intended to study hippies and non-hippies from New York City's East Village and the YMCA centers in New York define their program as one that should provide some information on which to base a program of preventative activities in the various Y centers.

One applied program sets up a "community" organization in which youths are members rather than patients and serves as a locus of free-time activity in order to help the community meet the various needs of teen-agers. One result of this report is that the NIMH did fund a conference of leading researchers in September 1967. One of the findings was that those attending agreed "that evidence of persisting psychological effects from long-term use of LSD was minimal." Despite this finding the NIMH report continues to refer to the taking of LSD as a problem:

> . . . researchers demonstrated the possibility that a mind-shaking drug like LSD precipitates prolonged anxieties, depressive state and psychotic reaction. This has been amply confirmed by clinicians. In addition those who use the drug ostensibly were eventually impressed by the "bum trips" and "flashbacks" that could occur unpredictably.

Certainly the data produced by the conference sponsored by the NIMH do not confirm those statements quoted from the introduction to their description of LSD research actually funded by the agency.

There is currently no research funded that attempts to explain the effect of hallucinogens on consciousness and explore the interesting fact reported by Dr. Gordetzky[47] that tolerance is so rapid that regular consumption is impractical. (People develop tolerance quickly and lose it just as quickly.) Dr. Gordetzky has many doubts concerning the research that has found increased chromosomal breaks with LSD. He says, "questions of technique, control groups, sample size, normal levels of chromosomal breaks and the possible effects of other currently used drugs have all been raised"[48] about research that has shown such breaks. He concludes that there is no reason to feel at this time that LSD is specifically involved.

3. STIMULANTS

Research of the stimulants (xanthines, such as caffeine, theobromine and theophylline cocaine, and a large number of sympathomimetics) suffers from the much-quoted report and mistake on the general effects of cocaine by Sigmund Freud. In 1885 Freud published a highly enthusiastic report on the effects of cocaine.[49] He remarked, "A writer who for weeks before had been incapable of any literary production was able to work for 14 hours without interruption after taking 0.1 grams of cocaine hydrochloride."[50] Heightened functional capacity appeared much more regularly as a symptom of the action of cocaine. Part of Freud's research was the rigorous testing of the effect of cocaine on muscular response, and he found that "ingestion of 0.4 grams of cocaine hydrochloride increases the effective work of one hand by two or three kilograms."[51] In the same article, he goes on to praise cocaine as an effective antagonist to morphine. A person who had presented the most severe manifestations of collapse at the time of an earlier withdrawal (from morphine) now remained able, with the aid of cocaine, to work and to stay out of bed and was reminded of his abstinence only by shivering, diarrhea, and occasional craving for morphine. "No cocaine habituation set in; on the contrary, an increasing antithesis to the use of cocaine was unmistakenly evident," he goes on to say. "I have no hesitation in recommending the administration of cocaine for such withdrawal cures in subcutaneous injections of 0.03 to 0.05 grams per dose, without any fear of increasing the dose."[52]

As we now know, cocaine turned out to be a much more complex drug than Freud believed it to be at the time. His enthusiasm in this matter may have affected the entire course of drug research. At numerous scientific meetings, when someone has reported on a positive effect of a psychoactive drug, a discussant invariably recounts Freud's early enthusiasm and later disillusionment. Although some form of cocaine had been known in Europe since the time the Spaniards returned from the initial conquest of South America and brought coca leaves back with them, there is no record of specific findings until 1883 when Dr. Von Assenbront reported that the Bavarian soldiers overcame fatigue and exposure after receiving small amounts of cocaine hydrochloride.[53]

Amphetamine itself was first prepared in 1887 and methamphetamine in 1927. The drugs were in general medical usage between 1930 and 1960 without arousing much concern. The recent preoccupation with speed freaks—the nonmedical usage—has led to much interest in research in the stimulants, which is now taking place. This is in spite of the fact that there was considerable concern about medical usage earlier and questions as to how dangerous a drug the amphetamines were. At the end of 1969 the NIMH was funding eight research projects which were all or in part related to the amphetamines.[54] As some of them were comparative research with other drugs, particularly the barbiturates, they do not stand on their own. In these projects, animals—geese, rats, dogs, mice, hamsters, and pigs—are being studied. These animals are being watched to determine if there is a persistence of drug-taking behavior after the removal of conflict or after brain stimulation; also investigated are the questions of self-administration and methods of self-administration, various aspects of physical and psychological dependency (again as noted by self-administration), neurophysiological concomitants of chronic amphetamine intoxication, the effects directly on the central nervous system (although the relationship between the central nervous system of chicks and that of humans is not directly reported on), and the question of hypersusceptibility to subsequent doses following enhanced response level, as well as the impact of the amphetamines on pregnancy in mice.

Another project obtains urine samples from two human populations, acute psychiatric inpatients and university infirmary inpatients, to see if a chemical detection method for the presence of ten widely used stimulants and appetite-depressant drugs can be developed. The study is intended to discover whether the occurrence of unsuspected stimulant drug abuse is found in a psychiatric population and to provide preliminary information regarding the incidence of stimulant drug abuse in college students.

In contrast to all the other classes of drugs, amphetamines are the one group of drugs that clinical research indicates does result in impulsive and violent behavior. Weil[55] contends that this is consistent with their pharmacological instability. He states:

> Amphetamine dependency is more serious than narcotic dependency because it is inherently less stable. When a person begins using a tolerance-producing drug, he must soon face the problem of trying to stabilize his use in order to keep his life from being disrupted. More than any other class of drugs, the amphetamines foil users' attempts to reach equilibrium with his habit because they induce such powerful and unrelenting tolerance. Consequently, users develop erratic patterns of use, such as "spree shooting" alternating with barbiturates and eventually with heroin.

Clinical observers[56] agree that there are at least two types of amphetamine dependency that develop: (1) The very bizarre, speed freak, hippie use of enormously high doses, usually intravenously. Gordetzky[57] believes that eventually all these people develop paranoid psychoses; (2) the so-called housewife syndrome, in which certain users of amphetamines begin because of either a desire to lose weight, a mild depression, or simply the need for a lift in the mornings to get started in a day characterized by housework and young children. The latter has never been involved in research. Whatever psychological research is going on simply tries to indicate the kinds of pathology that either results from enormous doses of amphetamine or causes people to begin to use the drug. The more general question of drug use in the population at large, which relates more to ordinary avenues of introduction, such as the medical profession, advertising, and so on, is not included in any of the NIMH projects or any other research that is currently being done on amphetamines.

4. NARCOTICS

Although specifically the concept of narcotics refers to opiates, a wide variety of drugs have at one time or another been listed as narcotics. It is well known that marijuana is classified legally under narcotics, and at different times such drugs as coffee have been declared a narcotic. In effect the term "narcotics" has come to have a nonspecific meaning that implies danger, addiction, and nonmedical uses. "The very word narcotic has taken on sinister meaning in American culture. There is probably no field—save perhaps religion and politics—so replete with popular misinformation and purposeful misrepresentation. It is enough that a substance be called a narcotic to draw away aghast."[58]

Probably more money is being spent in research on narcotics (in the more specific sense of the opiates) than on all other drugs together. The reason for this is the enormous investment in clinical research[59] on addicts attempting to withdraw from heroin, morphine, or the like, who go to treatment centers for methadone maintenance. The largest program is in New York City and is headed by Dr. Vincent Dole and Dr. Marie Nyswander, who began the push for methadone maintenance and have done most of the original clinical research. Many other cities have equivalent centers and are trying a whole variety of methadone programs.

The magnitude of the NIMH commitment to opiate programs can be gathered from the figures: $3,149,000 in fiscal 1969 alone. They funded numerous civil commitment programs as well. No exact figures are available for the amount of money invested in the

Fort Worth Clinical Research Center and the Lexington Clinical Research Center, but certainly more than $12 million was invested in each of these operations. The aim of the opiate programs across the country has basically been a comprehensive approach to management of the addict. The centers vary in their approaches but uniformly attempt to operate within a community to set up liaisons with judicial and rehabilitation agencies and specifically try to support and guide the addict as well as his family. They all hope for the addict to go through periodic examinations and to find his way to complete abstinence or, at the very least, methadone maintenance. While some provide group psychotherapy and educational and vocational programs, they vary from community to community. Of the more specific research projects, as opposed to treatment programs funded, only one would fit into the category of psychological research. This program is designed to show that the pathologies of extreme delinquents, such as addicts, make them poor partners in any task needed to support and sustain group life, and that they turn to drug use as a method of achieving shared relations.

Of 26 other studies funded by NIMH, only one could be considered sociological. This one has to do with the movement of young ghetto dwellers into an identity as an addict. The paucity of psychological and sociological research funded directly by the NIMH reflects the massive investment in clinical research centers. Many of the activities of the centers may be more directly sociological and psychological than is evident in the report available to us. From the "Drug Abuse" report it seems that the trend is to specialize in clinical pharmacological studies of a series of narcotic antagonists, drug metabolism in kinetic studies to establish a mathematical model for drug dose-response curves and a method of analyzing these curves, experimental psychiatric studies on the effects of drug use on sleep, the biochemical and pharmacological properties of analgesics, and the neuropharmacological effects of morphine on electroencephalograms. Also a number of animal studies using monkeys try to find the specific brain structures involved in the addiction syndrome. Investigators are studying the development and tolerance of physical dependency in mice, just as another granted project studies a differential rate of opiate-seeking behavior in aggressive and nonaggressive white mice. Self-administration in rats is also being studied.

A great deal of money and effort is being put into the study of narcotics by the NIMH. It is impossible at this point to evaluate the validity and worth of the investigations or the sort of things that are being investigated. It is easy to criticize what is being done but hard to prepare the kind of research that would produce information to help with essential decisions. However, it is fair to say that from the tone of the report, as shown by the opening statements that lead into the section on narcotic addiction— "While narcotic addiction appears to be epidemic in our urban slums among economically deprived young people, it is in fact an epidemic problem afflicting people at every level of our society"[60] —it does not take into account the different quality of use mentioned earlier in the discussion of the numbers game of narcotic addicts; that is, the attempt to describe drug use purely on a quantitative basis. For instance, during the period of 1952 to at least 1968 the addict population remained stable at about 55,000 to 65,000 and, in ratio of addicts to population, declined slightly.[61] If one goes over the figures, the remarkable thing is not the constancy of the addict and his habits, but rather that the addict deserts his habit quite easily. Kolb and DuMez[62] estimate the number of addicts in 1892 at 246,000. By 1915 this figure had declined by 31,000 to 215,000, and by 1922 it declined by another 105,000 to 110,000. Four years later the number fell still more, so that it was reduced to 100,000. In 1935 there was an estimated increase to 122,000, but three years later this had decreased by 96,000 or 79,000, depending on whether one reads the 1938 or 1939 report of the Federal Bureau of Narcotics (FBN). In 1938 they estimated that there were 26,000 addicts in the nation, and in 1939 estimated 43,000. The sensational increase in addiction between 1939 and 1955 or 1957 totaled 17,000 or 1,000 persons, depending on which year one takes as the closing date, because in 1955 the FBN estimated 60,000 addicts in this country, but in 1957 estimated only 44,000.[63]

Kolb and DuMez cite the estimate of the special narcotics committee of 1919, which was one million addicts in the United States.[64] Using the FBN figure for 1928 of 100,000 addicts, it would mean that 900,000 addicts deserted the use of their drugs within ten years.[65] Obviously research can be done that would aid us in understanding the extent to which the narcotic addict can desert his dependency more readily than has been previously supposed. Research could also, of course, be done on the ways in which statistics and figures are collected. Moreover, greater knowledge about the tenacity of addiction might help the public understand what addiction is and lead to a more informed attitude toward policy.

5. SEDATIVE-HYPNOTICS

Barbituric acid was synthesized in 1863;[66] the acid itself is not a central nervous depressant. The first active derivative, barbital, was not reported until 1902,[67] and was not introduced into medical practice, as Veronal, until a year later.[68] Within a few years there was a literary reference to chronic barbiturate intoxication and the occurrence of withdrawal convulsion in Germany.[69] Seven years elapsed between the first use of a barbiturate in a clinic and a qualifying report of the dependence potential of this class of drugs published by Isbell,[70] in 1950, who demonstrated through a series of controlled experiments in man that the abuse of barbiturates induces physical dependency. In 1970, Carl Essig,[71] the Chief of the Neurology Section of the National Institute of Mental Health Clinical Research Center, Lexington, Kentucky, reported, "The basic neurophysiological and neurochemical mechanisms underlying the barbiturates withdrawal syndrome are unknown."

The sedative-depressive drugs are discussed last in our report because they include alcohol and a whole list of other drugs in general usage. The alcohol-barbiturate class, like the opiates, produces both psychic and physical dependency. In the alcohol-barbiturate group are the paraldehydes and chloral hydrates, as well as newer sedatives that seem to have clinical effects like the barbiturates.

Controlled experiments on the treatment of withdrawal from the newer sedative drugs have not been performed in man. The probability of cross-dependence between barbiturates and these drugs makes it likely that the principles of barbiturate withdrawal treatment can be applied to nonbarbiturate sedative agents. It is also thought that pentobarbital can be used for this purpose, but diphenylhydantoin (Dilantin) or phenothiazines are not recommended.[72]

The prevention of sedative-hypnotic drug misuse has been defined by an AMA Committee on Alcoholism and Addiction as a role a physician might take "in establishing a potentially dangerous type of therapy even though it does not always lead to significant tolerance or physical dependence."[73] This AMA committee also listed the ways in which physicians might contribute to the misuse of sedatives. Thus, a statement was made against the prolonged and unsupervised administration of barbiturates for symptomatic relief often without adequate diagnosis or knowledge of the patient's past experience with medications or attitudes toward drugs. This same statement is also applicable to the other sedatives listed in this presentation. Other committee recommendations were as follows: that physicians resist any patient's demands for increased quantities of drugs; that he not shift the patient to another or newer sedative in the erroneous belief that such agents have no abuse potential; and that he not write refillable prescriptions for barbiturates or their substitutes without thought of cumulative effects, additive action with other depressants, or the possible establishment of strong psychological or physical dependence.[74] In addition to these AMA committee recommendations it is well for physicians to avoid prescribing sedatives to narcotic addicts, sociopaths, some alcoholics, and those known to refill prescriptions sooner or more frequently than specified. Perhaps clinicians

can play a more important role in preventing the misuse of sedative-hypnotic drugs in a larger and less devious group of patients
variously referred to as "anxious," "psychoneurotic," etc. The
prevention of moderate degrees of sedative-drug intoxication is an
important public health consideration, not only because of the
social implications of such impaired behavior but because moderate or periodic states of intoxication might lead to continuous
abuse and physical dependence. Thus, the effect of depressant-drug
intoxication on automobile driving, work performance, and social
interaction should be considered by the doctor when he prescribes
such drugs.

Not alone is the abstinence syndrome far more serious with this
class of drugs than with those associated with opiate withdrawal.
Convulsions, temporary psychosis, and death are not infrequent
complications. Even drugs considered mild tranquilizers such as
meprobamate (Miltown, Equanil) have been known to cause
coma and death following both excess dosage and abrupt withdrawal. Barbiturates are often implicated in accidental self-poison-
ing because tolerance of lethal dose does not develop as fast as
tolerance of the hypnotic doses.[75] Essig[76] reports a similar
situation with a so-called minor tranquilizer. The minor manifestations of their withdrawal are also like those of barbiturate
abstinence.

Despite the rigorous presentation of official medical concern
about barbiturates and the impressive reports as to potential difficulty, there are only two projects specifically listed by the NIMH[77]
that are principally concerned with barbiturates. A colony of
barbiturate dogs has been established to study drug preference and
social effects of drug dependence. The question raised by this
research is whether more dominant and fearless animals self-
administer as much of the drug as those that are more fearful.
Then, upon withdrawal, it will be determined whether abstinence
was severe in those monkeys or dogs who had shown the most
marked drug effect and whether they were necessarily those who
self-administered the higher daily dose.

The other project concerns a study of rats' hypersusceptibility to a subsequent dose of barbiturates once a tolerance level has been established. This research is intended to obtain some indication of the mechanism for delayed alteration and responses. It is hard not to speculate that the paucity of research in the sedative-hypnotic group is a strong indication of both the moral bias of research in drug use and the lack of understanding of the concept of the influence of set and setting on such drugs. After all, alcohol is a sedative-hypnotic and is the most used drug in this country. We have no wish to get involved in the fervent moral question brought up by so many marijuana smokers as to whether it is more or less moral that one uses alcohol rather than marijuana. In fact, the sedative-hypnotics as a group are the most used drugs; a user develops tolerance, withdrawal, and a whole variety of abstinence syndromes, as well as physiological damage related to their use. Nevertheless, there is relatively little research about the barbiturates and there is relatively little concern that we know so little about their action.

CONCLUSION

The sedative-hypnotics best illustrate the two issues: morality and influence of set and setting, and how little they are considered in the entire complex of drug research. It is not that the research per se is poorly organized or executed. Every project is a building block to increase our knowledge. It is certainly true that the accumulation of knowledge in these areas may lead to change in legal controls and social attitudes toward one drug or another.

But there is a problem in drug research when it is pursued essentially from the point of view of pharmacological action. Although there are research projects that investigate the extent and patterns of use, and the psychology of users, most projects revert again and again to the drug itself. In one way or another, scientists are trying to derive a method of predicting individual response to a psychoactive drug from consideration of the drug. They accept intellectually the proposition that drug, set and setting are interdependent in shaping the drug response; but they proceed, if one can deduce from the research done, as if the one factor, drug, is more determining than the others.

There should be greater interest in the "high" state itself and in the forceful fact that every culture that anybody ever studied (except possibly the Eskimo) has found some way to get high and has felt it important to have this experience. What's more, the experience has had important social ramifications and is deeply connected in many cultures with social rituals of importance. It has made little difference whether the drug of choice was alcohol, some form of hemp, or one of the opiates or cocaine; the particular culture that has adopted the drug has shown an intense desire to acquire both personal and social relationships through the drug experience.

Trouble begins when certain individuals in a social setting which rigidly defines social irregularities predominate over ritualized and regularized drug use. Lacking a consensus of approval, a society makes drug-taking an antisocial activity rather than one that conforms to the interest of society. Liquor, the pipe, joints, pills, no longer work as well, as drugs become a personal neurosis or a focus of social conflict. It is at this point that more frequent and compulsive use may occur with less and less reward. It can be argued, of course, that for certain disturbed persons this compulsive response will always be predominant. Little research proceeds from this anthropological point of view to help us understand the potential social factors that would create strongly negative set and setting. Thus, we only speculate on the likelihood that under negative conditions of set and setting users will be drawn into drug abuse rather than encouraged to explore the positive social potentials of use.

Considerations of the high itself (the influence of consciousness, the relationship of positive or negative social setting) have been little explored. The focus for research has been on the narrower considerations (of the pharmacology, biology, or sociology of the drug itself), leaving the field wide open to those who come at it, equally narrowly, from the opposite point of view.

It is hardly surprising that many people would like to investigate the concept of altered states of consciousness.[78] The emphasis on subjective experience leads toward a variety of directions—some interesting, such as current efforts to train patients with heart block to try to learn to control the sympathetic nervous system. It can also lead to preoccupations with magic, astrology, and tarot cards. It is not an uncommon human characteristic for one narrow preoccupation to leave the way open for its opposite. When research denies so much of human consciousness, it is not surprising that those emphasizing the side denied will move into the void and gain credence and respectability otherwise withheld from them.

Research simply cannot be convincing if it is conceived on the basis that drugs may not produce pleasure without a compensating harm. This ethic is as valid in its own way as the belief in spirituality, but no more so. When an effort is made to superimpose either view and when research becomes one of the devices to do so, we have moved far from the scientific tradition. The purpose of this critique of research has been to broaden the perspective from which drugs are considered. It has been repeatedly demonstrated that attitudes play an essential, important role in shaping opinions, not only in terms of the final social control, but also in limiting the horizons of scientific investigation. Drug users have told us again and again that they are experiencing things different from what they had been taught. Those who have studied the issue have found that myth and misconception play an enormous role in our entire view of drug use. We have tried to show the change in the educational experiences available to the generation now growing up through television and other technical, social, and psychological events, just as we have tried to be clear about the fact that the essential nature of man is unchanged.

5

THE BRITISH EXPERIENCE

Britain, unlike the United States, has always permitted addicts to obtain and use drugs legally. A noncriminal approach to addiction has minimized social costs from both use of drugs and efforts to prevent that use. No black market in heroin has developed; addict-related crime is largely unknown; and the police have not had to intervene in the lives of drug users. In 1965 there were still fewer than 1,000 addicts known to the government.

In 1964, with new patterns of drug use emerging, the "drug problem" suddenly burst on the British scene. The rate of new addiction rose dramatically, while the age of addicts fell. The total number was small (a few hundred), but the very fact that an increase, chiefly among young people, had occurred was perceived by the public as a major social problem. At the same time thousands of other people began to use cannabis,* LSD, and other drugs. Almost overnight, drug use became a cause of anxiety, confusion, and eventually social conflict. The role and powers of the police expanded, and charges that they were abusing their powers increased. To an American observer, the British response to drugs in the late 1960s was indistinguishable from the emotions

* *Cannabis sativa* is the plant from which marijuana (the leaves and flowering tops) and hashish (the resin) are derived. In England it is predominantly used in the resin form. In this chapter we use "cannabis," to refer to any form of marijuana.

and tensions that drug use had provoked in Americans. Both nations were bewildered by this new phenomenon, and became increasingly anxious when their efforts and ardent hopes for a solution proved fruitless.

Beneath the similarities, however, the British experience remains distinctively different from the American. Contrary to reports that the British "system" has failed or has been replaced,[1] the medical model has managed to ride the storm and come to grips with the new problems of addiction. Where it has faltered, its mistakes have been no worse than those in America and, because of social and historical circumstances, much less costly. The most intractable problems have arisen not with heroin, but with non-addictive drugs such as cannabis and LSD. In this area the British have been as irrational as the Americans, and as the 1970 Misuse of Drugs Bill shows, the problems there have been a repeat, in British style, of conflicts found in America.

The British experience has several lessons for those interested in developing a coherent, effective system of drug control—for example, the feasibility of providing addicts with drugs legally. But the British experience also confirms that an exaggerated, noninstrumental approach, where law functions primarily as a symbol, is bound to be self-defeating.

THE BRITISH SYSTEM—
THE MEDICAL MODEL

Both British and American drug laws were formulated in response to international treaties signed early in this century. The Dangerous Drugs Act of 1920 made it a crime to import, export, manufacture, supply, or possess without a license opiates, cocaine, or cannabis. The maximum penalty is ten years' imprisonment. In 1964 the Drugs (Prevention of Misuse) Act regulated for the first time the possession of amphetamines and hallucinogens. However, these drugs were treated more leniently (a maximum penalty of two years' imprisonment for possession, as opposed to ten under the Dangerous Drugs Act), and the act did not penalize sale of these drugs.

The chief difference between the American and British systems—and it is a significant one—is the legal position of the addict. Because the British medical profession defended its right to prescribe drugs to patients as it saw fit, drug addiction has always been treated as an illness, not a crime.

It is interesting to compare attitudes toward medical discretion in the United States and Britain. Both started from roughly similar positions. By 1900 each country had a sizable population of persons addicted to opium, largely as a result of uncontrolled patent medicines in the United States and of the use of laudanum (a mixture of opium and alcohol) in Britain. Both countries were active in the first international drug conferences that led to the Hague Convention in 1912. The signatories were obligated by this treaty to enact domestic legislation that controlled the opium trade. The resulting laws—in America, the Harrison Narcotic Act of 1914, and in Britain, the Dangerous Drugs Act of 1920—were identical in substance. Each proscribed the same acts of unlicensed export, import, sale, manufacture, and possession. The British penalties, providing a maximum of ten years, were in fact more severe than the five-year American maximum. Each law excepted doctor's prescriptions in the normal course of professional practice.

In the United States public perceptions of the addict changed abruptly after the passage of the Harrison Act. The doctor's right to prescribe was eroded by a succession of court decisions, and gradually doctors relinquished all control over the treatment of addicts. The problem became one of controlling crime. This initial definition of drug use as a criminal matter has influenced all subsequent policy decisions and public debate on the subject.

The question of the medical treatment of addicts was resolved differently in Britain. When a conflict over the legality of giving addicts drugs arose between the police and the medical profession, the question was referred for clarification to a committee of eminent physicians, known as the Rolleston Committee. In 1926 they recommended that narcotic drugs be lawfully prescribed to addicts where good medical practice required. Though never formally enacted into law, this became the foundation of British drug policy.[2]

The Rolleston Committee saw drug addiction as a medical problem to be treated like any other illness. Treatment was left to the individual doctor, informed by the committee's guidelines. No necessity or authority for police interference with the doctor-patient relationship existed. The recommendations also ensured that the British law, in most respects identical with the American, did not imbue prevailing attitudes toward drug use with hate and condemnation. In the eyes of the law and the public, drug addicts were sick people in need of medical treatment, not social menaces deserving harassment and jail.

The British system worked quite simply. A person who for whatever reason was addicted to drugs went to his physician and, if found to be addicted and in need of drugs to prevent discomfort, received a prescription. Often the prescription was covered by the National Health Service and cost no more than thirty cents. The Home Office kept informal records of the number of addicts, though neither addicts nor doctors were required to report. Drug inspectors periodically inspected pharmacists' and doctors' records. Some police activity occurred with cannabis and opium, but from 1945 to 1960 drug arrests never exceeded 300 annually (some of these were merely technical offenses). Britain, whose population was one-fourth that of the United States, had no more than 500 known addicts. The majority of these addictions were therapeutic in origin, and they clustered in the over-30 age bracket. With cheap legal supplies, a black market in heroin was unknown. There was no supply of heroin to initiate new users, and addict-related crime was nonexistent. The medical model, in short, was a rousing success.

The critical importance of the medical profession in maintaining this system is illustrated by the government's attempt in 1955 to ban all manufacture of heroin.[3] It appears that this move was inspired by American attempts at a worldwide ban on heroin. The reaction of the medical profession was overwhelmingly negative. Two important medical rights had been infringed—the right to prescribe a drug that doctors felt had a legitimate medical use, even for nonaddicts, and interference with a medical prerogative without consulting the profession. Furthermore, it was felt that the addiction situation would deteriorate. Faced with a politically strong profession, the government eventually backed down and lifted the ban on heroin manufacture.

In the late 1950s pill-taking caught on as a fad among certain youth groups. The Brain Committee (a committee of physicians convened by the Minister of Health but known popularly by the name of its chairman, Lord Brain) was appointed in 1958 to review "in light of more recent developments" the Rolleston guidelines and the necessity to extend them to "cover other drugs liable to produce addiction or be habit-forming." In 1961 the Brain Committee reported[4] that

> . . . the incidence of addiction to drugs . . . is still very small and traffic in illicit supplies is almost negligible, cannabis excepted. This is mainly due to the attitude of the public and to the systematic enforcement of the Dangerous Drug legislation.

The report found "no reason to think that any increase was occurring" and again emphasized that "addiction should be regarded as an expression of mental disorder, rather than a form of criminal behavior."[5]

BREAKDOWN OF THE MEDICAL MODEL— THE BRAIN REPORT

By 1964 the conclusions of the Brain Report were out of date. The public became aware and then alarmed by a growing addiction problem. In an atmosphere of emergency, the Brain Committee was recalled in July 1964 to reconsider the prescribing of addictive drugs. This time the Committee found an alarming increase in the use of addictive drugs and in abuses among doctors prescribing them. It learned[6] that from 1959 to 1964 the total number of known addicts had risen from 454 to 753, the number of heroin addicts from 68 to 342, of cocaine addicts from 30 to 211. Even more alarming, unlike former British addicts, most of these new addicts were nontherapeutic in origin (328 of 342). Also the age of addicts had dropped drastically. In 1959 only 50 of 454 addicts had been less than 35 years old, and by 1964 nearly 40 percent were, 40 of them being under 20.

Why had this upsurge in addiction occurred? The Committee again found a "black" market nonexistent, but did discover a thriving "gray" market, dependent on drugs legally prescribed by doctors. It appeared that a small number of doctors had been prescribing legal, but excessive, doses of heroin to addicts. The addicts then used the excess to recruit friends to heroin use or to make a profit from other users who were reluctant or unable to have a doctor prescribe for them. In 1962, for example, one doctor had prescribed almost *600,000* tablets of heroin to addicts.[7] The same doctor on one occasion had prescribed 900 tablets of heroin to one patient, and three days later prescribed another 600 "to replace pills lost in an accident." Other doctors had each issued single prescriptions for 1,000 tablets.[8] Considerable, if less spectacular, quantities were also prescribed over a long period of time.

While in perhaps two cases (the notorious Drs. Petro and Swan), the physicians were overprescribing for gain, the situation arose primarily out of the medical profession's own reluctance to deal with addicts. Indeed, the Brain Committee found that the overprescribers "had embarked on the treatment of addicts out of a sense of duty because they felt that the treatment facilities elsewhere were inadequate."[9] Addicts did not make good patients. They were often unruly, clamored for higher doses, and were difficult to cure. Many doctors believed that their disease was the result of weakness, and for that reason felt more concerned about the organic maladies of other patients. The medical profession, in short, was prejudiced against addicts, and few doctors would treat addicts at all.

The problem arose when the few doctors who were willing to treat addicts opened their rolls to all addicts unable to obtain treatment elsewhere. In one year two of these doctors each had 100 addicts on his list, and they became known to all London addicts. They justified their prescribing of heroin as necessary to prevent a black market, to treat addicts who were rejected elsewhere, to publicize the lack of treatment facilities, and to cure addicts by providing maintenance doses. The Brain Committee found that these doctors had "acted within the law and according to their professional judgment."[10] But overprescribing was inevitable in this situation. A typical consultation between addict and doctor resembled a union negotiating session rather than a professional consultation. The addict, knowing he could make enough money to live on by selling heroin at £1 a grain, would exaggerate his need to the doctor. The doctor, aware of this ploy, might prescribe half as much as he asked. Through acting, bluffing, and persuasion, the addict would eventually squeeze a few extra grains from the overworked physician who had a waiting room full of addicts.[11] Or an addict might supplement his supply from another doctor. There was no time to observe what doses were needed, obtain other medical opinion, or call the addict's bluff. With so few doctors willing to treat addicts, excessive prescribing and the resulting "gray" market were inevitable.

The Brain Committee's solution was to retain the medical model with modifications to control overprescribing. Restrictions so severe that addicts were prevented or discouraged from obtaining drugs legally would encourage a black market in heroin. To avoid this, the Brain Committee proposed restricting heroin and cocaine prescriptions to addicts, but did not limit the doctor's right to prescribe these drugs to ordinary patients. Doctors, by law, would need a license to prescribe heroin and cocaine to addicts. Only doctors on the staffs of special treatment centers attached to psychiatric units of hospitals and providing inpatient and outpatient treatment to addicts would be licensed. A doctor who disregarded these regulations could be struck off the register. The report still urged that "the addict should be regarded as a sick person . . . and not as a criminal, provided he does not resort to criminal acts."[12] Second, it reaffirmed the autonomy of the medical profession: "Doctors should retain the right to prescribe, supply or administer any dangerous drug required for other patients in the treatment of organic disease."[13] Some doctors resented even this limited restriction on their traditional prerogatives; but on the whole, it appeared a reasonable compromise, and was not strongly opposed.

Two other recommendations further strengthened the operation of the medical model. One provided for the "notification" of addicts to a central authority at the Home Office by any doctors coming into a professional relationship with them. Centralized records would prevent the same addict from obtaining drugs from more than one treatment center, and would provide epidemiological data. The second recommendation was to set up a mechanism to discipline doctors violating the prescribing restrictions.[14] Rather than make noncompliance a crime, a medical tribunal usually concerned with professional matters would adjudicate whether a doctor had unlawfully prescribed heroin or cocaine to an addict. If a violation was found to have occurred, the sole sanction was the removal of the right to prescribe the restricted drugs to nonaddicted patients.

The Brain Committee recommendations, sensible and dispassionate as they seemed, did not guarantee an immediate solution to the heroin increase or to public anxiety, nor was there unanimity on the soundness of the committee's approach. There was first of all the problem of implementation, which the committee had noted with its qualification that "our proposals are dependent on such treatment facilities being readily available at short notice."[15] For a while government delay and political jockeying made problematic the opening of the recommended treatment centers, and increased the likelihood of a black market developing to handle addicts' needs. Finally in 1967, two years after the report, the Dangerous Drug Act of 1967 was passed, incorporating the principal recommendations. However, despite a feverish public pulse, it was not until May 1968, the law's effective date, that the treatment centers were first opened. In the meantime, the problems referred to in the report had continued. In 1965 the number of addicts had increased to 927, with 134 under 20 years of age on heroin. The figures for 1967 were 1,729, with almost 400 under 20 taking heroin.

Furthermore, it was feared that the new restrictions on prescribing would not prevent the development of an American-style black market. Many young addicts might not voluntarily go to the treatment centers. Some experts suggested that greater powers, such as compulsory confinement of addicts during withdrawal be granted the government. It was also thought that the restrictions might divert users to other drugs and simply transfer the heroin problem elsewhere. Finally, maintenance doses for the young seemed out of keeping with the Rolleston philosophy of providing drugs only after other cures had been tried and had failed. No attempt had been made to cure many of the younger addicts.

Soon after they opened, it seemed that the treatment centers had avoided the problems feared and achieved some success in controlling the spread of heroin addiction. Dr. Dale Beckett, a doctor in charge of a treatment unit, reported in a television interview:[16]

> I think they've been very effective indeed. . . . One had the fear that two opposite things might have happened: firstly, that there would have been so little heroin prescribed that the illegal black market would have become established, and this of course would have led to enormous difficulties in society. The opposite extreme would have been the gross overprescription of heroin, because of the relative inexperience of the psychiatrists in the treatment centers, but again this really hasn't happened. What seems to have happened is that a happy medium has been struck, and a little less heroin is now being prescribed than was prescribed previously.

Another doctor from a treatment center in London, when asked whether the treatment centers were working, answered:[17]

> It depends on your aims. Ours were to control the spread of heroin addiction and control the amount of heroin on the market.

In this regard, we've been successful, I believe. I've seen only a few cases of heroin addiction. We have seen a spread of methadone and barbiturates.

The treatment centers have been able to hold down the spread of heroin addiction. The cure of existing addicts, however, is another matter altogether. It soon became clear that the outpatient clinics were only the first step in that process. The Advisory Committee on Drug Dependence has commented on the outpatient clinics and rehabilitation:[18]

> We consider that rehabilitation begins with the first contact of the addict with the outpatient clinic. We are concerned that in some quarters these centers are being regarded as mere prescribing units without any positive objective. Outpatient clinics are also rehabilitation clinics. Their object should be to encourage the addict to accept hospital admission for withdrawal and to make use of the opportunity which prescribing gives to build a constructive relationship with the addict. For this purpose longer and more frequent visits by the addict are desirable than would be necessary if maintenance were the sole objective. . . . We visualize the outpatient clinics as being strategically placed to form the focal point for the whole process of rehabilitation.

If this process were to be successful, there had to be adequate staffing of a full therapeutic team, including social workers; hospital beds had to be immediately available for addicts willing to be admitted; and hostels providing short-term accommodation for homeless addicts on outpatient treatment had to be established.

THE NEW DRUG SCENE

The steady increase in heroin addiction after 1963 profoundly altered public perceptions and attitudes toward drug use. The medical approach had shielded drug use, both physically and psychologically, from public attention. Drug addiction had been generally perceived as a minor health problem, affecting a few hundred unfortunate people who had accidentally acquired drug habits and who caused no major difficulties.

Suddenly, almost overnight, drugs escaped from the clinic into the street, and then into the consciousness of a startled, unprepared public. Junkies became familiar inhabitants of the mass media. They were visible late at night in Piccadilly Circus and were reputedly plotting the subversion of young people.

Traditional ideas about addiction no longer applied. The new addicts were not therapeutic in origin, but were seeking kicks and thrills. They were associated in the public mind with seaside riots among mods and rockers, with the emerging youth culture and rebellion. An older addict expressed the resentment felt by many nonaddicts:[19]

> Just a drag [the new addict], you know, because they don't take drugs because of some need or personal defect. It's just a case of exhibitionism with them, you know, the fact that "I'm a registered addict, take me," kind of thing. They go around with the hypodermic sticking out of their top pocket kind of thing, and just advertising the fact that they're on drugs, you know.

Finally, protection by the medical profession was no longer assured. In fact, the loose prescribing habits of doctors were one of the causes of the problem. When illegal methadrine, methadone, and barbiturate use became problems, again the medical profession was responsible. Bewildered and impotent, the public was confronted with a new social problem that seemed to threaten the very roots of society.

The rhetoric used to describe the drug situation captures much of the fear and anxiety disturbing the public. Invariably, addiction was likened to a bubonic plague, spreading at epidemic speed. Each addict was a "carrier" of the disease, liable to "infect" four or five other young people: newspapers reported how a single youth was the pathogenic agent responsible for the 30 addicts in Crawley New Town.[20] To heighten the alarm, "experts" speculated on the number of addicts expected in the next few years. The more conservative estimate[21] was 11,000 by 1970 or 70,000 by

1975. Inspector Terence Jones,[22] a police specialist in drugs, commented:

> The disease is spreading and it seems likely that in the not too distant future every town in the country will be infected. . . . Estimates have been made that by the 1980s there could be a million addicts.

Another writer summarized the situation in these terms:[23]

> There has hardly been another social problem which has aroused as much public attention as drug addiction in the course of the last twelve months. All the media of mass communication have combined in unleashing a veritable torrent of reports, comments, and suggestions. Drug addiction and drug abuse have been discussed and debated in virtually every forum of published opinion. Only those most directly affected—the addicts—have remained relatively inarticulate. . . . Public discussion has been characterized by a sense of foreboding, if not of impending disaster. Wild estimates have been made about the number of addicts which Britain will have in ten years' time. It seems as if the measure of alarm is only equaled by the degree of perplexity which accompanies the search for an answer to the problem. It is sometimes difficult to tell whether the debate and the publicity have not assumed an almost independent existence—a dynamic of their own. . . .

The full flavor of the public atmosphere in the late 1960s is best illustrated by three typical news stories concerning drugs that received wide circulation, but little verification. The first was a report, which gained wide currency, that there was "Chinese" heroin in Soho.[24] For a public concerned about addiction, and particularly the emergence of a black market, the very presence of imported heroin was ominous. By identifying it as "Chinese," and associating the drug in the public mind with the sinister world of opium dens, the report intensified worry and apprehension. The report turned out to be a complete fabrication; no evidence of foreign heroin was ever produced.[25]

A second story related the discovery of a new drug "many times more powerful than LSD" and "easily manufactured by any graduate chemist."[26] This story was actually referring to the hallucinogen STP (dimethoxy-4-methylamphetamine), then being used by a small number of people in the United States, and which was much less easy to prepare than the story claimed. Newspapers and politicians publicized STP in a way calculated to confirm the public's worst fears of a new drug about to engulf Britain.

In the third story a research psychologist who had founded an organization to promote cannabis research and law reform was described as "the world's most dangerous man."[27] To be objective, there were in 1968 greater dangers in the world than the possibility of easing the cannabis law. This characterization, however, and its predictable impact on the millions of readers aroused by the threat of drugs, is typical of the drug situation at this time.

Besides these and other deliberate scare stories in the press, there were some genuinely frightening aspects of the new drug scene. For example, there were the mercurial fads in drug use, which made it almost impossible for officials and legal policy to keep abreast of the latest developments. The public was threatened with wave after wave of drug use by users who were willing to switch drugs at will to stay ahead of the authorities. In 1967, for example, methadrine became a new problem. This was the fault of the medical profession: after the Brain Report many doctors had substituted methadrine for the cocaine usually prescribed to addicts with their heroin. Soon addicts were switching over entirely to methadrine. Although the drug is more dangerous than the heroin and cocaine it replaced, there were no legal powers to stop doctors prescribing it. When the supply of methadrine was finally cut off in 1969, mandrax became popular, another stimulant then legally prescribable. In 1970 barbiturates appealed to users seeking an injectable drug. The possibilities seemed endless, and the public felt that firm action must be taken.

These fears were made worse by the tendency already noted in the American context to see all drugs as equal threats and to exaggerate greatly the power of drugs. Newspaper stories almost invariably referred to "drugs," which could mean anything from cannabis to mandrax, without differentiating which drug was involved. Reports of cannabis offenses often referred to "junkies" and the "junkie menace," a lumping together of two radically different problems. The distortion and exaggeration are evident in the account of an Oxford undergraduate convicted of possessing cannabis. She ran "a junkies' paradise," and had enough cannabis to supply hospitals "for sixty years."[28] The public belief in progression and in the enslaving, destructive power of drugs—attitudes familiar from our discussion of the United States—intensified the atmosphere of crisis.

Public fears focused on the increase in heroin addiction highlight the British response to the drug scene. It was grossly disproportionate to the real dimensions of the problem. While the upward trend continued for the next few years (see table), the

NUMBER OF BRITISH ADDICTS*

Year	Total Addicts Known	Morphine	Heroin	Methadone	Other
1960	437	177	94	68	150
1961	470	168	132	59	189
1962	532	157	175	54	224
1963	653	172	237	59	294
1964	753	171	342	62	339
1965	927	160	521	72	413
1966	1,349	157	899	156	564
1967	1,729	158	1,299	243	574
1968	2,782	198	2,240	486	684
1969	2,881	345	793	1,687	457

* This table is based on data supplied by the British Home Office.

number of reported addicts never exceeded 3,000. By 1969 the rate of increase had dwindled, and the number of heroin addicts actually decreased by 1,450—many were being maintained on methadone in the outpatient treatment centers. When in 1965 heroin became a major issue, there had been an increase in the past two years of 300 users. Seen as an increase of 200 percent it was considerable; but in absolute terms, it was not a shattering blow to public health. In 1965 there were an estimated 350,000 alcoholics in Britain,[29] and weekend drinking alone caused 28,000,000 lost man-hours on Mondays. In the same year 35,000 people died of lung cancer.[30] Compared with heroin use in America, the increase was a mere flutter. A few blocks in Harlem contained more addicts, at considerably more cost, than all of Britain. Also, it was not clear whether the new addiction figures reflected an actual increase in numbers of addicts or were simply a more accurate count. Many addicts had postponed "registering"— going to a doctor themselves for drugs—for many months; it signified psychologically that they were "hooked,"[31] a state they were able to deny they were in as long as they got drugs from friends. Finally, without taking account of population growth and greater stress from social change, the mere fact of an increase was misleading.

Even if it is agreed that the public health dangers of addiction were greatly exaggerated, other features of the situation fanned the temperature of public concern. One was the knowledge that non-medical drug use of all kinds had risen drastically. Heroin addiction was merely the tip of an iceberg. Youthful drug use was thought to be expanding at a frightful rate, from "purple hearts" (amphetamines) in West End coffee bars and clubs to cannabis and, soon after, experimentation with LSD and heroin. The public became aware not of a single heroin or cannabis subculture, but of multiple drug subcultures, through which young people freely moved. Nor could drugs be dismissed as part of the London scene or an aspect of mods and rocker delinquency. All classes had their users. The nephew of a former prime minister died of a drug overdose at Oxford. In public schools and universities large numbers of students were found to be using drugs. At the same time, sales of medically prescribed drugs were increasing at an unprecedented rate. In 1966—one of the peak years of the "drug crisis"— four million prescriptions for amphetamine substances and fifteen million for barbiturates were issued.[32]

Public concern was also aroused by the conviction and selfrighteousness of young drug users. They wore bizarre clothes, grew their hair long, and challenged the authority of their parents. Both youth and drug use were inextricably associated with an emerging culture and life-style that clashed with traditional ideas. The drug users refused to acknowledge the wrongness of their drug use. In Gusfield's term, they were "enemy deviants."[33] They attacked the norm; they transgressed, and heaped scorn and ridicule on its backers. This generated great hostility and anxiety in the older generation: not only were young people committing illegal acts that threatened the nation's capacity to "get on with" pressing national problems, but they were proclaiming the desirability, indeed the righteousness, of doing so.

International Times, the newspaper of the alienated young, and R. D. Laing articulated the full depth of the attack launched by the young. *International Times* delineated an underground counterculture slowly flowering under the decadent, sterile forms of the old "bomb culture."[34] The counterculture had boundless energy, its own leaders, clubs, art forms, and encompassed all that was new and vital in an increasingly sterile society. Postindustrial capitalism, *International Times* argued, could not even provide basic social services, much less satisfy spiritual longings and the need for personal fulfillment. Drugs, which helped provide those experiences, were outlawed and their users suppressed because the spontaneity they inspired demonstrated the establishment's bankruptcy. R. D. Laing, in his *Politics of Experience*, states even more explicitly that the boundary of the real, and the right of adult society to define that boundary, was the issue. A decadent order incapable of satisfying basic human needs was maintained by a psychic dictatorship. The establishment defined consciousness arbitrarily, but in such a way that constructs such as an ego and the virtues of a scientific, mechanistic capitalism were essential. Drugs and psychic disruptions like schizophrenia toppled the ego's battlements and catalyzed creative, spiritual energies repressed by the dominant culture. They were thus tools in the political battle for consciousness.

In the face of such justifications of drug use, the public not unnaturally perceived users as determined to destroy society. Drug use threatened social chaos on two counts: it either turned people into addicts or made them cultural revolutionaries.

A third feature of the situation arousing public concern was the confusion surrounding the whole subject of drug control. Although few people condoned heroin use, there was considerable disagreement about the harmfulness of other drugs, and particularly over the role that the law should play in their control. The inflated urgency of the drug problem made firm opposition to all drugs seem the best and simplest approach. Doubts that some drugs could be used safely had to be stifled, because they threatened the whole edifice of strict prohibition.

Cannabis use, in particular, was ambiguous. It appeared to be a causative factor in addiction, was identified at law with heroin, and was extremely popular among young people. A tough position against its use was thus required. On the other hand, since there were legitimate doubts about its harmfulness, and more and more respectable people were using it apparently without ill effects, the possibility of a ten-year jail sentence seemed unwarranted.

The confusion surrounding cannabis was manifested by the events following the publication of a full-page advertisement in *The* (London) *Times* of July 27, 1967. The ad called the cannabis laws "immoral in principle and unworkable in practice" and demanded a reduction in penalties and legal differentiation from heroin. It cited the growing numbers of users, the paucity of evidence of ill effects, and the growing social costs of a law violated by thousands. Its signatories included psychiatrists, two Members of Parliament, and a Nobel Prize winner. The public heaped abuse on *The Times* for allegedly encouraging drug addiction, and a parliamentary debate on the ad followed. It is easy, however, to see how the *Times* ad could further the public consternation. Appearing a few months after the Dangerous Drug Act of 1967 enacted into law the second Brain Report, the ad undercut the bulwarks being constructed against heroin. It revealed the exaggerations in the public response to the drug problem and confused the public further by arguing that some drug use should be acceptable. Moreover, it suggested the possibility that the young people were, after all, right. In stressing distortions in the law, it raised doubts about the propriety of any legal control over drug use. The dominant mood was expressed by Mr. Channon in the Commons debate when he urged that an inquiry into cannabis take place "because we require urgent public action, and action which will convince young people."[35]

On the heels of awareness that a "drug problem" existed came urgent demands for action to halt "the spreading tide of drug use." Existing statutory controls seemed blatantly inadequate. They contained loopholes for overprescribing doctors, and were unable to cope with the fast-changing fashions of drug use. Moreover, inconsistencies and disparities in the treatment of drugs like cannabis, LSD, and the amphetamines undermined respect for the law, while the absolute nature of certain offenses and the enforcement practices of the police were criticized as unfair. Unfortunately, such wide-ranging questions as these are not best solved in an atmosphere of crisis. As we shall see, the public's fear, confusion, and growing demand for certainty about drugs strongly influenced the action taken.

As we have mentioned with regard to addiction, the public mood had facilitated government acceptance of the Brain recommendations, and prevented the normally strong medical profession from resisting limits on their prescribing authority. Indeed, in this climate it is surprising that stronger measures against doctors or addicts were not included in the Dangerous Drug Act of 1967. The act merely enacted the careful recommendations of the Brain Report that doctors be licensed to prescribe heroin and cocaine.

But prescription by an unlicensed doctor was not made a crime. It only initiated a cumbersome administrative procedure before a medical tribunal which could eventuate in removal from the medical register. By contrast, American doctors had been systematically harassed in the decade after the Harrison Narcotic Act for their prescribing, and today are subject to stiff penalties for not reporting addicts to authorities. Similarly, addicts were subject only to the inconvenience of obtaining their prescriptions at a treatment clinic rather than at their doctor's office. Some voices urged compulsory commitment of addicts,[36] but these had little support, while in the United States at that time millions were being spent in confining addicts to treatment "hospitals."

For Britain, however, despite its nonpunitive elements, the Dangerous Drug Act represented a novel departure that might have been impossible in a less anxious moment. For the first time the prescribing practices of the powerful medical profession were being restricted by the government. Also, the government had to assume responsibility for treating addicts, a problem hitherto in private hands. In this atmosphere acceptance of a relatively benign and rational solution to the problem of addiction can perhaps be explained by the political power of doctors, the shortage of medical facilities, and the attitude, ingrained from years of the medical model, that addicts were, after all, sick people. Toward cannabis users and others who claimed that the law was arbitrary or unfair, no such constraints prevented the public from venting its wrath. The remainder of this chapter describes the impact of those attitudes on the other issues of drug control that the explosion of drug use had uncovered.

THE WOOTTON REPORT

As we have said, cannabis, the opiates, and cocaine were regulated under the same act and subject to the same penalties. A single act of possession or sale of cannabis in any quantity could, like heroin, bring a ten-year jail sentence and a £1,000 fine.[37] Moreover, a person could be prosecuted if someone without his knowledge smoked cannabis on his premises. Strong drugs like LSD and methadrine were subject to the lighter penalties under the Drugs (Prevention of Misuse) Act, which did not make even sale a crime. And barbiturates were not illegal at all.[38] Legal restrictions also made cannabis research difficult, if not impossible.

As the number of cannabis users increased, these provisions became a major cause of controversy. They also undermined the credibility of the law and alienated many young people from the legal system. Indeed, the pattern of convictions under the Dangerous Drug Act revealed an emphasis on prosecuting cannabis users: [39]

CONVICTIONS FOR DRUG USE

Year	Cannabis	Opium	Manufactured Drugs	Total
1964	544	14	101	659
1965	626	13	128	767
1966	1,109	36	208	1,353
1967	2,393	58	573	3,024
1968	3,071	73	1,099	4,243

In 1967, nine out of ten offenses were for possessing less than 30 grams.[40]

The *Times* ad sharpened the controversy surrounding the drug. As we have seen, the government responded by having the Advisory Committee on Drug Dependence study the question and make recommendations. A subcommittee chaired by Baroness Wootton prepared a report that was endorsed by the main committee and submitted to the Home Secretary in December 1968. The Wootton Report, however, was not able to dispel the confusion or hammer out a consensus on the question of cannabis. Indeed, it intensified the cannabis controversy and gave added weight to charges leveled at law. Since this incident reflects the interplay of social attitudes, we will examine the report and the reaction to it in detail.

The Wootton subcommittee was composed of twelve members. Lady Wootton was an energetic, highly respected life-peer who had made valuable contributions in the fields of sociology, law, and economics. Among its other members were an assistant commissioner of Scotland Yard, a magistrate, a research sociologist, and four doctors. For the purposes of the cannabis study, two noted pharmacologists were added to the committee. Over the course of eighteen months it heard witnesses, discussed findings, and surveyed the existing body of knowledge. Although legal restrictions prevented original research, it heard a wide variety of witnesses, including the president of the United Nations Opium Board, drug users, and experts with wide experience with cannabis.

The report concentrated on three topics: (1) the effects of cannabis in different cultures; (2) its role in the current drug scene; and (3) the legal provisions relating to its use. Noting the uniqueness of its work for the United Kingdom and the uncertainty surrounding certain aspects of cannabis use, the committee nevertheless found that it could, on the available evidence, form "a reasonably clear picture of the use of cannabis in the United Kingdom."[41] In light of the evidence before it, it agreed with the conclusions of the Indian Hemp Commission (1893–94) and the LaGuardia Report (1944) that "the long-term consumption of cannabis in *moderate* doses has no harmful effects."[42] It then summarized the clinical features of the drug and described the general configuration of use in the United Kingdom in terms of use, users, supply, and effects. Contentions that cannabis use produced psychosis or violent crimes were examined and found to lack empirical support. With regard to progression to heroin, the committee concluded that "it can clearly be argued on the world picture that cannabis use does not lead to heroin and . . . a risk of progression to heroin . . . is not a reason for retaining control."[43] The committee also compared cannabis with other drugs in common use, such as alcohol, nicotine, caffeine, barbiturates, and tranquilizers. While it was not able to make any definitive comparison, it did note that social attitudes toward drug use were changing. It concluded[44] from the available evidence that

> An increasing number of people, mainly young, in all classes of society are experimenting with . . . [cannabis], and substantial numbers use it regularly for social pleasure.
> There is no evidence that this activity is causing violent crime or aggressive anti-social behavior, or is producing in otherwise normal people conditions of dependence or psychosis, requiring medical treatment.

The experience of many other countries is that once it is established cannabis-smoking tends to spread. In some parts of Western society where interest in mood-altering drugs is growing, there are indications that it may become a functional equivalent of alcohol.

In spite of the threat of severe penalties and considerable effort at enforcement the use of cannabis in the United Kingdom does not appear to be diminishing. There is a body of opinion that criticizes the present legislative treatment of cannabis on the grounds that it exaggerates the dangers of the drug and needlessly interferes with civil liberty.

The Wootton Committee, however, was not prepared to give cannabis a totally clean bill of health. It cited a number of imponderables concerning its chronic pharmacological effects, its mode of operation in the body, and problems in detecting its presence. As a drug capable of altering mood, judgment, and functional ability, cannabis was clearly as potent as alcohol, and could be fairly considered a dangerous drug. Accordingly, public health required restrictions on the availability and use. For this purpose, the committee concluded that there was no alternative to the criminal law and is penalties.

Although the Wootton Committee explicitly rejected "legalization" of cannabis for personal use, it did find that the dangers of the drug had been greatly exaggerated and that, accordingly, a reduction in penalties was in order. Cannabis users, it found, were often treated harshly and, in view of the relative harms, unfairly. It attributed this treatment to the harsh judgment contained in the law and the legal identification with drugs like heroin. In 1967, for example, of the 2,734 persons arrested for cannabis offenses, two thirds had no record of nondrug offenses. Nine out of ten offenses were for possessing less than 30 grams. And yet a quarter of all offenders went to prison, including 17 percent of first offenders. Accordingly, the committee recommended a reduction in penalties and a statutory separation from the opiates. Since a quantity limitation or presumption of intent created administrative problems in distinguishing between possession for personal use and sale, it was decided that

> The only practical way to legislate for the situation over the next few years is to retain the principle of a single offense, namely, unlawful possession, sale or supply of cannabis or its derivatives. This offense should carry a low range of penalties on summary conviction but a substantially higher range on indictment. If such legislation were brought in we would anticipate that the police would proceed on indictment only in those cases in which they believed that there was organized, large-scale trafficking. Offenses involving simple possession and small-scale trafficking would, we hope, be dealt with summarily.[45]

> . . . our main aim . . . is to remove . . . for *practical* purposes, the prospect of imprisonment for possession of a small amount and to demonstrate that taking the drug in moderation is a relatively minor offense . . . and not . . . an antisocial act or evidence of unsatisfactory moral character.[46]

On summary conviction a fine of £ 100 and imprisonment for up to four months could be imposed. The prison sentence was felt necessary to deter small-scale suppliers who would not be deterred by a fine. However, the right to a jury trial was assured, and the judge's power to suspend sentence would mitigate even this possibility of jail. Sentences on indictment were reduced to be two years' imprisonment and an unlimited fine. The fine was to be reserved only for large-scale traffickers. Sentences, however, were to be kept under review, and changes made if the objective of preventing prison terms was not achieved, or other relevant information developed. Mr. Peter Brodie, the police commissioner, and Mr. Michael Scofield, the sociologist, filed reservations to these recommendations. Mr. Brodie thought that deterrence of the large-scale trafficker likely to be attracted by an increasing demand for cannabis would occur only if imprisonment was certain and recommended that the sentence for possession of substantial quantities not for use be five years. Mr. Scofield, on the other hand, believed that rather than have the question of imprisonment for personal use depend on a magistrate's discretion, a maximum fine of £50 should be allowed. On summary conviction for possession of less than 30 grams, he recommended that no penalty be imposed.

The Wootton Report* thus tried to bring the law closer to the practical realities and dangers of cannabis use by dissociating it legally from heroin and reducing penalties for personal use. Although information about the drug was far from complete, a convincing case for its relative harmlessness existed. Since further study and increased use might reveal dangers, particularly with chronic use, it was essential to guard against any encouragement of the practice. For the interim, however, the possibility of jail and the association with other dangerous drugs was undesirable. Accordingly, the Wootton Committee chose to lessen the ill effects of the law, while maintaining societal disapproval of the drug and strict control of its use. The penalty recommendations, in fact, merely recognized the pattern of current sentences, which in 1967 were fines that averaged £37.[47]

The Wootton Committee thus chose to tread a careful middle-of-the-road path that protected public sensibilities while reducing the greatest costs and injustices of the law. It firmly rejected legalization, but also refused to condemn cannabis users. Its final position was remarkably similar to the American Medical Association's 1968 report on marijuana, which, while recognizing dangers, strongly urged a reduction of penalties for users.

THE RECEPTION OF THE WOOTTON REPORT

On January 9, 1969, the report was published. In terms of attention and emotion, the reaction was explosive. Rather than quieting the cannabis controversy, as the Brain Committee had done with heroin, the Wootton Report intensified polarization and deepened the public's need to cling to a distorted view of cannabis. To

---

* It also discussed research, premises offense, education, control of synthetic cannabinols, and power of search and arrest.

maintain this view in face of the contrary findings of the Committee, the public resorted to avoidance and denial mechanisms which twisted the facts and recommendations of the Report into a more palatable meaning.

The press, with a few exceptions, capitalized on the public fear with bold headlines and strident editorial comment. The *Express's* headlines read "Storm over Pot-Smokers Charter," and quoted an unnamed psychiatrist as saying that the Wootton Committee "must be mad and haven't read the textbooks."[48] The *Mail* and *Sketch* called the result "sadly muddled, and unconvincing," and saw it as "an official bid to take another step along the permissive society's road."[49] The *Sketch* suggested "the best thing to do with the report is dump it in the waste paper basket."[50] The *Evening News* printed a letter from a female addict who blamed her addiction on cannabis. All papers carried Dr. Elizabeth Tylden's comment that "the report was a junkie's charter and was merely haggling over how long it takes a drug to kill someone."[51] These papers invariably refused to accept the Wootton Committee's finding that there was no causal connection between cannabis and heroin. Most editors found the Wootton Report's reasoning "tortured" or "unconvincing" for failing to draw a clear-cut boundary. If cannabis wasn't so bad, it was argued, why wasn't it legalized. If there was a possibility of harm, why encourage its use by lowering penalties.[52] An intermediate position, adapted to the ambiguity of the situation, seemed intolerable.

During a period of two weeks, the issue was kept at boiling point. Newspapers reported the drug alarms then sweeping Sweden over, not cannabis, but stimulants. Several articles reported that the World Health Organization, then holding a convention, was opposed to the Wootton Report, while it actually supported reduction of penalties and objected only to legalization. The Wootton Report had tried to dissociate cannabis from other drugs, but the media grouped all drugs together. Numerous articles mentioned a "worldwide increase in drug-taking," discussing methadrine, heroin addiction, and reports of increased cannabis use in the same breath.[53]

On June 23, Mr. James Callaghan, the Home Secretary, took part in a debate in the House of Commons on the Wootton Report. Both Conservative and Labour members, led by Callaghan, rebuked the Wootton Committee. This debate further revealed the devices employed to maintain the prevailing view of drug use when a conflict arises. Most frequent were simple assertions contradicting the report, without citing other evidence. Mr. Quintin Hogg quoted a newspaper report claiming that cannabis produced "moral and social decay," aggressiveness, degradation of the personality, "misery, crime and unhappiness."[54] Few speakers would accept that a distinction between cannabis and heroin was valid, despite the report's contrary findings. The Home Secretary, for example, devoted the major part of his speech to discussing other drugs. He spoke of the dangers of an "easily manufactured" drug ten times more potent than LSD, cited statistics about the rise in heroin addiction, and alluded to methadrine abuse. He claimed that "it is simply not possible to say that those who smoke cannabis do not move on to heroin."[55] Another discrediting ploy was to charge the report with advocating legalization, although it clearly rejected that alternative. The Home Secretary's mind boggled at "the thought of licensing the sale of cannabis by the local tobacconist, off license . . . thereby creating centers where people will start on one drug and very easily move on to another."[56]

The Wootton Report, it will be recalled, refuted the progression theory and mentioned the possibility of future legal distribution only if forthcoming research showed no harm from the drug. When the report's recommendations were actually discussed, it was solely in terms of their symbolic overtones. Callaghan[57] rejected the report:

> I cannot reconcile the view that the wider use of cannabis should not be encouraged with the proposal that legislation brought in to reduce the existing penalties for possession, sale, or supply of cannabis would be bound to lead people to think that the government take a less than serious view of the effects of drug-taking. [Cheers] That is not so.

In his view, any liberalization of the law was a symbolic capitulation to the drug users and the values they represented, and therefore had to be rejected. The advocates of legal change were "another aspect of so-called permissive society, and I am glad if my decision has enabled the House to call a halt in the advancing tide of so-called permissiveness."[58] Perhaps Parliament was most disconcerted by the report's failure to eliminate ambiguity with a clear-cut black-and-white solution to the problem. The need for absolute and utter certainty was evident in the persistent description of a reduction of penalties as "a step in the direction of legalization," in Callaghan's refusal to acknowledge the special position of cannabis, and in the claim that another law would only confuse the public. Distinctions among drugs and their effects would conflict with the view that all drug use was a serious social threat. In a final effort to discredit the report, Callaghan accused the committee of being "overinfluenced" by the "pot lobby,"[59] and treated its conclusions as those of the lobby.

The response to the Wootton Report reveals a public so terrified by drugs that its reason and better judgment are overcome. In contrast to the careful, moderate, well-reasoned report, the reaction of the press and Parliament is hysterical, illogical, and untruthful. The Wootton Committee is maligned and its conclusions ignored, misstated, or denied. Dominating the public response is the need to condemn drug use, apparently at all costs—to express the societal judgment that drugs are immoral and undesirable and, above all, to avoid any public action that could signify permissiveness toward drug use. The narrow question of the law and its reform became the arena for symbolizing a social judgment, which could not be compromised.

POLICE POWERS

Another problem awakened by the drug issue was the question of police powers and abuses in enforcing the drug laws. With a mounting public outcry over drugs, the role and powers of the police had expanded greatly. This development was new for both the police and the public. Although since 1920 (the first Dangerous Drugs Act) drugs had been officially a police matter, in practice there was little drug use to be concerned with. Arrest statistics for drug offenses, at a time when the most punitive American legislation was being enacted, showed minimal police activity: [60]

ENFORCEMENT OF DANGEROUS DRUGS ACT*

Year	Cannabis	Opium	Manufactured Drugs	Total
1950	86	41	42	169
1955	115	17	37	169
1960	235	15	28	268
1963	663	20	63	746
1964	544	14	101	659

* The figures represent convictions, except for 1950 when arrests are listed.

After the second Brain Report, however, police took a renewed interest in drugs. Specialized drug squads were organized. The police saw a gap that they alone could fill. From 1965 to 1969 there was a 500 percent rise in the total number of drug convictions: [61]

DRUG CONVICTIONS—1965–69

Year	Cannabis	Other Drugs Controlled Under Dangerous Drugs Act	Drugs (Prevention of Misuse) Act, 1964	Total
1965	620	124	958	1,702
1966	1,109	248	1,216	2,573
1967	2,395	631	2,486	5,512
1968	3,071	1,765	2,957	7,793
1969	4,683	1,412	3,762	9,857

Along with more stringent enforcement came charges that the police were using their powers arbitrarily or unfairly. Young people, in particular, criticized the police for discriminating against them because of their appearance. Complaints also came from other quarters. The home of Lady Diana Duff Cooper was raided by the police (no drugs were found),[62] and *The Times*[63] printed an outraged letter from a London schoolteacher who had been stopped and searched on the street while walking with her teen-age son. There were also allegations of "planting" and corruption.

For Britain these charges have special significance. The British policeman, traditionally regarded as honest, occupies a special position of respect that is increasingly rare in the United States. Police abuses in drug enforcement threatened to alienate certain segments of the public, and introduce hostility into their relationship. Occurring in a period of national adjustment, when young people and immigrant groups were testing the integrity of social institutions, and "law and order" became a political slogan, this was a serious matter. With doubt cast on the propriety of police actions, the whole question of the balance struck by the drug laws between individual liberty and law was thrown open.

The issue is, of course, familiar from American experience. The difficulty of enforcing the drug laws tends to undermine police respect for legal restraints. The police are burdened with enforcing society's moral judgments, yet because such crime is consensual, and values of liberty and fairness equally demanding, the police lack the means for doing so. Jerome Skolnick finds the difficulty inherent in the nature of law enforcement in a democratic society:[64]

> Underlying this [problem] is a more general and fundamental issue growing out of the concept of law enforcement. This issue is the meaning and purpose of law in a democratic society. The idea of law enforcement in such a society, taken seriously, suggests that legally constituted institutions such as the police exist not only to preserve order, but to serve the rule of law as an end in itself. On the other hand, the circumstances of the operational environment, with its associated requirements that the police maintain order, might develop a very different conception of law in police, a conception without articulation or explicit philosophical justification, but existing nevertheless.

The police demand greater powers, or bend existing rules past the point of legality, to enforce laws that their own conception of order and perception of public need appears to require. The resulting practices often engender complaints from individuals, courts, or citizens, and create conflict with the police. The debate on police powers is often imbued with emotions arising from the issues originally creating the need for those powers. The desirability of police limitation then becomes a debate on drugs. The danger is that in staunchly defending the police, values central to democratic order and the rule of law are eroded. Both the American and British experiences suggest that as long as the public assigns to the police the job of enforcing its moral predilections and to this end is willing to tolerate incursions into democratic values—in Leslie Fiedler's words, "a few not quite Kosher searches and seizures"[65]—the relation of police and citizen will be subject to conflict and hostility, and police adherence to law will be undermined.

In Britain many of the problems arose out of the power granted the police in 1967 to stop and search persons suspected "on reasonable grounds" of possessing drugs illegally. This provision had been added to the 1967 Dangerous Drug Act on July 21, during Second Reading in the House of Lords, after most debate had already occurred. The broad police power to stop and search people had been opposed several times in the past. In 1967 the police were not even empowered to arrest drug offenders, unless they were about to abscond or had no fixed address. It is interesting to note the problems that the Lords perceived warranted chancing the "slight possible risk of misuse" which these novel powers created:[66]

> The Association of Chief Police Officers have recently made a full review of the adequacy of police powers in relation to the drug problem. They feel strongly that to deter pushers and enforce restrictions on unauthorized possession of drugs, the police everywhere should be given power to stop and search suspected persons and vehicles. The government recognize fully that to extend police powers in this way is a serious matter, but we must

balance the seriousness of the drug problem against the potential for infringing individual liberty.

The Government believe that there is a strong public demand that young people should be protected from the pushers and peddlars who exploit them. And we are convinced that the best way of affording that protection is to enable the police to play their part, by giving them the powers to stop and search. . . .

As the noble Lord said, we must do our best to stop this traffic if we can. When I say "stop" I am not talking about dealing with addicts; I am talking in particular about stopping the pushers getting new clients. At the moment the police have not the powers to do what they ought to do. A great deal of pushing, particularly in the earlier stages, is done on the street corner. The policeman may be watching, but he may not be close enough to see what is being passed. He knows very well what is going on, but there are difficulties about arrest and search. Therefore, it is absolutely essential to stop this pushing. The number of "pushers" is growing very fast, and it is essential that the police should have these powers. I seldom think that anything which is done by this Government is ever right, but because of this new clause, I forgive them all their sins.

A year later, during its investigation of cannabis, the Wootton Committee became aware of a growing hostility to the police resulting from these powers. It recommended "as a matter of urgency" that a public inquiry be made into them.[67] In addition to abuses of the power to search—growing out of the vagueness of "reasonable grounds" and the tendency of some police to use the power against the young or unconventionally dressed—there were complaints about mass searches in youth clubs, planting of drugs on suspects, corruption, arbitrary denial of bail to drug offenders, and a variety of other matters relating to enforcement of the drug laws. The situation, according to the National Council of Civil Liberties (NCCL), was as follows:[68]

The widespread public enthusiasm for controlling the "drug problem," which, in fact, comprises many different problems, places great pressure on the police force to take action and in the process to minimize the importance of respecting civil liberties of drug users, suspects, and members of the public alike. . . . The individual police officer is conscious of and shares public alarm. He is open to the temptation to bend the rules to secure the conviction of an individual he honestly suspects of having committed a drug offense.

A subcommittee of the Advisory Committee on Drug Dependence, under the chairmanship of William Deedes, a Labour MP, was convened in 1969 to study the subject. Its members included Police Commissioner Brodie, a magistrate, Scofield, Lady Wootton, and Professor Glanville Williams, a noted authority in criminal law. Their report, released in May 1970, illustrates again how the need to condemn drug users overrode the other interests to be balanced in a democracy.

Release and NCCL, two civil rights organizations, presented the Deedes Committee with evidence of incidents in which powers of search, arrest, and bail had been misused by the police. It appeared that the police concentrated on cannabis (72 percent of drug offenses in 1968), and that most of those arrests were for possession of small amounts (49 percent for possession; nine tenths of cannabis cases involved 30 grams or less). The legal profession supported strict controls over police powers and questioned the need for broad powers over cannabis offenders.[69] The police, on the other hand, pointed out:[70]

> While the new provisions for stop and search were too recent for detailed assessment, it would be extremely difficult without them for the police to carry out the intention of Parliament to suppress drug addiction and drug peddling and to honor international agreements on drug offenses. The police felt strongly that proper account should be taken of the alarming increase in drug dependence in the United Kingdom, the pervasive influence that could be exerted upon impressionable young people by a minority kindly disposed to drug taking, and the increasingly sophisticated methods and expertise of offenders. They were concerned that any limitation of powers would encourage a more rapid growth in the number of offenses and be interpreted in many quarters as official

acknowledgment that the misuse of drugs should not be treated too seriously.

However, there was no evidence that these powers increased the arrest of drug pushers or that searches helped in curtailing addiction.

The committee's report shows a sharp division between the majority and minority over the existence and solution of problems raised by enforcement. Scofield, Wootton, and Williams agreed that abuses existed and doubted whether the drug use justified a broad infringement of liberty. At the very least, they wanted some means to restrict these powers and make the police more accountable. The majority approach was described in Scofield's dissent:[71]

> Whenever allegations of malpractice or injustice were brought to the notice of the sub-committee, time and energy were spent attempting to show that these allegations were not true. In the event it is usually very difficult to ascertain the truth or falsity of such allegations. My view is that our energies should have been devoted to devising a legal framework and administrative procedures so that the allegations could not even have been made. The question we should have asked is not "Did it happen?"—but "Could it happen?" If there is a source of misunderstanding between police and public, our object should have been to devise a safeguard so that the police are not even exposed to the accusation.

Instead, the majority repeatedly fell back on the gravity of the drug problem, the difficulties of enforcement, and their feeling that the public was willing to relinquish some measure of liberty in order to stop drug use:[72]

> It is true that the advent and availability of these substances pose severe dilemmas. The difficulties are great; so, as far as our present knowledge goes, are the dangers, especially for the young. There must be protection against these dangers. That calls for a law which has to be enforced. The test is our will to enforce that duty.
> We believe that the general body of the public appreciate and

accept that enforcement of the drug laws cannot be carried out without police inquisitiveness. . . .

. . . The public wish to see the drug laws enforced. . . .

In their acceptance of the need for search powers, the majority did not consider the more general effect of broad police discretion on legal authority, nor recognize that the police practices could be a major source of alienation. Nor did it attempt to restrict the rise of this power, or provide remedies for its abuse. England does not recognize the exclusionary rule of evidence, whereby illegally seized evidence may not be admitted in court. Thus, the victim of an illegal search has no practical remedy for correcting the wrong. The majority also refused in the face of very strong evidence to acknowledge bail abuses. It did recommend that no one be searched solely because of his appearance.

The Deedes majority report suggests that their primary purpose was to reassure the police and public that there was strong support for the fight against drug use. This desire led them to overlook distinctions among drugs and the purposes for which they may be used, and to dismiss the importance of police relations with the young and other social costs. Again the majority, like Callaghan in the debate on the Wootton Report, approached the law as a symbol. Whether or not these powers actually helped stop addiction or harmful drug use, it was necessary that nothing be done that "could be interpreted . . . as official acknowledgment that the misuse of drugs should not be treated too seriously."[73] The flaw in this approach was summarized by Dr. Malleson, a member of the Advisory Committee and a witness before the Deedes Committee, in a letter to the chairman of the Advisory Committee:[74]

> The problem presented to society by the misuse of drugs is a serious one. But it is not so serious as to justify what is, for practical purposes, the removal of all rights for the protection of individual privacy from a substantial section of the population. This deprived section is, in effect, one-third of our young people —the less conformist third. The position is to be contrasted with

the refusal of the adult community to accept comparable curbs on its own dangerous unlawfulness in the matter of random breathalyser tests.

. . . If it is held that massive infringements of individual liberty are to be accepted as permanent, their gravity should have been recognized and major counter-balancing innovations proposed. . . . Our society is becoming more divided; we cannot afford to have drug control laws which only drive further divisions between young people and adult authority.

MISUSE OF DRUGS BILL

Many of the new problems of drug control in Britain resulted from an inflexible and fragmentary legislative approach. The Dangerous Drugs Act of 1920, supplemented by frequent amendments, was called upon to solve the drug problems of the 1960s, when both knowledge and attitudes toward drugs had greatly changed. Inevitably this statute would appear arbitrary and inadequate to deal with problems unforeseen at the time of its passage. In rejecting the Wootton Report, the Home Secretary had alluded to these difficulties and made a plea for a new drug code:[75]

In the light of recent experience and the challenge ahead, there is a clear risk that each new fashion of drug-taking will find new gaps in the defences, which will only be plugged, too late, by voluntary steps or by ad hoc legislation. Therefore, I suggest to the House . . . that it would be better to have a single comprehensive code which would rationalize and strengthen the Government's powers and also enable them to act flexibly in the difficult and dangerous problems that are likely to arise in the years ahead.

In March 1970, the Labour government introduced the Misuse of Drugs Bill, which granted new powers to the government and departed in several significant ways from the old structure. This law is the product of the debate, Advisory Reports, and public attention centered on drugs for five years since the second Brain

Report. Again, in the paradoxical treatment of different drugs, the ascendancy of public emotions is revealed.

THE BILL

Like the Dangerous Drugs Act, the bill makes it unlawful to import, export, manufacture, supply, or possess the scheduled drugs unless licensed to do so. The process by which this is done is new. Scheduled drugs are broken down into three classes, according to their relative harmfulness. For the first time all controlled drugs are included under one statutory scheme. Class A drugs include opium, heroin, morphine (and other narcotics), cocaine, synthetic cannabis, the hallucinogens LSD, STP, DMT, and DET, and injectable amphetamines. Class B includes all forms of natural cannabis, certain narcotic substances with a codeine base, and certain amphetamines. In Class C are stimulants considered to be less dangerous than the amphetamines of Classes A and B.

The government is given power to add or take away drugs in any class. This power was lacking under the old structure and created problems in dealing with new drugs. Penalties vary with the class of drug and the act committed. For the first time possession and supply are made separate offenses, with different penalties. Production or supply of Class A or Class B drugs is subject to fourteen years' imprisonment and an unlimited fine. The penalty for possession is seven years (plus fine) for Class A drugs and five years (plus fine) for Class B drugs. Class C drugs merit five years (and fine) for production or supply, while possession brings only two years (and fine). These sentences are new in several respects. The maximum penalty for supply and trafficking has been increased for all drugs, while that for possession of some drugs, like cannabis, reduced. The penalties for possession and supply of LSD and injectable amphetamines are greatly increased. Other provisions for the first time make it a crime punishable by the same fines as trafficking, for a physician to disobey an order or regulation issued concerning the prescribing of drugs. These orders may be directed to the prescription of whole classes of drugs, or they may be directed to a physician considered to be "prescribing, supplying, etc., controlled drugs in an irresponsible manner." The government can issue these directions without delay and suspend a doctor pending a final determination. This prevents a doctor who has been found to be overprescribing from continuing to prescribe pending a lengthy appeal. The doctor's rights are protected by a hearing and appeal from an adverse decision.

Other provisions of the Dangerous Drug Act remain essentially unchanged. It is still a crime to knowingly "permit or suffer" production or supply of controlled drugs and the smoking of cannabis on one's premises. However, the penalty has been raised to the maximum for trafficking for each class of drug. Existing police powers of search and arrest are unchanged. *Mens rea,* or knowledge, is specifically required for all offenses. Also, there is a provision making research easier. Finally, the Advisory Committee on Drug Dependence is continued as the Advisory Council and Expert Committee on the Misuse of Drugs, to advise the government on new drug problems and needed changes in the law.

ANALYSIS AND EVALUATION

The bill is an improvement in three respects. Most important is its power to control overprescribing by doctors. As we have seen, both heroin and methadrine became problems because physicians had prescribed irresponsibly. The 1967 Dangerous Drug Act attempted to close the gap by restricting the prescription of certain drugs to licensed doctors and by granting the medical profession responsibility for policing itself. But under that act it was not an offense to prescribe without a license, and the act covered only drugs listed in the Dangerous Drug Acts (opiates, cocaine, cannabis). Thus, when methadrine became a problem the government lacked statutory authority to restrict its prescription. It was obliged to work out an informal agreement between manufacturers and hospitals—hardly a satisfactory procedure for rapidly changing drug problems.

Similarly, the medical profession's discipline of its members was clumsy and slow. Pending a final determination of his case, a doctor may continue to prescribe. Dr. Petro, a notorious over-prescriber, was able to prescribe 24,000 30-mg ampules of metha-drine in a single month after he had been found remiss, but before a final appeal had been made.[76] By allowing the government to order a doctor to stop prescribing certain drugs, or prohibit all prescriptions of a drug, the bill facilitates the quick, effective action necessary to deal with drug problems.

The power granted in the bill to add or delete drugs in the scheduled classes was also sorely needed. When new drug fads came to light, the government could not readily bring them under control without enacting new legislation.

The final advantage of the bill is its attempt to classify drugs according to their relative danger and to distinguish between possession, and supply and production. For the first time cannabis is classified separately from heroin, and powerful drugs like methadrine are put in a more appropriate class. Differentiation of drugs is necessary to dispel the tendency to think of all drugs in the same terms, and thus obstruct measures suitable for one drug but not for others.

While the bill closes existing loopholes in the medical model, its chief defect is the contradictory treatment accorded nonmedical or recreational drug use. The premise of the bill is that any nonmedi-cal drug use is drug *misuse,* for which severe penalties, including prison, are warranted. The punitive nature of the bill is evident in the classification of different drugs, the subtleties of which are not reflected in the penalty structure. For example, production and supply of Class A and B drugs are subject to the same maximum penalty, a result hard to reconcile with a scaling by "relative harm-fulness." Thus, sharing a pipe or joint of cannabis with a friend is theoretically punishable by the same penalties as trafficking in narcotics or overprescribing methadrine. It is doubtful whether a single LSD session is more of a threat than amphetamine dependence, yet possession of the first may be punished by two years more in prison than the second. And barbiturates are not included in the bill at all. The change in cannabis penalties—the maximum for possession is half of the present ten-year penalty—is not much of a reform when compared with the Wootton recommendations. Casual users of cannabis—the great majority of drug users—would still find this bill arbitrary, discriminatory, and out of line with existing knowledge. Particularly punitive are the high penalties for the supply of cannabis, and the increased penalty for allowing cannabis to be smoked on one's premises. Thus, under the bill, one risks fourteen years' imprisonment by allowing a friend at a party to smoke cannabis. This penalty is the maximum for the most serious offenses under the bill.

These contradictions indicate an underlying confusion about the goals of drug policy. As we have seen, the drug explosion of the 1960s treated addicts and pot smokers quite dissimilarly. Addicts were allowed to obtain and use drugs, while cannabis users were jailed. Yet cannabis is a less dangerous drug. The bill continues this discrepancy and increases reliance on the police for enforcing nonaddictive drug use. Thus a cannabis user is "misusing" a drug and risking a long prison term, while a heroin user is neither "misusing" his drug nor committing a crime, as long as he obtains the drug from a doctor. The special status of addiction, however, is not consistently maintained in the treatment of addicts guilty of offenses under the act. No alternative to jail exists for addicts, even if their offense is related to their addiction. The *Observer* commented on this feature of the bill:[77]

> The Bill proposes to continue the practice of dealing with drug-takers as criminals, rather than as social deviants in need of various kinds of help that they are unlikely to get in prison. Nobody would seriously propose that alcoholics could be successfully deterred by prison sentences; why, then, should drug-takers? For legislation today to offer no remedy for social deviants other than imprisonment and to propose to regard every schoolboy who experiments with pot as a criminal is a piece of social nonsense.

By failing to look at the roots of the problem and to suggest remedies more in keeping with modern knowledge, Mr. Callaghan is in danger of accidentally helping to spread the fashion of looking sympathetically on those who see in drugs a socially useful form of escape, a harmless means of easing pains and releasing tensions, or a meaningful act of rebellion against society. . . . What is needed is a much more scientific and humane approach. . . . in so far as the bill offers no alternative to prison as a means of deterrence or treatment, it must be regarded as largely a waste of time and, possibly, even as a harmful measure. Its passage would be likely to put off the pressure of more radical measures possibly for another decade—a decade which may be decisive in determining whether the current fashion is to become an accepted part of our way of life.

The Misuse of Drugs Bill represents another exercise in symbolic lawmaking. Introduced a few months before an election campaign in which a main issue was "law and order," it was hailed as a hard-line approach to drug users and drug pushers. Indeed, the penalty structure confirms its tough stance on drug use, particularly on cannabis. The penalties, in particular, must be viewed as symbolic. Even at the time of the Wootton Report, the average cannabis user was usually being fined, rather than going to jail. The proposed penalties are unlikely to influence the sentencing of drug users, although they do provide a new weapon against major suppliers and unscrupulous doctors. More important, however, is the societal judgment, expressed through the new law, that drug use is automatically drug misuse—an immoral, antisocial act. The law functions as a symbol to reassure the public that the line against the chaotic and disorderly (symbolized by drugs) is firmly drawn and staunchly defended.

Resort to the police model, however, exacts a price. In this case, it is the acceptance of extensive police powers, arbitrary treatment of different drug users, erosion of the rule of law, and a growing alienation from legal authority. In the haste to condemn, the threat from drugs is exaggerated and the social costs of the laws are overlooked. In Britain a policeman may now search and detain a person on the street or enter his home and seize papers that he suspects are involved with cannabis use. The security gained against drug users has been offset by a decreased security against the official power of the state. Even where the state is benign the precedent is dangerous, and the possibility of injustice increased.

The British experience is curiously paradoxical on this point. It accepts the idea that serious social costs may flow from an ill-considered and emotional heroin policy, but denies that any costs could accrue from policy toward other drugs. Until such paradoxes are faced and resolved, the drug issue and the controversy it provokes will persist in disrupting the fabric of social life.

CONCLUSION

Although this survey of the British experience with the drug controversy is necessarily cursory, it is enough to show that national character difference is not the crucial variable in the success or failure of drug programs. Whenever the relative success of the British in dealing with heroin addiction—small number of addicts, little crime connected with drug use, fewer deaths—is cited in American discussions the automatic arguments against it are that (1) the British system is not working anyway, and (2) it only works because of the essential law-abiding nature of the average Britisher and his good relationship to the police.

Certainly the British system is imperfect in that the medical facilities for treatment and rehabilitation of addicts are grossly inadequate. Also, the British have come no farther than we in assessing addiction-prone people and devising fresh approaches to preventing addiction. Nevertheless, on any terms the situation is better in England. The rise in the number of addicts is numerically small, and considering the enormous amount of publicity drugs have received, it is astonishing that the number isn't larger. This applies also to the United States; there must be a sizable portion of young people, perhaps as high as 6 to 10 percent of the entire population, who, when there is a lot of shouting, *must* find out what the shouting is about. Hence, under the recent mass-media pressure a large rise in addiction can be seen as the moderate success of the largest advertising campaign in history.

The absence of drug-connected crime in England changes the entire embiance of the society. By any subjective or objective criteria one can imagine, the streets of London are safer than those of any large American city and drug policy is one important reason. On July 26, 1970, Sir John Waldron, London Police Commissioner, could confidently state in his annual report, "People can still walk abroad in London at night with little fear of being molested."[78] Can you imagine what the police commissioner of New York City feels upon reading that?

Under the British system of licensed addicts, the heroin received is officially quality-controlled, as is the equipment to administer it. Almost all the gray-market heroin comes from the same source, so that the horrid uncertainty as to dosage which plagues the American addict and was a principal factor in the 1,100 addict deaths in the United States in 1969 simply does not exist. This does not mean that there are *no* drug-related deaths in England any more than the availability of clean needles and syringes means that there are *no* cases of infectious hepatitis. Addicts are often strange people. Much overdosing, both in the United States and in Britain, represents conscious or unconscious suicidal attempts. Addicts also tolerate frustration poorly and, in their haste, do not take careful precautions to ensure sterile injections. No doubt the addict personality type is similar in both the United States and Britain, and results differ only because the control systems are different.

The medical and social problems of drug use that have developed in the United States in the past decade have also developed in Britain. This enables us to dismiss the "national character" argument. We prefer to make little here of the racist nature of an argument that implicitly holds that the relatively homogeneous, Anglo-Saxon, rational English can handle a problem that the melting-pot, racially mixed, minority-group-plagued United States cannot. The important thing for us to notice about the British experience is that a long time ago, in 1920, they elected a medical model when the United States elected a police model. The drug-using population was essentially the group we think of as dependency-prone on psychological and sociological grounds. Given what we know now, it can be seen that the medical model worked far better.

However, once both countries were faced with a social drug problem—whether pills, joints, or LSD—both panicked. They identified drug use with a host of other issues—long hair, dirt, social irresponsibility, promiscuity, degeneration of values, political destructiveness, violence, crime, and indolence—and reacted with hysteria. We found the same public attitudes in the United States toward the social drug issue as we found in Britain, and the development of the legal position outlined in this chapter represents the same preoccupation with moral control based on ideas of harmfulness that we find in the United States.

One more development—and one of the saddest—that indicates that differences in national character amount to less than might have been thought is the changing attitude toward the police. Alan Brian, in an essay in the *New Statesman* called "From Bobby to Fuzz,"[79] outlined the changing attitude of the British public, particularly the young, toward the police. It indicates that once search and seizure laws are adopted and differential law-enforcement procedures become frequent, even a mutual trust as strong as that between the average Britisher and the bobby can break down. Cannabis bedevils British society and its most trusted social institutions in much the same way marijuana has the United States.

The United States is more vulnerable. It is larger, more diverse; it has the Vietnam War; and with 50 percent of its young in institutions of higher learning, as opposed to 10 percent of the British, it has a far greater problem of student unrest. Perhaps the British can make the best of these advantages. With a working medical model already in operation, Britain is in a good position to lead in thinking through and putting into practice the changes we advocate.

6

THE DRUG LAWS

Since the early twentieth century Americans have relied on criminal sanctions to stop drug use. Reliance on the law, however, has not stopped drug use nor drug-related harm, but has provoked controversy and impeded efforts to deal with drug misuse.

The confusion and controversy surrounding the law are the result of a conflict, as yet unresolved, between using the law to protect order and health and using it to express a moral judgment. Laws are enacted to protect health, safety, and order by penalizing harmful conduct. We usually think of drug laws in this vein. Without penalties to deter drug use, it is thought that crime, violence, personal injury and eventually social chaos will occur. Accompanying this goal is one with a decidedly moralistic bent: all drug use, whatever its consequences, is wrong. Criminalizing drug use thus reinforces moral feelings and protects a moral code increasingly under attack.

As long as the law hovers between the goals of morality and utility, the law will foment controversy without lessening the damage of harmful drug use. The two goals are often incompatible. The first, that of treating and rehabilitating drug users, may recognize that some drug use harms no one or even is functional for the user, and thus contradicts the criminal treatment on which the second depends. In attempting to achieve both aims, one or the other inevitably suffers. With the present laws the desire to condemn and punish has taken precedence over the need to treat. Drug use is thus more damaging than a regime concerned solely with health would allow, and as a further consequence, the drug laws engender conflict, rather than consensus, about the place of private drug use in modern society.

In this chapter we see that the most controversial features of the drug laws—the ones related to indiscriminate condemnation of all drug use—are least justifiable on grounds of protecting the health and welfare of users or anyone else; we then discuss the functions that such laws serve.

THE MORALISTIC ELEMENTS OF THE DRUG LAWS

Certain features of the drug laws provoke hostility and resistance and bring the law into disrepute; they are central to a system that condemns out of hand all drug use. Yet these features are least justifiable as necessary to protect the health and safety of users or the public. We examine several areas in which the law, while avowing concern with health, has actually tried to condemn all drug use.

OVERINCLUSIVENESS

A drug policy concerned with preventing harm from drug use would concentrate on those drugs that produce harm, and those instances or patterns of use that actually or are likely to cause harm. The present laws are overinclusive in two ways: they treat all drugs, and all uses of a drug, as if they were equally damaging.

Yet it is well known that the depressant, stimulant, analgesic, hypnotic, hallucinogenic, and tranquilizing agents in illegal use differ vastly from one another in pharmacology, psychic effects, motives for use, and consequences for the user. Use of one drug may seldom be harmful; another may be harmful only in clearly defined circumstances; and to use a third may be courting serious risks.

The laws take no account of the relevant distinctions in the potential for harm of various drugs and the circumstances of use. Even where legislative or historical accidents have produced disparate categories, the legal judgment is clear: all private drug use is criminal, whatever its actual effects on the user and others.

The monolithic view has produced some absurd results and given credence to claims that the law is arbitrary. Under existing state and federal laws a drug is classified as either a "narcotic," a "dangerous," or a "harmful" drug. First came "narcotic," which for years has been a convenient catchall for all drugs of public concern. Today "narcotic" remains in the language and minds of millions of people as the generic term for drugs and drug use. The term was introduced into state law by the Uniform Narcotic Drug Act. In 1928 the FBN, working through the Commission on Uniform State Laws (a body of lawyers that drafts and recommends legislation for uniform enactment in each state), drafted the act. The act defined "narcotic" to include the opiates and cocaine. With no convincing evidence of dangers, the commission had decided against including marijuana. It did permit each state the option of including marijuana in its definition of "narcotic." Over the years, 48 of the 50 states adopted the uniform act.[1] All defined narcotic to include marijuana, as well as a hodge-podge of nonnarcotic substances ranging from LSD and amphetamines to airplane glue and paregoric.

The uniform act proscribes a number of transactions involving "narcotic drugs," with the penalty determined by the class of transaction rather than by the drug and its potential for harm. For example, all sales of "narcotics" are subject to the same penalty, without regard for the particular drug sold or the features of the sale. Any exchange of drugs, including gift, is defined as sale. Thus, a doctor relieving an addict's withdrawal symptoms with methadone, a professional heroin importer, an addict selling a five-dollar bag, a student sharing a marijuana cigarette with his roommate, or a woman passing one of her own sleeping pills to her husband are guilty of the same crime and subject to the same penalties. Assuming that each transfer threatens harm to a valid state interest, the degree of harm and the seriousness of the harm vary so greatly that essential distinctions are blurred. Instances of actual harm are overlooked when all are included in a single category.

In recent years some states and the federal government passed legislation creating a new category of "harmful" or "dangerous"[2] drugs to deal with drugs that seemed to present problems different from narcotics. Offenses involving these drugs are generally treated more leniently than "narcotic" offenses; and in many cases, an act involving a "dangerous" drug is not criminal, whereas with a "narcotic" it is.

Although this category suggests a differentiation among drugs and their effects, the refinement is hard to substantiate. The logic of different drug classifications has not been consistently followed. Rather than introducing clarity, the new category has more often compounded the confusion and contradictions of the laws. To begin with, a separate class for "dangerous drugs" was largely a historical accident. With the federal laws, for example, dangerous-drug legislation resulted from the inability to fit the regulated drugs into the framework of narcotic and marijuana tax statutes enacted several decades earlier. Where states have chosen to enact a new category for such drugs as amphetamines and barbiturates, rather than expand the list of "narcotic" drugs (which other states have chosen to do), it appears that the characteristics of their users, mainly middle-aged adults, rather than sensitivity to the inconsistencies of the narcotic label have been the motivating factor. A control scheme attuned to the varying potential for harm would not treat leniently drugs that can be extremely dangerous, while harshly penalizing less dangerous drugs. Amphetamines and barbiturates, for instance, produce tolerance, severe withdrawal syndromes, psychosis, high toxicity, and violent or impaired behavior, yet are treated more leniently than marijuana, which has none of those effects. A further anomaly has been added by putting LSD into the dangerous-drug category, while continuing to regard marijuana as a narcotic.

Under the Drug Abuse Control Amendments of 1965—the first federal regulation of stimulant, depressant, and psychedelic drugs —personal possession was not even penalized, and unlicensed sale or manufacture was subject to a one-year penalty, while marijuana and heroin received mandatory minimum sentences of five years. Such disparities confused even the federal drug police. In 1968 they testified before Congress that differential treatment increased their problems. Congress attempted to rectify the anomaly by increasing the penalty for sale of dangerous drugs to two years and imposing a maximum penalty of one year in jail for personal possession. Yet the confusion remains. LSD is still subject to the same treatment as amphetamines and barbiturates, while marijuana, the most widely used and least dangerous of illegal drugs, merits more severe sanctions. As a final flourish, THC, the more potent synthetic of the active ingredients in marijuana, was legally grouped with the dangerous drugs.

Classification schemes based on the relative harm of various drugs has become the current legislative vogue, and is hailed as drug reform both in the United States and in England. The Controlled Substances Act, passed in 1970 and now being urged upon the states by the Justice Department, and its British counterpart, the Misuse of Drugs Bill, classify all regulated drugs in five different groupings under one heading. This is widely thought to be a substantial reform, but it is unlikely to alter the dominant tendency to think of all drug use as an undifferentiated phenomenon. Aside from inconsistencies in the relative rankings of the drugs, the fact that all uses of the regulated drugs, whatever their effects, remain criminal indicates that dealing with damaging drug use is not the sole concern of the law.

Except for overt poisons, it is rare that every use of an illegal drug represents the same degree of danger to everyone. Yet under the law all uses of a drug are proscribed, no matter that the motives for use vary tremendously. Peyote or LSD may be used in religious ceremonies by organized cults or individuals; in carefully controlled settings, by experienced, aware individuals, with expert supervision; or as an adjunct to psychotherapy. It may also be taken in the search for yet another kick by a prepsychotic, a depressed teen-ager, an adult, or a youth seeking peer group approval. Even opiates, when they are provided regularly, may help people to function and be productive: doctor-addicts, the romantic poets, and the ordinary British addicts are the most obvious examples.

The most basic flaw in a system that penalizes without regard to harm every act of use or possession is its clash with the fundamental safeguard of Anglo-American jurisprudence that only the occurrence and not the potentiality of harm be penalized. The vast majority of criminal statutes act *post facto*—they penalize conduct after it has caused injury. A system whereby an intention to steal, say, was made a crime might, assuming detection of intentions were possible, be an efficient way of preventing theft. Yet the price of such efficiency would be the nightmare of thought control, and the injustice of arresting people who, despite their intention, never actually do steal. Where the law penalizes actions prior to the occurrence of actual harm, as with the crimes of attempt, conspiracy, drunken driving, etc., the law occupies an anomalous position, and, as the debate over indicting Dr. Spock and the Chicago Seven for conspiracy shows, is criticized when used too frequently. Such crimes are limited to conduct that is clearly preparatory to, and certain to produce, an undesired harm. With conspiracy, for example, an actual overt act in furtherance of the unlawful design must be shown to have occurred to prove the crime. Nor does one "attempt" murder merely by harboring a desire to kill his wife, buying a gun, and waiting in ambush by the garage as she parks the car. Some further act that shows beyond a doubt the intention and likelihood of its completion is required. Similarly, a high degree of probability that harm will result underpins intoxicated-driving statutes. Some may be able to negotiate the road quite ably when intoxicated, but there exists massive evidence that most people cannot. We assume quite reasonably that drunken driving is likely to produce accidents. In all these instances, no matter how direct the causal chain between conduct and eventual harm may seem, we are extremely hesitant to prohibit an act short of actual harm.

The drug laws ignore these limitations—because, of course, all drug use is generally believed to be harmful in itself and to lead to worse harm. This unfounded belief is clearly evident in the conclusion drawn by the judge in a famous test of the constitutionality of the marijuana laws when a witness stated that "no drug (marijuana or otherwise) is harmless."[3] He concluded from this that "marijuana should be prohibited."

Because some uses of a drug may be harmful, it does not follow that all uses are, or that every use must be prohibited to avoid those few harmful ones. Prohibition of all use is justified only when the evidence shows that most uses of the drug are likely to be damaging, or that it is impossible to use the drug with discrimination. Even then, it does not automatically ensue that criminal sanctions are the most efficient way of preventing harm from drug use. The vice of the present system is that we approach dangerously close to the penal code of Lewis Carroll's Red Queen, where the virtue of punishing likelihoods, and intentions is proclaimed as "all the better," since punishment before the harm obviates the harm that would otherwise have occurred. Total condemnation of all drug use is not necessary if our object is to prevent damage, but it is essential if our real intention is to express a moral judgment.

PUNISHMENT

Drug penalties are among the most severe on the books. Only murder, rape, and kidnapping receive equivalent treatment. In many states armed robbery, manslaughter, and a variety of other violent crimes are often treated more leniently than drug-selling.

Yet there is no evidence that the extreme penalties actually deter people from using drugs in a damaging way or, indeed, from using drugs at all; and there is growing evidence that excessive penalties cast the law into disrepute. The length of penalties, the practice of punishing a single act as multiple offenses, mandatory minimum sentences, and civil commitment programs are difficult to justify in health terms, but they are readily understandable as the wages of sin.

The length of drug sentences is punitive in a relative and absolute sense. In relation to other social harms—such as violence to people or property, injury or death resulting from automobile accidents, and the high infant mortality rates in the black ghetto—the harm from drug use appears minimal. Usually there is no tangible victim, and self-inflicted harm ranks low in the hierarchy of social interests. Thus, drug sentences are objectionable because frequently nothing has been done deserving retribution; and when there is harm, the Draconian penalties are out of all proportion.

The federal sentences, until recently, averaged 2 to 5 years for simple possession of marijuana and narcotics, 5 to 10 years for first offense of sale or possession for sale, 10 to 40 for a second sale offense.[4] The Controlled Substances Act, while reducing all possession penalties to one-year imprisonment, created a new category of "dangerous special drug offender," who may receive up to twenty-five years' imprisonment. Persons convicted of a "continuing criminal enterprise," as defined by the act, may receive up to life.[5] New York in 1969 made a life sentence mandatory for possession or sale of more than sixteen ounces of heroin, morphine, cocaine, or opium. Texas allows from one year to life for simple possession of any amount of marijuana. Some states punish sale to a minor of a narcotic (including marijuana) with life imprisonment, and Georgia allows the death penalty. Some states would permit the incarceration for life of a 21-year-old college student who shares a "joint" with his 20-year-old roommate.

Ancillary drug activities are often treated more strictly than use or possession. Merely being in the company of one possessing narcotics illegally could result in a five-year prison term in Massachusetts, while simple possession draws three. A doctor who treats a drug-dependent patient without notifying state authorities risks several years in jail and loss of his medical license. In some states, removing the label from a prescribed medicine is an offense. Most courts tend to place a broad construction on the prohibited actions. Sale, punishable in most states by a mandatory minimum penalty of five years' imprisonment, has in Illinois, for example, been interpreted to apply to buyers as well as sellers.[6] Thus, one can be convicted of "sale" of a narcotic by buying drugs for another. Fleeting possession of minute nonusable quantities of a drug is as criminal as possessing large quantities. While there are factors that often prevent adherence to this rigid schedule, high penalties and jail sentences are imposed often enough to cause serious concern. Although there have been noticeable changes in recent years, judges often think that marijuana is as dangerous as heroin because of their equivalent legal treatment, and they sentence accordingly. In other cases, a well-informed and humane judge will have no discretion at all to tailor the sentence to the particular offender.

Some idea of how seriously courts view drug offenses may be gleaned from the following cases involving marijuana: A college sophomore, found in Virginia with less than 25 grams of marijuana, received the statutory minimum of 20 years' imprisonment. In Seattle, Washington, a man sold a marijuana cigarette to a minor and is now serving a 20 to 40 years' prison term. Twenty to forty years was also the sentence imposed on a Cleveland 20-year-old who sold a police informer a quantity of poinsettia alleged to be marijuana. Lee Otis Johnson, a black activist in Houston, was recently sentenced to 30 years' imprisonment for allegedly giving one marijuana cigarette to an undercover agent. And Timothy Leary now faces a 10-year prison term in California for possessing less than one ounce of marijuana, a penalty that few of the 40,000-plus marijuana offenders receive. High sentences are more the rule with heroin and similar drugs. Half the federal prisoners from 1954 to 1964 were drug offenders, serving average sentences of seven years.[7] And in England, an enlightened jurisdiction by comparison with the United States, a study showed that judges were sending 17 percent of marijuana first offenders to jail, 90 percent of whom possessed less than 30 grams.[8]

A single act of possession or sale of a drug may be dealt with as the commission of several crimes, and consecutive sentences may be imposed for them. Under the former federal law one instance of possession could also constitute unlawful importation and failure to register under the tax act, while transfer of a drug for remuneration was also prosecuted as illegal possession and unlawful importation. With a 5-year penalty on each count, an act otherwise penalized by a 5-year term could result in a 15-year sentence. In many states, the possession of one marijuana cigarette may be prosecuted as three crimes: possession, possession with intent to sell, and being present where a drug is kept, with separate penalties imposed for each. It is hard to see what purpose this practice serves other than providing another club to hit the drug user.

Many statutes require a judge to impose a minimum jail term in every case. Discretion to sentence according to the background and character of the defendant and the circumstances of the case has been removed because it is feared that the judge might not be punitive enough toward drug offenders. Congress, in 1952 and 1956, provided mandatory minimum sentences for most drug offenses. Judges were not permitted to suspend sentences or grant probation. The right to parole was also severely limited.[9] They had no choice but to sentence every seller to at least five years in jail, and every user to a prison term.

In actual operation, mandatory minimum sentences have had an opposite effect. Limitation of judicial discretion actually amounts to a transfer of that discretion to the police and prosecutor. Their decision to arrest and prosecute becomes simultaneously a sentencing decision if guilt can be established. It is highly questionable whether the sentencing function should be performed by officials whose role in the criminal process is detecting violations and initiating prosecutions. This undermines the checks and balances built into the system, and gives inordinate weight to the subjective decisions of police and prosecutors.

Judges have been unhappy with this arrangement for several years. With no flexibility possible in sentencing, defendants are less willing to negotiate guilty pleas. One effect of minimum sentences has been to increase the number of jury trials in drug cases and add to court backlogs.[10] Convictions, however, have not risen accordingly. To avoid a mandatory jail sentence judges have construed the law of search and arrest liberally, thus acting to frustrate the legislative purpose of punishing drug offenses with high sentences. If a conviction is obtained, a long prison sentence follows, increasing the number of drug offenders in prison, but at the same time prosecutors are loath to bring cases to court. Similarly, prison authorities are frustrated. Rehabilitation is a futile hope when a man cannot be paroled no matter how well he behaves.

Despite these criticisms, the question of sentencing discretion is not rapidly yielding to a more rational view. The reforms of the new federal law have been offset by the severity of the "dangerous special offender" category. While some mandatory minimum penalties have been removed, John Ingersoll, head of the Bureau of Narcotics and Dangerous Drugs, has urged this reform as necessary to ensure that drug offenders are in fact punished, a recognition that minimum sentences have backfired.

These features of drug sentences are difficult to support in the absence of evidence that penalties actually do prevent drug use, harmful or otherwise. Legal sanctions, along with drug availability, peer-group pressure, education, and family background, are one of many variables that influence the decision to take a drug. The dismal failure of alcohol prohibition and the current wide use of psychoactive drugs suggest that the threat of punishment is by no means the most significant factor.

The marijuana laws, in particular, are widely and openly flouted, sometimes by thousands of people simultaneously. Where people have refrained from using the drug, few give the law as a reason. Kaplan comments:[11]

These reports are, of course, subject to all the frailties of a person's evaluation of his own motives. Nonetheless, if believed, they show that some of the non-users had abstained because they were morally opposed to the use of any intoxicants; some because they feared the effects of marijuana; some because they had "better things to do" with their time; some because they were afraid of something that might reduce their resolve to give up cigarette smoking; some because they hadn't gotten around to using the drug; and finally some, a very few, because they did not know where they could obtain the drug without too great a risk of apprehension. In a sample of students at Cal Tech, fewer than twenty percent of the non-users of marijuana regarded the law as a major reason not to use the drug. Of these, eleven percent stated that they wished to avoid the risk of legal or security-clearance problems, while eight percent as a matter of principle wished to avoid doing what was illegal.

Law students, with their vested interest in obeying the law, are one group that would be expected particularly to be deterred by sanctions, yet a survey of University of California law students entitled "Casing the Joint" found that in 1969, 73 percent of the student body had risked arrest, imprisonment, and refusal of admittance to the bar to smoke marijuana.[12]

Two limitations of criminal sanctions further weaken the power of the law to deter: the chances that the criminal activity will never be detected and, if it is, that no punishment will be imposed. The threat of punishment is an abstraction, lacking substance unless there is a high probability that it will be applied in a particular case. But the drug user knows how improbable is his arrest. He may not even know anyone who has ever been arrested. He knows that nonusers cannot readily detect drug intoxication. He also learns to control his "high" to avoid suspicion by nonusers. He will use the drug only at certain times and places, may not keep a supply on the premises, and refuse to obtain drugs even for friends. But even if he is detected, actual punishment is still highly problematic. At present few marijuana users go to jail. If they are students, middle class, reasonably cooperative, and repentant, the case will probably be continued without a finding and eventually be dismissed if no further drug involvement occurs. At worst, they will be put on probation and given a suspended sentence. In Houston, for example, juveniles know that they can chance three or four arrests for marijuana before a finding of delinquency will be made.[13] In a recent survey of drug arrests in Massachusetts, the Massachusetts Bar Association[14] found that of 600 people arrested for drug crimes, only 6 were jailed.

In addition to the abstract nature of the sanction and the forces mitigating its imposition, the satisfactions derived from drug use further diminish the deterrent effect of the law. For the addict, the physical satisfaction of avoiding withdrawal is overwhelmingly compelling. If he will rob, steal, and prostitute himself to stave off the pain of withdrawal, it is absurd to think that the threat of legal punishment will induce him to undergo it. The non-dependent user, though not compelled like the addict, also finds the drug experience worth the risk of imprisonment, simply because it's enjoyable. Skolnick[15] suggests the following procedure to determine whether the threat of punishment is likely to dissuade a person from private conduct he finds pleasurable:

> One way of putting oneself into the position of the potential offender is to translate the abstraction of such terms as "opiate addiction," "marijuana use," "homosexuality," into the reality of an already experienced everyday behavior. For example, the lawmaker might ask himself how he would respond to penal sanctions forbidding the smoking of cigarettes, the drinking of coffee, sexual orgasm, or any other commonly practiced activity which, if "excessively" indulged in, *might* lead to social and personal harm.

Since 1962 many states have enacted statutes that allow addicts to be committed either civilly or in lieu of punishment to treatment centers for long periods. Yet even here, where the law purports to rehabilitate and treat, in operation it works out as punishment. While hailed as a new departure in drug control and a humane shift from a police approach, these programs are indistinguishable from a frankly punitive approach and, in some cases, are worse. Governor Rockefeller commented after legislative endorsement of his committal program: "We are really facing up to the tragic social scourge of narcotics addiction. We will get the pusher and the addict off the streets."[16]

Indeed, the desire to "get the addict" off the street, and for long periods—often longer than sentences for criminal convictions—rather than rehabilitation, seems to have been the overriding purpose of these laws. In California, legislators and police strenuously opposed the commitment statute until it was pointed out how it provided another, indeed a heavier, weapon against the addict. Stanley Kramer,[17] the former research director of the California program, thinks the civil commitment procedures most "uncivil," and finds that they are neither rehabilitative nor nonpunitive:

> The program is placed in the hands of the California Department of Corrections. Since its inception the program has been virtually indistinguishable in operation from a prison program. The physical facilities are prisonlike and the institutional rules are prison rules. Psychiatrists and psychologists have played only the most peripheral role in the program. Originally, release was granted through the same paroling authority which acted for the prison system. . . . Thus a situation has been created in which a large number of people, who have been declared addicts or in imminent danger of becoming so, are being incarcerated intermittently over many years, most spending more time locked up than free, in a program administered and carried out by correctional personnel. By calling the commitment civil, changing the lexicon from penal to therapeutic and offering five meetings a week in groups of sixty, some feel the state has met its obligation under *Robinson*.

CAVALIER LAWMAKING

The legal policy of penalizing all drug use and possession has not resulted from clear and convincing evidence that drug use is damaging, and that the damage can be best prevented by criminal law. Accident, distortion, or disregard of information, and an almost naive acceptance of any charge about the evil of drugs, dominate the lawmaking process.

Alfred Lindesmith[18] has described the less than rational process by which it became established in America that heroin addicts were dread criminals:

> The present program of handling the drug problem in the U.S. is, from the legal viewpoint, a remarkable one in that it was not established by legislative enactment or by court interpretations of such enactments. Public opinion and medical opinion had next to nothing to do with it. It is a program which, to all intents and purposes, was established by the decisions of administrative officials of the Treasury Department of the U.S. After the crucial decisions had been made, public and medical support was sought and in large measure obtained for what was already an accomplished fact.

Other striking examples of the liberties that lawmakers have taken with facts have occurred in connection with the prohibition of marijuana and LSD, two drugs central to the drug controversy.

At different junctures in the history of marijuana control, different claims about the harmful effects of the drug have been put forth to justify legislative action. Upon closer examination, the substance of one claim has evaporated, only to have a new one take its place, and criminal prohibition is maintained.

Federal prohibition of marijuana occurred after three days of congressional hearings in 1937. Howard Becker[19] has described how the Federal Bureau of Narcotics under Harry Anslinger created a marijuana problem in the press, drafted the bill, and called the hearings leading to the passage of the Marijuana Tax Act. The chief argument advanced in favor of control was that marijuana produced insanity and led to violent crime. The Senate report[20] described the danger in these terms:

> Under the influence of this drug marijuana the will is destroyed and all power of directing and controlling thought is lost. Inhibitions are released. As a result of these effects, many violent crimes

have been committed by persons under the influence of this drug. Not only is marijuana used by hardened criminals to steel them to commit violent crimes, but it is also being placed in the hands of high school children in the form of marijuana cigarettes by unscrupulous peddlers. Its continued use results many times in impotency and insanity.

The method of proving these claims left much to be desired. They quoted hearsay statements of an anecdotal nature, relating incidents of murder or violence that were allegedly the result of marijuana intoxication. One witness, for instance, stated: "I believe in some cases that one marijuana cigarette may develop a homicidal maniac probably to kill his brother [sic]."[21]

A study by Kaplan, in *Marijuana: The New Prohibition,* analyzes each report and finds inadequate the evidence that marijuana was the cause. In most cases the source was a newspaper or magazine story in which a police officer or an arrested suspect reported marijuana use before the commission of a violent crime.

The poor quality of the evidence was pointed out to Congress by Dr. William C. Woodward, who had previously participated in an investigation of marijuana with the Commission on Uniform State Laws:[22]

> It has surprised me that the facts on which these [newspaper] statements have been made have not been brought before this committee by competent primary evidence. We are referred to newspaper publication concerning the prevalence of marijuana addiction. We are told that the use of marijuana causes crime.
>
> But as yet no one has been produced from the Bureau of Prisons to show the number of prisoners who have been found addicted to the marijuana habit. . . . informal inquiry shows that the Bureau of Prisons has no evidence on that point.
>
> You have been told that school children are great users of marijuana cigarettes. No one has been summoned from the Children's Bureau to show the nature and extent of the habit among children.
>
> Inquiry of the Children's Bureau shows that they have had no occasion to investigate it and know nothing particularly of it.
>
> Moreover, there is in the Treasury Department itself, the Public

Health Service, with its Division of Mental Hygiene. . . . That particular bureau has control at the present time of the narcotics farms that were created about 1929 or 1930 and came into operation a few years later. No one has been summoned from that bureau to give evidence on that point.

Informal inquiry by me indicated that they have had no record of any marijuana or cannabis addicts who have ever been committed to those farms.

The Bureau of the Public Health Service has also a division of pharmacology. If you desire evidence as to the pharmacology of cannabis, that obviously is the place where you can get direct and primary evidence rather than the indirect hearsay evidence.

Congress disregarded Woodward's criticism, dismissed him as an uncooperative witness, and passed the law.

When in the late 1940s it became clear that marijuana was not the monster claimed in 1937, the rationale for prohibition shifted. At the original hearings, Commissioner Anslinger entered into this exchange: [23]

Congressman Dingell: I was just wondering whether the marijuana addict graduates into a heroin . . . user?
Anslinger: No, sir; I have not heard of a case of that kind. I think it is an entirely different class. The marijuana user does not go in that direction.

For the first time the link to heroin addiction, previously denied by Anslinger, began to appear as a reason for criminal penalties. There is evidence that the FBN officials switched the main danger of marijuana from instantaneous murder, rape, and insanity to the "schooling it provided future addicts." Jerry Mandel[24] observes in a study of the genesis of the escalation argument that "in less than three years, at least nine mass media articles on narcotics listed the only danger of marijuana to be its propensity to start 'heroin users.' " Again, there was scant evidence for this newfound danger. The FBN was claiming an upsurge in heroin addiction in the postwar period, but there was no way to relate that development to marijuana use, nor could physiological or chemical connection between marijuana use and heroin experimentation be shown. The only proof appeared to be the widely accepted "fact" that most heroin addicts had used marijuana sometime previously to their addiction. The high incidence of opiate addicts of a rural or medical origin belies even that "fact."

In any case, the relevant question is what proportion of marijuana users become addicts, not what proportion of addicts first used marijuana. We would probably find that 100 percent of addicts first used tobacco, alcohol, and even milk, but these are not responsible for heroin addiction. The best statistics on this subject came from California, where marijuana use has grown more rapidly than elsewhere. But these figures show no corresponding rise in heroin addiction. In fact, marijuana use is quite prevalent among both college students and North Africans, two groups with very low rates of opiate addiction. The evidentiary picture is summed up in a report to the British Home Office on the dangers of marijuana, which put the matter in these terms: "It can clearly be argued on the world picture that cannabis use does not lead to heroin addiction."[25]

Advocates of marijuana prohibition still rely on the escalation argument, but they have supplemented it with a new list of dangers, including dangerous driving and psychological dependence. As the focus of attack on the marijuana statutes has shifted from the legislatures to the courts, such claims are increasingly aired. Attacks on marijuana statutes have been mounted on several constitutional grounds, from freedom of religion and privacy to cruel and unusual punishment. In one way or another they at least force courts to apply minimum standards of cogency to the evidence. The results to date suggest that courts are only slightly more rigorous than legislatures in evaluating the alleged dangers of marijuana. In *Commonwealth v. Leis,* the Boston marijuana trial, twenty experts presented evidence on the harm versus the harmlessness of marijuana. Both the lower court and the state supreme court held the marijuana laws to be valid on the ground that the legislature could reasonably think the drug harmful. In its reasoning the higher court demonstrated the power that conjecture and speculation so often exercise over hard fact in dealing with drugs. The court's handling of the escalation argument reveals a confusion about the meaning of "cause," which led it into a contradictory position:[26]

> Essentially the experts do not point to any evidence of direct, causal relationship between the smoking of marijuana and the use of more dangerous drugs. The studies that do exist discount the once prevalent belief that the smoking of marijuana inevitably leads to the use of more dangerous drugs. However, *it is not necessary to show such a direct, causal relationship.* There is considerable evidence that marijuana *does lead* some people to use of more dangerous drugs. The progression from marijuana to heroin or LSD is a frequent sequence. [Emphasis added.]

In this passage, the court distinguishes between "inevitably leads" and "direct, causal relationship," on the one hand, and "does lead" and "progression," on the other, and then concludes that this distinction is legally significant for purposes of showing evidence of a relationship between marijuana and other drugs. However, the distinction between causation and progression is not apparent, and the court makes no attempt to defend or explain its position. It ends contradicting itself by deciding the evidentiary issue in favor of the state, after recognizing the lack of evidence of causation.

A similar fuzziness appears in the court's summary of the grounds for its decision:[27]

> We do not think that the present unavailability of or inability to collect absolute, statistical and scientific proof that the smoking of marijuana (1) triggers "psychotic breaks," (2) leads to the use of more dangerous drugs and (3) causes automobile accidents prevents the legislature from acting to prohibit its use. . . . To prevent psychotic breaks, to guard against the use of more dangerous drugs and to eliminate a cause of automobile accidents are valid state interests.

In this passage the court has actually avoided the evidentiary issue that was the point of the trial. The precise question is whether there is evidence of the harms listed. Discounting the necessity of "absolute, statistical and scientific proof" does not remove the need for some other kind of proof of harm—indeed, that is precisely the question before the court. The court's statement that the putative harms are valid state interests is no answer, for the question still remains as to whether there is evidence that the use of marijuana threatens those interests. Essentially, the court bases its conclusion on the mind-altering and time-space-distorting capability of marijuana. It equates altering mental processes with automatic causation of harm, when the question to be answered was whether marijuana, conceded to be a mind-altering drug, could reasonably be said to produce those harms.

The court in *Leis* also relied for its decision on the recently advanced contention that marijuana use may produce auto accidents. Once again we see a new threat from marijuana replacing the old, unprovable arguments. In this case the assumption is that since marijuana has a definite mind-altering effect, it necessarily impairs driving ability. To the defendant's claim that no evidence existed of a link between marijuana and auto accidents, the *Leis* court reasoned that the properties of marijuana that preclude easy detection of its use "undoubtedly account for the unavailability of statistical data."[28] Rather than considering the lack of data a sign that a causative effect in accidents was nonexistent, the court found:[29]

> However, there is agreement among the experts that marijuana causes an alteration of sensory perception, a degree of psychomotor discoordination and an inability to concentrate. All of these effects of marijuana would interfere with the operation of a motor vehicle.

Again, the question of whether these effects actually interfered with driving (the precise issue before the court) was not pursued.

The weakness of the court's logic was underscored a few months later when Alfred Crancer[30] at the University of Washington published the results of an experiment testing the effects of marijuana and alcohol on a simulated driving course. A "regular" dose of marijuana produced the same number of errors that driving uninfluenced by any drug did. Only alcohol was shown to have a significant effect on driving ability. While this experiment does not settle the question, it points up the weakness of the court's reasoning.

A California law passed in 1965, as the psychedelic movement was cresting, illustrates the instinctual response permeating LSD and other drug legislation. A bill prohibiting the manufacture, sale, importation, or possession of LSD and DMT passed the senate 33–0 with virtually no debate and went to the Criminal Procedures Committee of the state assembly. Testimony in the committee was generally restrained, with most witnesses in favor of regulation but divided on the need to ban personal use and possession. When the committee failed to clear the bill, the press launched a blistering attack on their "irresponsible" action. William McGlothin[31] describes the ensuing events that eventually led to the enactment of the bill:

> Attorney General Lynch stated that LSD and other hallucinogenic drugs "present the most crucial drug problem which the United States has faced"; Governor Brown, Ronald Reagan, and various other political candidates announced that they favored passage of the bill, and a Los Angeles *Times* editorial expressed amazement that the committee was unaware of the LSD menace. The committee chairman . . . defended the action by pointing out that Federal law already prohibited manufacture and sale, and that further state laws should await the findings of an interim study group which has been established.
>
> In the following week, the committee defeated a move to reconsider the bill, and the attacks from law-enforcement agencies and the press mounted to new heights. The Los Angeles County District Attorney, Evelle Younger, was quoted on daily radio and TV newscasts concerning the need for LSD controls, and the Los Angeles *Times* ridiculed the committee for considering such things as "motivation" for use of the drug. At the beginning of the third week, another move was made for reconsideration, and this

time the beleaguered committee removed the possession clause from the bill and sent it to the assembly floor. Their action was attacked as a "watering down" of the bill, and District Attorney Younger initiated a campaign to have the possession feature restored. This was promptly accomplished by a vote of 44–24, and the final bill passed the assembly by 63–5.

The Los Angeles *Times* editorialized that the legislature had acted properly, stating that "LSD not only can cause serious harm to the user but can also lead to very serious criminal acts," and naively concluded that the "action will keep it [LSD] in the laboratory and the hospital where it belongs." Attorney General Lynch capitalized on the victory in his political campaign: spot radio announcements pictured him as the man who protected the state from LSD and also fought the menace in Washington. As a postlude, the governors of California and Nevada vied for the honor of being the first to formalize an anti-LSD bill; the former claiming to have signed a few hours earlier, while Nevada's Sawyer claimed primacy on the grounds that California's law was not to be effective until 90 days after the legislature adjourned.

The federal LSD laws, in a curious reversal, also illustrate the ascendancy of emotion over logic and reliable data. The Drug Abuse Control Amendments of 1965 attempted to regulate the manufacture, sale, and distribution of LSD by criminal penalties, but exempted possession of the drug for personal use. Possession penalties were thought to needlessly penalize otherwise law-abiding young people who were experimenting without antisocial tendencies. Fear of arrest might also discourage users from seeking psychiatric aid should they need it. Three years later President Johnson asked and received from Congress a law penalizing personal use and possession of the drug. No new evidence of drug effects had been unearthed in the interim. Use of LSD had, in fact, dwindled in response to rumors that it might cause chromosomal damage. The political need for a tough stand against crime and the unruly activists associated with LSD seems to have been so strong that the lack of firm evidence and the still-relevant arguments of 1965 could be ignored.

EVALUATION AND FEEDBACK

Francis Allen, dean of the Michigan Law School, has said:[32]

It is fair to say that one of the most serious deficiencies of the American legislative process is the failure to provide machinery for the routine collection of data adequate for evaluation of existing regulatory measures and consideration of new proposals. Nowhere are the consequences of these deficiencies more serious than in the area of narcotics control. For two generations we have engaged in a program of penal regulation profoundly affecting the lives and liberties of persons and involving public interests of greatest importance without reliable data on a host of matters indispensable to any sound audit of what we have been doing and to what we should be doing.

The deficiencies of the drug laws in this respect are manifold and lead to the conclusion that disapproval of drug use, rather than prevention of harm, is the chief concern of the law.

Most striking has been the dogmatic adherence to a police approach through recurring drug crises. Legislators simply increase the dose of legal firepower and turn their backs on the problem. When a new crisis appears, the cycle is repeated. This ostrichlike stance is due in part to the rigid assumptions governing drug policy. The unquestioned premise dominating dialogue and foreclosing consideration of noncriminal alternatives is that drug use is inherently bad, and only stern sanctions can stop it. One consequence has been a failure to experiment with ambulatory or maintenance systems of the British type. Another is the resistance that methadone programs have faced, even though they are one of the few bright lights on the treatment horizon. The limits of discourse were evident in the failure to examine first principles in the two presidential commissions and the White House Conference convened in the 1960s to suggest answers to the drug problem. No one questioned the ruling assumptions that total abstinence from drugs was the only goal of treatment and that criminal sanctions were the chief means of control.[33]

When heretical views have challenged these prevailing doctrines, orthodoxy has responded by distorting the evidence or attacking the challengers. The FBN, for example, seldom refers in its literature or regulations to the *Linder* case, the Supreme Court decision upholding the right of doctors to prescribe heroin to addicts; and when it does, it dismisses the result on the basis of a "technicality" in the indictment.[34] Appeal to the British system usually elicts the official response that "it was tried here and failed," referring to the narcotic clinics opened in 1919. The clinics are usually described as an "utter failure," even though some writers have shown that certain clinics, such as the one in Shreveport, were successful, while the fault of others lay in the administration and not the idea. Federal officials have castigated those who disagree with official policy as "self-appointed experts" or "doctors who have never seen a drug addict in their lives."[35]

Another notorious misuse of public power occurred when, after the FBN intervention, the publication of an AMA-ABA joint report, *Drug Addiction: Crime or Disease,* criticizing the policy of treating drug addiction as a disease and calling for limited experimentation in legal distribution of drugs, was delayed for two years. In the interim the bureau officially distributed its own report with a title, format, and color that made it hard to distinguish from the original.[36] On another occasion a federal agent was sent to the University of Indiana to try to halt publication of a book and intimidate a writer critical of the bureau's policies.[37]

Even if officials or lawmakers wanted to monitor and evaluate their programs, they would be hard-pressed to gather the necessary information. They would be blocked by a statistical system which can provide information neither about the extent of drug use nor about the impact of law on that use. Except in California, state statistics on drug crimes are deficient and incomplete. The number of arrests, convictions, and drug seizures is usually provided, but without distinguishing among different drugs or giving data on the costs or effects of the enforcement programs. Drug-seizure statistics, common and widely publicized, are meaningless even as an indication of law-enforcement activity, for there are no agreed criteria on how to measure the drugs or take impurities into account. Federal statistics are categorized according to drug, but as Mandel's excellent study[38] of drug statistics shows, changes in the legal definition of drug offenses, penalties, law-enforcement priorities, and search and seizure doctrine will influence arrest statistics without necessarily reflecting any real change in patterns of use. At best, drug statistics describe all the police can detect—the tip of the iceberg—and bear little relation to the larger mass of drug use. As long as drug use is a crime, it will be difficult and probably impossible to obtain data on drug-use patterns, social effects, and other factors relevant to policy decisions. On the other hand, a system of licensed distribution and legal use would permit the damage of shifting patterns of drug use to be monitored and indicate how public resources may best be allocated. A British law[39] passed in 1967 to restrict the prescribing of heroin to addicts by hospital clinics also required statistics on the addict population, to give a clear picture of the epidemiology and incidence of heroin use and provide a benchmark to assess policy. In the United States, despite chronic alarm over the existence of addicts, the total number of addicts remains a mystery. We cannot even say accurately that there are more heroin addicts now than there were ten years ago.

The sorry state of drug statistics prevents the evaluation of old policy and the establishment of guidelines for new ones. A basic question for policy makers is the effect of raised, lowered, or mandatory minimum penalties on the incidence of drug use and sale. A study commissioned by the American Bar Foundation to answer this question found that there was not enough information to tell one way or the other.[40] The New York State Narcotics Addiction Control Commission has spent some $50 million a year in "treating" addicts, yet because no follow-up has been done on the addicts,[41] no one knows whether the program has actually made any difference.

Feedback so far has usually been the "big case," such as Stony-brook, in which the police gain headlines from smashing a "dope ring." This usually reassures the public that the police are plugging the dike and that harmful drug use is temporarily under control. One study[42] of narcotic enforcement practices found such cases usually to be exaggerated, and of course no evidence for how the law was really working:

> The following day a story appeared in the local . . . newspaper with an eight column headline and front page pictures reporting that a one-and-a-half million dollar dope ring had been smashed. The size of the dope ring was reported in newspaper headlines according to the ultimate possible price of heroin on the black market. Actually the pound of heroin confiscated contained only 6 percent pure heroin. Such a quantity does go a long way on the retail market, but not nearly as far as the newspaper story suggested. . . . Another purpose served by exaggerated newspaper treatment of narcotic cases is to indicate to the public that "dope rings" are in common operation, but that the police are able to smash them. To a certain extent, however, the dope ring referred to in the newspaper article was itself "created" by the narcotics police. This is not to say that Charles Gomez was not a criminal purveyor of narcotics; but when law enforcement agencies themselves become major purchasers of narcotics, they make someone like Gomez a much more important-appearing dealer than he would have been had not close to $12,000 worth of narcotics been purchased from him by the state. In this sense, then, in the "big case," narcotics police are inevitably a part of the dope ring they themselves help to create.

If drug damage is to be minimized, a research and evaluation component must be built into each policy, whether it be appropriations for the police or a treatment center. The existing control framework appears too narrow for this purpose: new institutions and measurement instruments must be devised. Refusal to adopt such techniques will preserve the condemnation embodied in the law, but do little to lessen the damage of drug misuse.

THE FUNCTIONS OF THE LAW

The condemnation dominating the law does not prevent indiscriminate drug use, nor treat it when it does occur—the law's manifest purpose. But, as we shall see in the next chapter, it actually frustrates those goals and opens a Pandora's box of other ills. The gap between the manifest purpose of the law and its actual effects suggests that the law serves other functions.

ENFORCEMENT OF MORALITY

One function of laws against the use and possession of drugs is that they publicly sanction the feeling of most people that drug use is morally wrong, even when no one is hurt. John Kaplan,[43] an advocate of marijuana reform, has articulated this feeling: "Like many Americans of my generation, I cannot escape the feeling that drug use, aside from any harm it does, is somehow wrong." Professor Kaplan, however, was able to separate his moral views from his legal judgment. Since the marijuana laws created heavy burdens for the legal system, he urged that penalties be dropped. Most people, however, are unable or unwilling to keep law and morality distinct. If drug use is wrong, they reason, it is perfectly natural to have the law express that judgment and punish the immorality when it occurs. Indeed, the need to enshrine moral sentiments in the law often obstructs the desire to lessen the damage from drug use.

Moral entrepreneurs seldom acknowledge their moral aims. Usually they rationalize their goal in terms of public health and order. With drugs, it can be convincingly shown that public health requires controls over distribution and manufacture; but it is less clear that criminalizing personal drug use contributes to that end. In the first place, drugs, except when unavailable, rarely incite crime or violence. While indiscriminate drug use may damage the individual, and by extension consume public resources, most (our second group of drug users) seem able to use drugs without suffering serious damage. Finally, as we have seen, criminal penalties do not deter people, and jailing people is an odd way of helping them.

Even if we assume that the laws are meant primarily to protect a person from his own worst tendencies, the moral import of the law is clear. We tolerate and even encourage riding in airplanes and cars, we overeat, imbibe huge quantities of nicotine and alcohol, climb mountains, sky-dive, and race cars—all at great risk to health, productivity, and the well-being of others. Yet only when personal risk involves drug-taking is stern disapproval forthcoming. Such inconsistencies suggest that the drug laws enforce a morality based on the wrongness of private drug use. The code is rooted in indigenous American values and an almost religious view of the nature of man and his place in the universe. According to this code, private, recreational drug use is wrong and must be punished, either because it allows us to achieve undesirable psychic states, or because it is an unacceptable way of achieving otherwise desirable experiences.

In a culture committed to hard work, competition, aggressiveness, sequential thought, and postponed pleasure, the passivity, pleasure, and escape from discursive thought provided by drugs seem wrong. Likewise, where independence and the self-made man are ideals, it seems destructive, or at best unfair, to find happiness, pleasure, and insight artificially, without the industry that usually precedes and lends such states value. The strictness of the standard, which like Victorian sexual mores condemns a single departure, implies a view of man as innately evil. So strong are man's desires, and so vulnerable the wall he erects against his evil instincts, that once the forbidden fruits are tasted, he will fall prey to his appetites. Thus, one shot makes an addict, and one marijuana cigarette often is thought to cause personality disintegration.

The strength of these feelings was evident in the reasoning of the lower court in the *Leis* case, which found marijuana to be harmful because, among other things, it causes "a euphoric and unreal feeling of exhilaration . . . an abnormally subjective concentration on trivia" and leads "the user to lose perspective and focus his attention on one object to the exclusion of all others."[44] Such reasoning does not spring from a rational assessment of tangible injury to user or others. It rests on a subjective feeling that pleasure, contemplation, and inactivity for their own sake cannot be worthwhile, and are thus wrong.

It is not immediately apparent why the psychic states attained through drugs are undesirable. Even the bluest Calvinist knows some pleasures. If the court just quoted were consistent, it would permit laws banning television, van Gogh paintings, flowers, prayer, and mountain views. Indeed, such mental states are in some sense enjoyed and sought by us all. When they occur, they enrich our lives and are satisfying. Postindustrial society surely can survive without the same instinctual renunciation necessary in a frontier or developing culture. Indeed, as many historians have noted, we have left behind the era of production and moved into an era of consumption, with increased leisure for all, and a shifting attitude toward hedonism.

Nor is it natural for a technical culture whose material success is dependent on the manipulation of human and natural resources to recoil at the deliberate stimulation of desirable mental states. Drug use—the conscious alteration of consciousness—reflects the environmental control deeply ingrained in a technological society. It has been fostered by doctors and the pharmaceutical industry which, in teaching us that pills are a cure for pains, accustom us to think of our minds and bodies as objects for chemical manipulation. Applying their teaching to psychic pain, anxiety, or other moods should neither shock nor alarm. More pressing than condemnation is the need to acquire the knowledge and techniques for extracting the full benefits of drugs with none of their costs. Used wisely—a goal not yet attained—it is possible that drugs will allow us to soften the rough edges of an overly mechanical modern society. There might seem a paradox in using the enemy's own weapons to defeat him; it points to the necessity for responsibility and discretion in the use of drugs.

The morality embodied in the drug laws is one pushing men to higher standards of excellence than they themselves would choose or than the essentials of social living require. The distinction, in the words of Lon Fuller,[45] is between a "morality of aspiration" and a "morality of duty":

> The morality of aspiration is most plainly exemplified in Greek philosophy. It is the morality of the Good Life, of excellence, of the fullest realization of human powers. In a morality of aspiration there may be overtones of a notion approaching that of duty. But those overtones are usually muted, as they are in Plato and Aristotle. Those thinkers recognized, of course, that a man might fail to realize his fullest capabilities. As a citizen or as an official he might be found wanting. But in such a case he was condemned for failure, not for being recreant to duty; for shortcoming, not for wrongdoing. Generally with the Greeks instead of ideas of right and wrong, of moral claim and moral duty, we have rather the conception of proper and fitting conduct, conduct such as beseems a human being functioning at his best.

> Where the morality of aspiration starts at the top of human achievement, the morality of duty starts at the bottom. It lays down the basic rules without which an ordered society is impossible, or without which an ordered society directed toward certain specific goals must fail of its mark. It is the morality of the Old Testament and the Ten Commandments. It speaks in terms of "thou shalt not" and, less frequently, of "thou shalt." It does not condemn men for failing to embrace opportunities for the fullest realization of their powers. Instead it condemns them for failing to respect the basic requirements of social living.

When a person responds to frustration, anxiety, or unhappiness by taking a drug, we may think him inferior to a person who can without artificial palliatives sail through adversity; but we certainly should not *blame* him for failing to meet the highest standards of human excellence. People differ in personality, capabilities, and social circumstances. A rigid standard of independence, health, or the good seems unreasonable and impractical, however much we agree that the truly independent man deserves praise. Some simply lack the capacity to conform even when coerced; some choose other criteria of worth; and still others can attain their own brand of excellence only with the aid of drugs.

By enacting an aspirational standard into law and treating it as a component of duty, the drug laws dictate a congeries of values which in a heterogeneous democracy is the stuff of individual, not state, choice. The difficulties with denying the individual his own moral choices have been described by Herbert Packer:[46]

> The extent of disagreement about moral judgments is an obvious reason for hesitancy about an automatic enforcement of morals. There have been monolithic societies in which a static and homogeneous ethnic, religious, and class structure conduces to widely shared acceptance of a value system. But that is hardly a description of the reality of twentieth-century American society, or of its pluralistic and liberal aspirations. In a society that neither has nor wants a unitary set of moral norms, the enforcement of morals carries a heavy cost in repression. We don't begin to agree about the morality of smoking, drinking, gambling, fornicating, or drug taking, for example, quite apart from the gap between what we say and what we do. The more heterogeneous the society, the more repressive the enforcement of morals must be. And the more heterogeneous the society, the more foreign to its ethos that kind of repression is likely to be. Morals legislation is less likely to be socially damaging in, say, Portugal than it is in this country. In a society like ours, some tensions and some ambivalences are better left unmediated by the criminal law.

A SYMBOL OF POWER AND PRESTIGE

By enforcing a moral judgment about the wrongness of drug use the law also fulfills an important symbolic function. Laws operate both instrumentally and symbolically. In instrumental terms, laws are passed to influence behavior in a direction thought to be desirable. But passage or repeal of a law may also convey a meaning or signification totally unrelated to its instrumental aims. Often the two may conflict, with the unavowed and more powerful symbolic aim taking precedence.

For many years the drug laws have symbolized the limits of socially acceptable conduct and have marked off the deviant from the normal. Recently, with a new type of drug user and growing conflict over the drug laws, the law has come to symbolize more than a moral judgment.

One of the most significant social changes of the past decade is the emergence of youth as a critical social group. Youth, however, have been vociferously sacrilegious in their critique of social institutions. Not only have they aimed their shafts at government, foreign policy, the draft, corporations, and the universities; they have also flagrantly disregarded the sacred cows of traditional sexual and drug morality. Stung by this onslaught of revolutionary rhetoric, idealism and immorality, simultaneously an insult and a threat to their power, the older and more traditionally American social groups have fought back with all the weapons at their disposal. They have more money, power, and access to the political process, and thus have been able to use the lawmaking power to reaffirm the values and prestige damaged by the life-styles of the young. Inevitably the drug laws have been pulled into the conflict; firstly, because drug attitudes and use are sharply age-bound, and secondly, because the drug laws, with their moral implications, symbolize the divergent value systems and life-styles at the heart of the conflict.

The ability of a group to designate social norms and shifting structures of power, especially in a period of social conflict, as Gusfield[47] demonstrates in his study of Prohibition, indicates that the authority and the prestige of that group are still intact. Adherence to a criminal approach to drug use, despite its repeated failure and social costs, has thus come to symbolize that the insurgents have not yet won power. Thus, a pattern evasion of norms, whereby violation of the law is officially proscribed but unofficially tolerated, often exists, as with Prohibition and personal marijuana use. The important thing is that the law lends its prestige to the norms of one group without really affecting the practices of another.

Most drug legislation of the past seven years reflects this controversy and, indeed, cannot be understood without reference to the symbolic meaning that enacting or refusing to repeal a drug law conveys. We have described the anomalies in the scope and enactment of LSD legislation. While the case for banning all uses of LSD in health terms is difficult to sustain, the meaning of outlawing its use—exemplified in the down-to-the-wire race of the California and Nevada governors—is not. It states clearly and forthrightly that advocates of chemically induced utopias are deviants with no say in setting social norms. By the same token, enforcement of the law often has a symbolic impact far greater than its reduction of adverse drug effects. The first Stony Brook raid (200 policemen in 78 cars arrested a handful of pot smokers)[48] and Operation Intercept (search of everyone crossing the Mexican border) were reaffirmations—the one local, the other national—that drug users were not to be tolerated. With so many young people waving the banner of legalization, repeal of marijuana-possession laws would also signify a victory for the current out-groups. Such a concession would validate the critique levied by youth against the system, and correspondingly decrease the status and power of the establishment. It would also remove one club by which the older generation have maintained their moral and political hegemony. This view explains the often irrational opposition to marijuana reform, and the flagrant disregard by lawmakers of the law's social costs. Where legislators have heeded calls for reform, the legal changes have been minimal; changing the penalty from a felony to a misdemeanor makes little practical difference and in no sense departs from the view that marijuana users are deviant.

PSYCHOLOGICAL SECURITY

A third function performed by laws which, although unnecessary for health and order, condemn drug use is a psychological one. Maintenance of the drug laws in the face of growing criticism and dizzying social change reassures many people that their life-style and values have survived a serious threat.

Penal laws express society's view of the worth or desirability of behavior and, in doing so, confirm the righteousness of those members of society who share the views expressed in law. When conduct appears threatening, or when there is overt disagreement about its undesirability, it is doubly reassuring to see that standard embodied in a legal norm. The norm articulates social disapproval, announces a commitment of societal resources to eradicate the threat, and resolves doubts about what the standard should be. Now that drug attitudes and practices are thawing and the law increasingly attacked, a firm stance against drug use allays anxiety from two sources: (1) intrapsychic conflict and (2) social change.

Mr. Fry's fierce and tenacious attitudes toward drug use were, as we saw in Chapter 2, one way in which he mastered his own deeply felt but forbidden desires for passivity and pleasure. He felt better in condemning drug use because it represented a denial of feelings which he could recognize only at great psychic cost. Similarly, Blum[49] found the virulence of antidrug attitudes held by policemen to be a reaction formation against their own unconscious desires:

> We suggest that the projecting police officer—or citizen—is, in fact, threatened by his quite accurate but partially unconscious understanding of what some users do mean or intend by their drug use. That threat mobilizes the individual's feelings about past trauma of his own, trauma experienced at the hands of parental authority during the difficult stages of learning order and suppressing impulse. These individuals respond with disgust, anger, revulsion, and fear, and "cleanse" themselves by the standard human ploy of making the enemy external, that is, of scapegoating. What is an inner problem is externalized; a private issue is added to a public one. If these be the dynamics, one must conclude that police involvement in drug control—for some—is a central personal issue in which stamping out drug use is symbolic self-policing as well as the performance of public duty. The emotionally aroused police officer who calls these users dirty and hates them for their "self-indulgence" is quite an accurate diagnostician, even though the diagnosis is in the service of his own defense system.

We suggest that the stubborn reliance on criminal sanctions to control drug use, despite the failure and high costs, is also rooted in an unconscious desire for what drugs represent. A whole menu of psychoactive drugs, promising everything from instant ecstasy and mystical union to ultimate orgasm, has been dangled before a public, as have cohorts of "flower children" and others who have accepted the promise of drugs and dropped out of work, striving for joy, play, and closeness to nature. For one who presses his nose to the grindstone and denies his impulses for the sake of a secure social niche, the temptation is disconcerting. Above all, it must be resisted, but in so doing, one suspects that something good and worthwhile has been given up. Rather than resurrect old traumas, it is much easier to keep the desires forbidden under strong legal wraps. Acknowledging ambiguity in drug use means wrestling with that ambiguity, and thus intensifying the disequilibriums touched off by the drug issue. An uncrossable boundary that denies ambiguity is needed. This the law—society's authoritative pronouncement that drug use is deviant—provides.

The drug laws also help people feel better by creating a safe harbor of stability against the gales of change. The cliché that ours is an era of unprecedented change locates a source of anxiety whose full ramifications are yet to be charted. Most social scientists agree that the more pervasive the change—that is, the greater the dislocation of the past—the more anxiety and resistance it generates. Inertia and fear of the unknown combine to create a dislike of change. People are reluctant to abandon a known and safe pattern for an uncertain future, however much change may be needed.

In a world fraught with change and its attendant anxiety, a reversal in the social position of drug use is particularly disturbing. Old attitudes and perceptions must be reexamined, one's personal position redefined, and one's responses to related issues reconsidered. In addition, there is the unpleasant recognition that the values that created meaning, defined personal worth, and located the transitional point between good and bad no longer stand impregnable. Future anxieties magnify the uncertainties of the world, and leave one uninterested in the balance sheet of the law's costs and benefits, or the sufferings of untreated drug misusers. In this context, the law becomes a pillar of stability and certainty and provides a bastion for the public, perhaps the last, against the onslaught of change.

CONCLUSION: THE PARADOX
OF LEGAL CHANGE

Using law for functions unrelated to public health is, as we detail in the next chapter, a costly enterprise, and one that snares us in an insoluble dilemma. We are damned if we keep the present laws, yet their symbolic functions prevent us from taking steps in a new direction.

The situation has come about because the law, to fulfill its latent purposes, has focused increasingly on establishing the deviant status of drug use, and less and less on protecting users. The overinclusive, punitive, and other condemnatory features of the law, however, conflict with existing knowledge about drugs and, more importantly, conflict with the practice of millions of users who find drugs to be something less than the monolithic horror defined by the law. Out of this clash has sprung the controversy enveloping drug questions.

A shift in the law's emphasis from punishment to treatment would restore credibility on all sides and return drug use to a social setting in which damaging use could be dealt with effectively. The controversy would simultaneously diminish because, on the one hand, drug use would be officially recognized as a medical-social problem and, on the other, a sensible legal policy would allow the social consensus which the law's current vulnerability prevents.

The dilemma is that the unconscious needs served by the law and aroused by controversy obstruct the reorientation of the law that the interests of health require. The shift from condemnation to treatment requires a lowered commitment to the law's symbolic ends, yet only a reduced concern with the badness of drugs will halt its use as a surrogate. As long as the law makes drug use criminal, latent functions will be served. The legal change that would interfere with the notion of drugs-as-evil and lead to a less symbolic concern with the law is precisely what is needed, but the situation as presently structured does not permit this. Until this dilemma is resolved, the drug problem will remain with us.

7

THE COSTS OF
THE DRUG LAWS

Laws that penalize all nonmedical drug use have created serious problems, which in many cases are more disruptive than drug use itself. Not only have laws failed to cope with a revolution in drug use; they have also prevented the control of harmful drugs' effects, undermined the credibility of the legal system, and increased social unrest. Legislative reluctance to consider these costs is a major factor in the drug controversy.

Until the drug explosion of the 1960s, it was relatively easy to ignore the side effects of a punitive drug policy. The costs of the law were by no means negligible, but because of the size of the problem only a small number of people suffered. Equally important, before 1960 the social context was not such that the impact of these costs was magnified and transformed into fuel for social conflict. But with a dramatic increase both in drug use and in hysterical opposition to the practice, the social costs have risen. The drug laws today touch directly the lives of between 10 and 20 million people; in an already unstable social system, these laws further undermine the credibility and integrity of democratic institutions. If the system is to continue to function, these costs can no longer go unheeded.

Three issues are highlighted by the growing costs of the drug laws. First, it is clear that legislation on a particular social problem largely determines the nature and characteristics of that problem. As we shall see, many of the most dreaded effects of drug use are a chimera created by laws that define drug use as an antisocial activity. So the first question policy makers must ask themselves is not whether unregulated use of a certain drug is harmful, but whether the action they plan to take will make the situation better or worse.

The second issue is whether, in view of the law's costs, it is worth having the law at all. Every law has its costs; the point is to balance these costs against the benefits of the law. In the particular case we are discussing, the social and financial costs must be weighed against the law's success in reducing crime, violence, and the adverse effects of unregulated use. Where these benefits are minimal, hard to ascertain, or the subject of hot dispute, legislators should take pause.

The third important issue is the law's potential for intensifying or defusing the drug controversy. From its very beginnings in the international opium conferences in the early twentieth century, American drug policy has studiously ignored the side effects of the law. At the Shanghai Opium Conference in 1909, America forced through a decision for total prohibition in the face of opposition from Britain that this would open the door to abuses far worse than the drugs themselves.[1] The lessons of Prohibition—widespread corruption and an increase in the consumption of hard liquor—are also ignored by politicians who today demand more stringent drug control. The costs in terms of crime rates, police corruption, and human suffering, of fifty years of denying addicts drugs, go unheeded. Drug policy has been formulated and reformulated without reference to its efficacy or consideration of the social fallout. But failing to take into account the problems created by the law indirectly causes the situation to deteriorate; this in turn leads to the call for more and stronger laws. This is the vicious circle that we must break.

Before we discuss in detail the costs of present drug laws, one caveat is in order. To weigh accurately costs and benefits, we should express many diverse and intangible factors in terms that can be measured and compared; assigning numbers to such intangibles would grossly distort the most serious effects of the law. So we shall not try to convert the problem into dollars. Even without this ultimate precision, however, we believe that we can demonstrate clearly that the law creates burdens that far outweigh its benefits.

A COUNTERPRODUCTIVE DRUG POLICY

One of the most serious charges against present drug laws is that they are, in fact, counterproductive. Criminal sanctions against drugs use are justified on the grounds that drugs cause crime and physical and psychological damage. But in our opinion, laws defining drug use as antisocial have intensified the very trends the law was intended to curb and have inspired in drug users antisocial tendencies they might otherwise never have had. This is not to say that drugs never cause harm to individuals and society; merely that prohibition does not deal with the problem and in many cases exacerbates it.

DEATH

A minimal aim of any sensible drug policy (and therefore presumably of our current laws) should be to protect drug users from death. But under the present system, users are forced to buy their supplies on the black market, frequently buying dangerously adulterated drugs. The result is that heroin was the chief cause of death for men between the ages of 15 and 35 in New York City in 1969. In the 1960s there were 3,000 more deaths as a result of narcotic use than there had been in the 1950s, and the median age of death dropped from 35 to 23. Figures are expected to be even higher in the 1970s. Particularly disturbing is the number of teen-age deaths. One fourth of the deaths in 1969 were among teen-agers:

53 percent were under 25, and a number were 13- and 14-year-olds.[2]

There are two reasons for the high mortality rate, both arising indirectly out of the present state of the law. One is the unknown quantity of heroin in an illegal purchase. Dr. Michael Baden, deputy chief medical examiner of New York, observes:[3]

> Each shot is potentially fatal and each could be the last because the bags of heroin are distributed by so many different middlemen that the individual may get a varying quantity each time he uses it. If the next dose contains larger doses of heroin than the user has customarily taken, it can be his last—as the death statistics vividly demonstrate.

An addict is also at risk from contaminated heroin and dirty needles. Some 30 percent of deaths among addicts are traceable to tetanus, hepatitis, or bacterial endocarditis, all contracted from bad heroin or dirty syringes. Yet in most states heroin users are forbidden by law to purchase or possess a clean syringe, and it is impossible for them to be sure that their heroin is free of bacteria.

A drug policy concerned less with labeling addicts as social outcasts and more with minimizing the harmful effects of drug use could avoid these deaths in several different ways: it could provide addicts with standardized, pure doses of drugs, or at the very least make available clean syringes and immunization against tetanus and hepatitis.

CRIME

Drug use has long been popularly associated with violent crime. Indeed, this is a major justification for the policy of total prohibition. Yet evidence suggests that far from provoking criminal acts, the opiates, marijuana, and the hallucinogens actually reduce criminal impulses (other than the impulse to obtain the drug).

As the law stands, however, the addict user almost inevitably turns to crime to support his habit at inflated black-market prices.

Typical and notorious are the robberies by heroin users; they have become predators, ravaging our cities and suburbs for the where-withal for their next fix. These robberies amount to $3 billion a year in New York City, and $400 million in Washington, D.C.,[4] and this does not include the cost of the protective devices—window locks, television sets chained to the wall, etc.—that city dwellers are obliged to install. Where drugs are legally supplied to addicts, as they are in England, little of this crime occurs.

Addicts also turn to crime for reasons other than the need to pay for illegal drugs. The law defines the drug user as a criminal and a deviant, and he will frequently conform to this image. This is especially true once he has fallen afoul of the law. Criminal conviction is a particularly strong form of social condemnation. Conviction of a user may make both the user and others think of him as a criminal or "outsider." In this case, an individual who lacks support or who has personality difficulties will be confirmed in his negative image of himself, and this will make him more likely to turn to criminal activity.

Once a jail sentence has been imposed, an addict's future is marked out even more clearly. Prison brings him into contact with other criminals in a situation where their skills, ethos, and support are very readily transmitted. On leaving prison it is harder than ever for the addict to get a job and reenter the law-abiding world, and now he is equipped with skills for a criminal existence.

A significant factor in the user's assumption of the deviant role that is thrust on him by the law is his resentment at what he believes to be arbitrary or discriminatory treatment: he feels that he has been singled out for prosecution, while users of the same drug from different social strata, or users of socially accepted drugs, go free. Eldridge Cleaver[5] expresses this vividly:

> The others [black prisoners] I despised for wasting time in debates with the segregationists: why not crush them, put them in prison—they were defying the law, weren't they? I defied the law and they put me in prison. So why not put those dirty mothers in prison too? I had gotten caught with a shopping bag full of marijuana, a shopping bag full of love—I was in love with the

weed and I did not for one minute think that anything was wrong with getting high. I had been getting high for four or five years and was convinced, with the zeal of a crusader, that marijuana was superior to lush—yet the rulers of the land all seemed to be lushes. I could not see how they were more justified in drinking than I was in blowing the gage. I was a grasshopper, and it was natural that I felt myself unjustly imprisoned.

There is strong evidence that the practice of habitually flouting the drug laws has diminished the force of law in general, and in many thousands of youngsters has resulted in skepticism toward all legal authority. At Woodstock and other rock concerts, thousands of mostly young people have openly violated the drug laws and escaped punishment. Many college students have no compunction about supplying their friends with marijuana—a serious felony in every state. They have learned that the law can be violated at considerable profit and relatively little risk. There comes a point where regularly breaking the law with impunity reduces the power of the criminal sanction to deter, and the likelihood of behaving in a criminal way becomes greater. This was demonstrated at Stony Brook University. In the notorious 1968 police raid, when over 200 police arrested students for possessing marijuana, the students looked on in bewilderment. A year later, when police raided again, the students rioted, forcibly preventing the police from making arrests.[6]

Addict-related crime also erodes the respect for law among ordinary law-abiding citizens who buy stolen goods from junkies:[7]

> But I was confident that I'd be able to pick up a stolen bike when I wanted one. If you can't get anything you want at Alice's Restaurant try the junkie market. In the 4 years that I've lived on the Lower East Side I've been offered stolen steaks, cameras, clothing, car accessories, watches, jewelry, toasters, TV sets, and just about every other item that can be shoplifted or carried downstairs in a pillowcase. The price was always right.

On the whole, the buyers at the junkie market would protest their respectability. Faced with the easy price of the junkies' loot, however, their scruples fade away.

ADVERSE DRUG REACTIONS

One reason consistently advanced for denying individual choice over the use of drugs like marijuana and LSD is that they cause anxiety, depression, paranoid reactions, and sometimes more serious psychological disturbances. It appears now that psychoses do not occur so frequently as was originally thought, but undoubtedly these drugs can in some circumstances produce adverse psychological reactions. As we saw earlier in this text, the action of a drug depends on three things: its inherent pharmacological effect, the personality and psychological set of the user, and the setting in which the drug is taken. Since relatively few people experience adverse reactions, set and setting appear to be the key variables.

Part of the set and setting of nonmedical drug use is the prevailing public attitude that labels it an immoral and destructive activity. Thus, it must be practiced clandestinely and in an atmosphere of fear and suspicion. This contributes to toxic drug reactions in several ways. The novice user comes to marijuana with a fund of officially disseminated misinformation about intoxication, and one major source of adverse reaction to the drug is the violent anxiety novice users experience at an unexpectedly strong dose of the drug. At one time, half of the patients suffering from acute toxic reactions at the Haight-Ashbury Medical Clinic were novice users. Most of them were straight people over 25 years of age. David Smith,[8] director of the Haight-Ashbury Clinic, states:

> We have seen cases where the mild increase in heart rate that occurs with the early stage of marijuana intoxication was interpreted under increased sensory awareness as resembling the onset of a heart attack with a subsequent anxiety state.

Official warnings have threatened the marijuana user with insanity. The altered state of consciousness, sense of time, and sensory awareness, and the impairment of short-term memory and verbal facility may appear to the novice user to presage derangement. As long as marijuana is illegal and is reputed to produce psychosis, novice users will lack the knowledge of how the drug works, which would enable them to avoid toxic reactions.

The social setting increases the likelihood of adverse psychological reactions to marijuana by creating a negative mood or set in the user. This is especially frequent in the novice user and in those who are not full-time members of a drug subculture and fear the consequences of discovery. David Smith[9] describes this situation:

> In many cases, however, it is the marijuana use itself which creates the stressful situation. Since marijuana use in the United States is illegal and most of us have been exposed to strong warnings about its dangers, the novice experimenting with marijuana often finds himself in an emotionally charged situation. He may fear discovery and arrest with consequent loss of respect, loss of job, straining of family relations, and possible incarceration. He may harbor secret fears that marijuana intoxication will produce physical damage, will make him lose control and do things that he will not want to do, or will drive him insane. Such a strong negative attitude toward marijuana can, of itself, produce sufficient stress to create a state of panic when the influence of the drug is felt. The altered mental state produced by the drug seems only to confirm the fears, and a full-blown anxiety reaction develops.

With LSD, the social setting created by the law is even more crucial. Apart from the dangers of bad acid, the public hysteria about LSD (it "destroys the mind," "transforms the personality," etc.) may induce in the user fear, guilt, and other elements of a negative set.

LSD is indeed a powerful drug, and the length of its effect—between nine and fourteen hours—makes the physical setting particularly important. But most researchers are agreed that if one remains in an appropriate setting, with an experienced user as guide throughout the experience, panic or anxiety can be averted or handled calmly. The fact that the drug is illegal prevents even this minimal safeguard being taken. People take LSD as opportunity permits—some use it on the subway, while driving, or on the street, circumstances in which the drug's potential for psychic damage is most likely to be fulfilled.

The present law actually deters drug users who suffer adverse reactions from seeking medical help. A statute found in many states requires:[10]

> Every physician and every hospital treating persons suffering from the chronic use of narcotic drugs (defined to include all drugs, even marijuana and LSD) shall within 72 hours of the first treatment therefor furnish the Department of Public Health with a statement in duplicate containing the name, address, height, weight, date of birth, color of eyes, color of hair, date treated and the name of the narcotic drug the person used or suffered from. Such information shall be made available for the use of any agency of the Commonwealth or of the United States which may require it.

The result is self-medication, or no help at all. Self-medication can be disastrous—for example, Thorazine (an antidote to LSD) used with STP intensifies the latter drug's worst effects. Either way, the symptoms are aggravated.

MULTIPLE DRUG USE

The present drug policy, particularly with reference to marijuana, is frequently justified on the ground that there is an inevitable progression from the use of one drug to the use of more powerful and dangerous drugs. If such a progression did exist, laws directed against the "initiator" drug might well be in order. But much drug use today is multiple use: hallucinogens, stimulants, and depressants are often used simultaneously or sequentially, and progression has never been proved. Any progression from the use of one drug to another is more likely to arise because all drugs are illegal, for the following reasons:

Since all drugs are lumped together, and purveyors of drugs usually sell several different types, there are frequent opportunities to try new drugs. Also because of their illegal status, an immense glare of publicity surrounds drugs, and thousands of youngsters have decided to try them because they have been so repeatedly thrust in front of their noses.

Officialdom's very attempts to tighten up on marijuana have turned people on to other drugs. Operation Intercept in the fall of 1969 illustrates this. The Nixon administration attempted to cut off the supply of marijuana by initiating the largest search and seizure operation in American history. Everyone crossing the border into the United States from Mexico was stopped and searched. The supply of marijuana was sharply cut of, with the result that people who had previously used only marijuana turned to whatever drugs were available. There was an upsurge in heroin use among suburban, white, middle-class high school students shortly after Operation Intercept.[11]

The total prohibition of drugs, setting them all on an equal footing, has led to multiple use also by preventing education in the effects of different drugs. The official warnings suggest that every drug is almost indescribably evil, with the result that young users have come to disregard every official pronouncement on the subject. Educators are presented with a dilemma described well by Professor John Kaplan:[12]

> The difficulty is that the drug educator, along with warning students of the dangers of some of the extremely dangerous drugs that are sometimes used in the student culture, is required to discuss marijuana. Unfortunately, the issue of whether marijuana is more dangerous than alcohol will arise, and the educator cannot avoid the subject merely by saying that the penalties are too high. The students will press him again and again until he discusses the issue. He will then find himself in a very difficult position.
>
> He can say that, except for the chance of getting caught, there is no good reason to believe that marijuana, as used in the United States, is more dangerous to the individual than is alcohol. If he says this, the student will believe him, but he will then risk being charged with encouraging a violation of a serious nature and may lose his job.

Unfortunately, with the regrettable capacity of the young for overgeneralization, they will conclude that the educator may be equally wrong about amphetamines, LSD, barbiturates, and perhaps even heroin. The inevitable controversy over marijuana—which is, after all, by far the most widely used illegal drug among students—will then compromise the entire process of drug education. Many young people, after unfortunate experiences with LSD, have explained their rashness in trying the drug on the ground that "I knew our drug education program was lying about marijuana so I thought they were lying about LSD too."

A similar phenomenon may explain the spread of heroin among American soldiers in Vietnam. After the news media exposed extensive marijuana use, the army mounted a powerful campaign to stamp it out. The enlisted men quickly adapted, and turned to heroin, which was less bulky, odorless, and thus "safer" to use. Whether true or apocryphal, the oft-repeated statement by drug-using men was "I can salute with my right hand while I'm taking a hit with my left, and blow the smoke right in the old man's face, and he would never know."[13]

Multiple drug use, particularly among marijuana users, can also be explained by the subcultural atmosphere in which marijuana use takes place. Erich Goode[14] observes that "the most significant fact about marijuana use is that it is overwhelmingly a group activity; the drug, in other words, is highly 'sociogenic'—or 'culto-genic.'" The drug is used in a group setting, usually among intimates who share many of the same values and will come to share more and more as a result of progressive group involvement. Other drugs will be regarded favorably, and opportunities for taking them will increase.

It is unlikely that marijuana would be so highly cultogenic if it were legal. Its very illegality pushes drug users into a subculture in a number of different ways. Firstly, there is the need to get hold of the drug, which inevitably leads to contact with other people sympathetic to drug users. Secondly, because it is illegal, marijuana is a relatively scarce product which has to be used economically: there is a great sense of intimacy among marijuana users sharing a single "joint" or pipe. A third factor is the legal definition of marijuana users as deviants or criminals. The members of the subculture escape isolation and ostracism and reinforce each other in their choice of drug and their feelings of alienation from the system. A change in the law might well alter this situation. Erich Goode[15] observes:

> The less deviant and criminal marijuana becomes, and the more easily obtainable it is, the less its use becomes "special" and therefore significant. Under these circumstances, a detribalization occurs, and marijuana loses its subcultural impact, and its socializing power. And, possibly, the less susceptible users will come to favorable definitions of using the more potent drugs. Ironically, legalization might, for this reason, very well reduce the likelihood of users progressing to heroin and LSD.

LACK OF TREATMENT

The punitive approach of the law has left us unprepared to deal with the very real problems of drug misuse. Surprisingly little is known about addiction and its cure, as the conflict over whether addiction has metabolic or psychological roots shows.

Basic clinical data on marijuana and its effects were not collected systematically until 1968. No one has charted a dose-response curve, gathered conclusive evidence on marijuana's capacity to impede motor functioning, or described the circumstances in which use is likely to be dangerous. As a result, treatment of overdoses and toxic reactions is crude, no antidote exists, and society is lumbered with costs that could have been avoided. Standard treatment for the majority of drug addicts is still cold turkey in a jail cell. The work of such organizations as Synanon and Daytop is hampered by unanswered questions on whether an addict- or psychiatrist-run community is more effective, or indeed whether adjustment outside the community is possible at all.

Education, on which concerned citizens, officials, and politicians pin their hopes, is an unknown quantity. Compulsory education on drug abuse is now required by Massachusetts state law for the primary grades; drug police and advertising agencies have been enlisted; television and radio blare out the dangers of drugs. Yet no basic research has been conducted to discover whether these efforts are an economical use of resources, or whether, indeed, they may cause more drug use. Dr. Matthew Dumont, director of the Division of Drug Rehabilitation in Massachusetts, said:[16]

> We simply have no idea what are the effects of drug education. Whether drug education as we have known it prevents or stimulates the use of drugs is unknown. Our schools can't seem to teach anything effectively so there is no reason to believe they will have any more success with attempting to teach young people not to use drugs. Drug education, like all aspects of any approach to the drug problem, should be carefully and systematically analyzed and evaluated before it is put into use.

Another barrier to effective treatment is the lack of resources for dealing with adverse drug reactions. Again, let us look at the situation in New York. There are estimated to be between 100,000 and 200,000 heroin addicts in New York City, of whom 25,000 are thought to be teen-agers. Out of the city's budget of $6.6 billion in 1970, $13 million, or 0.2 percent, went for addiction service programs, and of that only $3 million is put up by the city.[17] On the state level, the Narcotic Control Commission in 1969 had less than 15,000 addicts in treatment, despite huge capital outlays for confinement centers. An addict seeking help cannot obtain emergency treatment and might have to wait a year to get into a methadone or therapeutic program. What does he do in the meantime? He might die, or as *The New York Times* reported:[18]

> One addict said he stole $55 from a waitress after a doctor at Bellevue advised him to "go to the Salvation Army and get a square meal." Another addict who could not get help at Metropolitan Hospital threw a garbage can through a bar window and stole $300.

For the 25,000 juvenile addicts, the situation is even sadder. Odyssey House, run by Dr. Judianne Densen-Gerber, is the only house catering to juvenile addicts. It cares for 135 children and is dependent on donations. The city has seen fit to issue it a summons for overcrowding.[19]

At the same time, law-enforcement funds increase steadily. In less than ten years the federal government has spent over $75 million on drug-law enforcement and tripled the number of enforcement personnel.[20] If figures on similar trends in all fifty states were ascertainable, a true picture of the extent to which enforcement diverts scarce funds from treatment would emerge.

OBSTACLES TO CONTROL

Drug control is obstructed by two features of the present drug laws. One is the public attitude nurtured by the punitive laws: the drug user is seen as a criminal, and punishment rather than medical treatment seems the most appropriate way of dealing with him. If not a criminal, he is viewed as a "junkie," who must be kept away from respectable people and not pampered in his wicked desire for drugs. Donald Miller,[21] chief counsel to the Federal Bureau of Narcotics and Dangerous Drugs, explains the bureau's objections to the use of methadone:

> The Bureau does have a vital role . . . to alert society as to the possible pitfalls and to caution against mass acceptance of a theory which could adversely affect our society by increased addiction. . . .
> Will there be any deterrence when potential users are assured that there will be no ill consequences from drug experimentation; indeed, that addicts may even receive preferential treatment? What will be the result of having no social stigma against addict-proselytizers in our communities?

Thus, the response has been, on the whole, punitive. Even the civil commitment programs that have sprung up since *Robinson v.*

California seem to have confinement rather than therapy as their chief purpose.

The second obstacle created by the law is the lack of funds for research into the use and effects of drugs. A vast body of information on the effects of marijuana exists in the minds of the millions of users, but it cannot be tapped because the drug is illegal. The legal and administrative hurdles that drug researchers must vault are many and high. Some drugs cannot be prescribed, even to research subjects; others are unobtainable. The technicalities of obtaining funds and permission are intricate and deter all but the most stalwart. One of the authors of this book spent nine months persuading federal, state, local, university, and police officials to allow him to conduct a simple marijuana experiment.

Even where funds are made available, legal restrictions on the research considerably diminish its value. There is a remarkable preponderance of studies of the effects of marijuana, LSD, cocaine, and heroin on animals; in the few involving human beings, the experimental settings are quite different from those in which marijuana use will ordinarily take place. These restrictions are rationalized on grounds of safety or to prevent the drugs from getting into the wrong hands. However, the extraordinary and severe difficulties some researchers have faced suggest to us that the funding bureaus prefer research that does not contradict official policy. Experiments showing that marijuana is a drug milder in its effects than commonly thought have been officially denounced as "dangerous" and "irresponsible"; the results have been distorted and the experiments have had to end.

COSTS TO THE LEGAL SYSTEM

Over the past ten years there has been a deterioration in the relationship between the citizen and society and the law. There are two elements in this turn of events. The first is the law-and-order controversy: the rising crime rate, the apparent disregard for the law which is becoming more and more commonplace, leads many people to believe that existing laws can no longer maintain the order necessary for personal security. The widespread violation of the drug laws has intensified this fear, and at the same time has goaded the police into certain practices contrary to the rule of law. Thus, citizens and police have become alienated from the law and from each other, the credibility and integrity of the legal system have suffered, and the problems of our complex society have become less susceptible to legal solution.

The second element in the deteriorating relationship between society and the law lies in the very complexity of the massive problems of a postindustrial society. They range from the tensions of world politics, a threatened environment, and the population explosion to new attitudes toward government, corporate responsibility, and individual liberty. Old institutions must be overhauled and new power structures evolved to meet the challenges of pervasive and continuous change. A legal system that can impose order without strangling innovation is essential, but as the influence of the law is eroded it is gravely handicapped in this task.

Against this background we turn to the problems that a punitive approach to drug use has created for our legal system.

DIVERTING RESOURCES

Increased demands are being made on our undermanned and overworked police force. The courts dispense a revolving-door type of trial-less justice, where 95 percent of cases are disposed of by negotiated guilty pleas and where trials in the lower courts sometimes last five minutes. This rough semblance of justice is further attenuated by high caseloads for probation officers and crowded jails. In New York City the backlog of criminal cases numbered over 200,000 in 1970. Some 177,000 arrest warrants for bail-jumpers were outstanding.[22] In a little over two years, drug enforcement added over 100,000 new cases to the workload of the courts. This system does not protect the public, or treat defendants fairly, and cannot rehabilitate its criminals. As the pressures on the system mount, failures of enforcement and arbitrary dispositions will become the rule, and genuine law and order an elusive goal.

The criminalization of drug use has added to the staggering burdens disrupting the law. In 1968, there were 34,000 adults and 15,000 juveniles arrested in California for marijuana alone, a figure ten times greater than that of 1962.[23] A study of the Los Angeles Police Department has shown that a simple marijuana arrest consumes six to eight hours of a policeman's time.[24] When arrests result from stake-outs, undercover work, or raids, the drain is even greater. And even so, nothing like full enforcement of the law is achieved. Many cities and towns are creating or expanding specialized drug units. Often this entails a reallocation of men from other units or monopolizes increases in manpower. In New York City, some 200 men were transferred in March of 1970 to drug units, making the drug police there 700 strong.[25] Federal drug police have tripled in number, while the Customs Bureau has recently added 300 men to deal with drugs.[26] An accurate estimate of the police time diverted by drug policy should also include time spent on theft, burglary, prostitution, and other crimes growing out of drug addiction. Complete accuracy is impossible, but it is estimated that in California in 1968 the drug laws consumed $75 million of police resources.[27] The national total in 1970 is estimated to be over $1 billion.

Leaving aside the questionable nature of the benefits of such numbers, in many instances police time appears to be wastefully employed. In Houston, as in many other major cities, numerous agencies suffer from overlapping jurisdiction and little coordination:[28]

> Both federal and state agencies are active in drug detection. At the county level the sheriff's department functions both within the city of Houston and in the rural areas of Harris County. Within the urban complex there is, of course, the Houston Police Department as well as smaller departments operating out of small communities in and adjacent to Houston. It is conceivable that an individual under suspicion of misusing drugs could be pursued

simultaneously by numerous police agencies. Thus, a person might attend a school located in the Village Police Department's jurisdiction and might live in a house located in the Houston Department's bailiwick. He would be subject to the sheriff's scrutiny as well as the State Department of Public Safety's concern and might even be under surveillance by the Federal Bureau of Narcotics and Dangerous Drugs. Five different enforcement agencies—each possibly acting independently and without knowledge of the others—would be focusing on one individual. . . . This overlap is presently resolved only by informal cooperation among the agencies. There is no law establishing enforcement priorities. Neither is there any formal organizational structure that helps minimize friction among the agencies.

Most arrests involve marijuana, perhaps the least dangerous of the illegal drugs. In California 40 percent of the marijuana violators were first offenders, and 60 percent of these cases were dismissed without trial.

The drug laws also burden the postarrest stages of the criminal process. In Los Angeles in 1968, 17 percent of the felony complaints issued in one six-month period were for marijuana.[29] Most of these cases never went to trial, but valuable prosecutorial time was used up. If a defendant elects a jury trial, he may have to wait up to a year; if he cannot make bail, he will remain in jail. In a case reported in 1970 a deaf-mute who had been mistakenly identified by an undercover agent as a drug seller was held without bail for five months.[30] Courts and prosecutors must prepare and hear the case. Probation officers file reports and supervise sentences. Appellate review may be sought. Finally, a prison term may be unavoidable. With mandatory minimum penalties for many drug offenses, drug offenders crowd state and federal prisons. Throughout the 1960s at least 10 percent of federal prisoners were drug offenders serving an average of five-year sentences.

We have reached two conclusions: First, an accurate cost accounting system is needed to ascertain the full cost of enforcing the drug laws. Second, even without a precise cost analysis it is clear that elimination of use and possession offenses would free the process to deal with more serious drug offenses and nondrug crimes.

EROSION OF THE RULE OF LAW

Perhaps the most serious legal cost is the effect on the rule of law. The rule of law, the basic feature of a democratic society, imposes legal restraints and orderly procedures on the state's use of power. It ensures that official power is exercised fairly, and it protects against the abuses of unfettered discretion and arbitrary power. Without the rule of law, individual liberty is at the mercy of the police. The drug laws offer in many respects a paradigm of official power operating outside legal control.

This situation arises largely because drug offenses are on the whole "victimless" crimes. Possessing or using a drug is usually a private act. Even drug sales occur in private with other consenting persons. Drug offenses seldom impinge so forcefully on others that they feel impelled to notify the police. Professor Herbert Packer[31] has outlined the consequences of victimless crimes for law enforcement:

> To the difficulties of apprehending a criminal when it is known that he has committed a crime are added the difficulties of knowing that a crime has been committed. In this sense, the victimless crime always presents a greater problem to the criminal process than does the crime with an ascertainable victim. But this problem may be minimized if the criminal process has at its disposal measures designed to increase the probability that the commission of such offenses will become known. If suspects may be entrapped into committing offenses, if without evidence that he has committed an offense, if wiretaps and other forms of electronic surveillance are permitted, it becomes easier to detect the commission of offenses of this sort. But if these measures are prohibited and if the prohibitions are observed in practice it becomes more difficult, and eventually there may come a point at which the capacity of the criminal process to deal with victimless offenses becomes so attenuated that a failure of enforcement occurs.

The policeman is presented with a dilemma. He is under pressure to enforce the law, yet lacks the tools to do so; he must devise techniques to provide himself with the necessary information. At this point, operational efficiency conflicts with the legal limits of police powers. For the policeman, the overriding value is the enforcement of the law. Perhaps understandably, he is less sensitive to the necessity of enforcing the law according to the Constitution, especially when that seems to impede law enforcement. One result of this situation is that a great deal of illegal activity goes on on the part of the police; another is that the legal limits to their powers are expanded. Both results are inconsistent with the rule of law, for the first disregards law, and the second removes larger areas of official action and power from legal scrutiny. In practice, therefore, essential democratic values are sacrificed on the altar of the drug laws, and this affects the power of the law to regulate our lives effectively.

SEARCH AND SEIZURE

The chief technique used by the police to detect drug offenses and obtain evidence for prosecution is to search a person or his property. Unless the policeman has a warrant or has arrested the suspect, he has no legal right to search an individual. In the case of *Mapp v. Ohio,* 360 U.S. 1, the Supreme Court recognized that the only practical means of enforcing this rule was by excluding illegally seized evidence. This situation has created considerable hostility between the courts and police.

A glance at some of the landmark decisions of the Warren Court in the area of criminal procedure reveals some of the practices resorted to by police in their efforts to enforce the drug laws. They have pumped stomachs, probed rectums, and arbitrarily searched people suspected of carrying drugs. It is not clear whether the exclusionary rule has eliminated most of the illegal conduct. Jerome Skolnick,[32] in an empirical study of police practices in a large norther California city, finds:

The practice of making an unlawful exploratory search of the room of a suspected criminal is, so far as I could tell on several occasions, accepted by both the Westville police and the state police. As one policeman commented: "Of course, it's not exactly legal to take a peek beforehand. It's not one of the things you usually talk about as a police technique. But if you find something, you back off and figure out how you can do it legal. And if you don't find anything, you don't have to waste a lot of time."

There is considerable evidence that the police will evade the constitutional imperative of probable cause before search by making an arrest and then lying in court about the circumstances in order to establish probable cause. Paul Chevigny,[33] in his study of police abuses in New York City, describes several incidents in which police search illegally, find drugs, and then testify in court that they saw the drugs first. In one case, the police simply barged into the apartment of a "hippie" on the lower East Side and found him and friends smoking pot. In court their testimony was that as someone was leaving the apartment, they saw the defendant holding contraband.

More frequently, the search occurs on the street. One patrolman in uniform stationed himself outside a "head" shop that sold cigarette papers and pipes. As individuals who appeared to have purchased these implements came out, he would stop and search them, in a nearby hallway. In court the officer testified that he actually saw a marijuana cigarette being carried or passed back and forth between two persons in a hallway. He lost his case when it was pointed out that the hallway had six high steps leading to it, and could not be looked into by a policeman standing in the street.

The particular vice of these illegal searches is the dishonesty induced in the police. From the policeman's point of view it is reasonable to stop and search someone he "knows" is using drugs. Indeed, to him the drugs then uncovered prove how reasonable the search has been. Yet, since *Mapp,* the law is different, and the policeman is caught in a bind between the law and his perception of his duty. To fit within the law, the policeman will commit perjury—a pattern of conduct one does not like to see in policemen testifying in court where the liberty of individuals is in question.

The police perjury resulting from this conflict is nowhere better evidenced than in the "dropsie" case—by now a familiar term to police, prosecutors, and judges in urban areas. In case after case the policeman claims that he was observing the defendant, who then dropped (whence the term "dropsie") or abandoned a small packet or object that contained drugs, whereupon he was arrested. In a typical dropsie case there will be no reason why an individual would openly discard an expensive drug in the presence of a stranger, especially if that stranger is wearing a uniform. In *People v. Bueche,* a typical New York drug case, the defendant, an addict of many years familiar with police practices, according to the police not only exhibited heroin "in broad daylight on a public street in full view of others, but would be so startled at the approach of a stranger in ordinary street clothes [the cop] that he would make his possession of contraband even more visible by throwing it down at his feet, and then stand there next to it, inviting arrest."[34]

An empirical study of police searches before and after *Mapp* corroborates the testimony of thousands of defendants that the police lie as a matter of course in "dropsie" cases. Sarah Barlow[35] found, after analyzing the arrest affidavits filed in Manhattan Criminal Court in drug cases, that the percentage of cases in which abandonment was alleged by all policemen rose from about 14 percent in 1961 to 31 percent in 1962, and for specialized narcotics police, it rose from 14 to 47 percent. During this same period the number of drug misdemeanor cases dropped about 30 percent for the police in general and 47 percent for the narcotics police. The unavoidable conclusion is that while *Mapp* did succeed in reducing the number of unlawful searches, if the police wanted to arrest someone on drugs, they would search him illegally and manufacture a "probable cause" situation in court.

Further support of the prevalence of suspicious dropsie testimony recently came from a judge of the New York City Criminal

Court who has been involved in hundreds of drug cases. Faced with the conflicting testimony of police and defendant, the judge observed:[36]

> Were this the first time a policeman had testified that a defendant dropped a packet of drugs to the ground, the matter would be unremarkable. The extraordinary thing is that each year in our criminal courts policemen give such testimony in hundreds, perhaps thousands, of cases—and that, in a nutshell, is the problem of "dropsy" testimony. The difficulty arises when one stands back from the particular case and looks at a series of cases. It then becomes apparent that policemen are committing perjury at least in some of them, and perhaps in nearly all of them.

A more recent study of marijuana enforcement in San Mateo County, California, uncovered questionable searches in fully one fifth of the arrests selected at random. The following are typical examples:[37]

> In one case officers stopped to question four young men parked at night in an exclusive residential area. One officer stated that when he requested identification from one occupant, "as he was leaning to one side to remove his wallet from his pocket, I was able to notice vegetable-botanical material underneath his foot on the floorboards." Twenty grams of marijuana were discovered when the car was searched. This was one of five cases in which officers claimed that from outside a car at night they were able to observe marijuana seeds, marijuana debris, or a single roach inside the car on the floor. In assessing the officer's explanations, it should be noted that the interior of an automobile is dimly lit, if at all, that the floor is generally covered with a dark carpeting or rubber mats, that dirt and other debris are usually present, and that seeds and particles of marijuana rarely exceed one sixteenth of an inch in any dimension.

> In four instances in the sample, the case for probable cause was based in part on the officers' testimony that they detected the odor of burning marijuana. That odor is distinctive. In one of these cases, however, the officer claimed to have detected it in an open

park; and in another it was claimed that the smoke came billowing out of an automobile in "great amounts" when a window on the passenger's side was lowered, even though this occurred some time after the door on the driver's side had been opened.

At times illegal searches turn into systematic patterns of harassment. Recently thirty-seven persons sued the New Jersey State Police for their alleged policy of searching, as a matter of course, long-haired persons who travel the New Jersey Turnpike, known to youths as "Bust Alley," in the hope of turning up drugs. To substantiate its charge that the "Fourth Amendment doesn't exist on the New Jersey Turnpike," the suit claims that thousands of persons have been illegally stopped for no other reason than their long hair.[38] Tolerance of such practices excites resentment against the law among those searched, especially when they are innocent, and, of course, encourages the police to operate illegally.

UNDERCOVER ACTIVITIES

There has been a noticeable increase in the use of undercover agents, spies, and informants by the police in their efforts to enforce the drug laws.

The undercover work takes several forms, engages valuable police time, and causes a resentful and suspicious atmosphere. Typical was a case decided in 1970 by the Massachusetts Supreme Judicial Court, in which a state police undercover agent was introduced into a teen-age group in a small Massachusetts town upset about its supposed drug problem. He repeatedly telephoned the defendant asking him to get him some drugs. Although a user of marijuana and familiar with the local drug scene, the defendant was not a seller. After repeated solicitations, he introduced his newfound "friend" to someone who was. Stupidly, the defendant stood between the cars of the seller and the agent and helped transfer the drug and money. He was prosecuted for sale and possession of a narcotic, and sentenced to five years imprisonment.[39]

In Houston a study[40] revealed that both police and school officials had engaged students as informers:

> In addition to receiving information from parents (some of whom do spy work of their own) and students who occasionally volunteer information, the Village Police have enlisted student informants for detection of drug abuse among high school students. These students are not paid for their work, but some of them . . . have been picked up by the Village Police and have agreed to cooperate rather than have charges filed against them. The student informants keep an eye out for the location of parties, who has drugs, and when sales are to be made. They make a buy from a student and report back to the Village Police. The practice . . . is not to arrest a seller after the sale to an informant buyer so as to preserve the anonymity of the informant but rather to let the informant stay friendly with the seller. When the seller arranges another sale to another buyer, the informant reports the time and place to the police and then they move in for the arrest. . . . One administrator admitted that he has two seniors that play undercover and that he is training two sophomores to take their place. . . . These two relay information back to him and make buys from other students not only from his school but also from students from other schools in cooperation with other school administrators.

> One school administrator was found to be quite active in law enforcement and seemed to enjoy the role. He had several students in the school acting as informants and had a couple more in training. One of his students was on loan to another high school for a law enforcement assignment.

Several universities have permitted or actively encouraged undercover police to pose as students to obtain information about drug activities. At Hobart, Fairleigh-Dickinson, and Cornell this has provoked a number of angry incidents.

Besides wasting police time, these practices raise several problems. First, there is little or no judicial control of police in these circumstances. The legal doctrine of entrapment offers little protection; it did not prevent the Massachusetts youth from going to jail. Second, the agent or informant will often have committed the same offense as the person arrested, yet he will not be punished. Third, student informants are exposed to violent retaliation for their role in law enforcement. Even more serious, the informant may use his position to satisfy personal grudges, or in an excess of zeal, encourage crime in the innocent. The Houston practice evoked these comments from the police:[41]

> The police admit that using juveniles in this way could be dangerous, and say they always get parental permission. So far, no student informant has been assaulted by a deceived seller. The police report that they have had difficulty at times keeping student informants quiet about what they are doing. Sources at the high school reveal that the Village Police are not always successful, for at least one of their informants is known because of his talking too much. There have been attempted frame-ups where one student has gotten mad at another, planted something on him, and informed the police. More than once the mad student has been a girl just jilted by her boyfriend. Village Police feel they have always caught these instances before charges were brought against an innocent person.

Another objection is that it is unethical to use juveniles to spy on one another. It generates suspicion and hostility which mar the friendly atmosphere of university or social gatherings and contribute to the negative set and setting of drug use. There have been cases where undercover agents have killed persons in dubious circumstances and escaped punishment.[42]

Besides, spying further alienates students from legal authority and can provoke violent reactions. At Hobart College in May 1970 police attempted to arrest five students on drug charges. They had received their information from a police agent who had infiltrated the campus. There was a violent confrontation between 50 policemen and 500 students, and when the police were trapped inside their cars, they were forced to free the arrested students and drop the charges.[43]

EXPANSION OF POLICE POWERS
AT THE EXPENSE OF PRIVACY

Many provisions of the drug laws make sense only as a means to enforce more basic prohibitions. For example, policemen will often justify the criminal status of illegal possession on the ground that it helps them to arrest pushers who are difficult to detect in the act of sale. The offense of being present where drugs are kept enables the police to dispense with having to prove which individual in the group was in possession. Addiction, a crime declared unconstitutional in 1962, enabled the police to prosecute addicts without having to prove either possession or sale. Rather than helping to enforce the provisions against sale—surely the most important target for drug laws—this category of crimes primarily affects users and innocent people who happen to be in their company.

The moral ferment about drugs makes courts and legislatures willing to expand police powers. For example, entrapment is almost null as a restraint on police activity, on the ground often reiterated by appellate courts that the police need such powers to counter the narcotic menace. More recently, postal officials have made it a practice to search mail and packages for drugs.[44]

When a drug "crisis" occurs, the usual response is to strengthen the policeman's hand. We have seen how in 1956 the Price-Daniel Act imposed long, mandatory minimum sentences for drug offenses, ostensibly to help the police catch drug sellers; in practice, however, it transferred judicial discretion over sentences to the police.

More recently, the police have been granted broad wiretapping powers in drug cases (a similar development has occurred in Sweden), and Congress has passed a provision allowing police with a search warrant to break into the home of any suspect without knocking or otherwise identifying themselves. The rationale for this is that it will prevent suspects from destroying illicit drugs before the police can enter. It is doubtful, in fact, whether this power will help the police to apprehend pushers, although it is sure to increase hostility toward the police. As Geoffrey Stokes,[45] of the Addiction Services Agency of New York City, points out:

> The logistical difficulties attendant to flushing a kilo of marijuana down the toilet, or of burning a similar amount of heroin, are such that the no-knock provision is simply not needed to reach the dealer, who would be likely to have substantial amounts of any illegal substance. Its inapplicability has long been recognized in New York State, which has had a no-knock provision for years. Manhattan District Attorney Frank Hogan's office reports seeking no-knock authority in only three out of 903 narcotics cases last year. . . . In fact, the no-knock provision is of use only against persons who are likely to possess a relatively small and easily disposable amount of a drug: that is to say, against typical younger activists like (and here the examples the police use of a drug charge in a political context are factual) Mark Rudd, Abbie Hoffman, Jerry Rubin, and Huey Newton. In short, the bill attempts to legitimize Stony Brooks, the kind of promiscuous midnight raid on a college dormitory which yields large headlines, but no progress against the forces which control illicit drug traffic in America.

Among current proposals for dealing with the drug problem in New York City is a plan for preventive detention of drug addicts suspected of crime. District Attorney Burton Roberts, of the Bronx, and Mario Procaccino, a 1970 Democratic candidate for mayor, would deny bail to a suspect who an arresting policeman has "probable" cause to believe an addict. If a urine test immediately after arraignment revealed heroin use, the suspect would either be committed to the State Narcotic Control Commission or, if charged with a serious crime, tried within 90 days.[46] If the accused wished to contest the finding of addiction, a judicial hearing would be held within four weeks to determine if there is probable cause to detain him without bail as an addict. The following objections to this plan were raised by a New York Supreme Court Justice and several lawyers:[47]

—A policeman would have the discretion to determine who might be an addict. Policemen are not qualified to do this. Moreover, they could interpret probable cause to harass suspected criminals who might or might not be either criminals or addicts.

—The plan would come into effect only after . . . the commission of a crime. To say nothing of the tens of thousands of addicts who are never caught.

—The facilities of the State Narcotic Addiction Control Commission have come under criticism recently as being more custodial than rehabilitative.

—If addicts were to be accorded all the guarantees of law, including the right to counsel at arraignment, the problem of getting lawyers in time would be substantial.

—Since the court system is woefully overloaded now, it is doubtful that it could really dispose of all addiction hearings within four weeks and trials within 90 days.

Undoubtedly this pattern will repeat itself in further calls for increasing police powers. Such powers have a way of affecting nondrug activities, particularly political activities. Once granted to the police, they are seldom relinquished. They intensify an atmosphere of police repression and remove more police activities from legal control. While such expanded powers have little impact on the extent or effects of drug use, they do reduce individual freedom and subvert the rule of law.

POLICE CORRUPTION

One serious consequence of victimless crimes is police corruption. One can only guess at the full extent to which the drug laws cause corruption. In 1969, seventy federal drug agents working in New York were dismissed for venality. This included extortion, theft from arrested drug offenders, and accepting bribes to arrest a pusher's competitors. In past months the Knapp Commission investigating police practices in New York City, has found widespread and pervasive corruption, much of which stems from drug enforcement. Single bribes as high as $10,000 to individual policemen have been reported. One member of a special unit in Harlem reported that he received $1,500 a month from drug pushers. Some officers sell the drugs found on arrested persons. Still others give informants orders for liquor and clothes in return for heroin and cocaine. The shocking extent of the corruption is summarized in the Commission's Interim report,[48] in which it agreed that:

> Narcotics police engage in various types and techniques of corruption ranging from extortion, bribery, contradictory court testimony designed to affect the release of a narcotics criminal, improper associations with persons engaged in drug traffic, and finally . . . involvement by police officers in the actual sale of marijuana.

A number of other illegal practices occur in the course of enforcing the drug laws. A frequent complaint is that the police plant drugs on a suspect and then arrest him. This allegedly occurs when they suspect him of being a drug offender but find no drugs on him, or when they want him arrested for personal or political reasons. A New York lawyer who has defended many drug cases reported complaints by his clients that the police often charge them with having less heroin in their possession than they actually have, and then sell the excess or plant it on someone they want to arrest.[49]

Chicago police officials testified during the Price-Daniel hearings:[50]

> *Lt. Healy:* . . . every time our men see these addicts on the street loitering around, they bring them in. That is how we get our information on the peddlers, from the addicts.

> *Mr. Speer:* You mean when you see an addict on the street, whether or not you suspect that he may have narcotics on him or in his possession, you arrest him and bring him in for interrogation?

Lt. Healy: We do, unless he has a very good excuse for being at that certain point.

Mr. John Gutknecht, former professor of law, the state's attorney, indicated that this police tactic was illegal and appeared mildly troubled by the violation of civil rights involved:

Mr. Gutknecht: In view of my background as a law professor, I am very jealous of civil rights, civil rights of individuals. One of the things I determined when I got in here was that I was going to be particularly careful about that. I must say this to you, that where narcotic addicts are concerned, I haven't any complaints, though I do know the police are a little prone to pick up these men. They have the protection of an ordinance, and I must say that the problem is so serious that even if we must admit some of their civil laws or civil rights are being violated, you have to go along with a certain amount of the fringe violation, if you see what I mean. . . . I think that you will also have to agree that . . . I in my capacity—and we both have civil rights laws to enforce—can, with our multiple jobs, get too excited if a known addict has been unlawfully arrested and then discharged, knowing that because he is a known addict the police have to take little extra measures.

Jerry Rubin claims that the police broke into his apartment, threw drugs on the floor, and arrested him. Allen Ginsberg has alleged that several of his friends have been asked by the police to plant drugs on him so that he may be arrested.[51] One of the most widely publicized cases of suspected planting, in combination with entrapment and undercover tactics, was the arrest of Professor Leslie Fiedler and his family. This well-known author, who is an English teacher at Buffalo, was accused of maintaining premises where others smoked marijuana. Fiedler, who claims never to have used marijuana, asserted that his arrest was contrived because he sponsored a student group working for the legalization of marijuana. It appears that a 16-year-old girl, a friend of Fiedler's children, was persuaded by the police to enter his house—already wired with eavesdropping equipment—plant marijuana, and inform the police.[52]

These practices are rife not only because of the policeman's low pay and long hours, so often quoted in extenuation; they are an inevitable consequence of the low visibility of drug-law enforcement. The drug police operate as an autonomous unit, and are seldom seen by the public when making an arrest. Frequently they cannot be made to account for their actions, even to police superiors.

The consequences of this endemic corruption should not be underestimated; it considerably lowers the respect in which the police, and by extension all legal authority, are held. To the extent that drug laws increase the likelihood of corruption, they impose a heavy cost on the whole criminal process and lower the cohesive power of the law.

ARBITRARY ENFORCEMENT

The drug laws are not administered impartially. People guilty of identical offenses are treated differently, according to their personal characteristics and the predilections of the officials dealing with them. This arbitrary treatment is a major source of hostility toward the police and legal authority, especially among offenders who belong to groups that, they feel, are subjected to discrimination.

The rule of law also suffers. The police base their decisions on subjective rather than legal premises, and for them too this results in a loss of respect for the law.

Perhaps the most arbitrary decision concerns whom to arrest. Zealous in their pursuit of street addicts, the drug police are more reluctant to arrest and prosecute well-to-do addicts. Lindesmith[53] points out:

> Judges of lower courts have sometimes commented upon the singular absence in their courts of well-to-do addicts, such as those from the medical profession. Such persons are sometimes prosecuted . . . but often they are not. Sometimes they may be

given a chance, or several chances, to cure themselves of their habits before they are prosecuted or the addict's doctor may be privately assured by an agent that no action will be taken against him if he provides the addict with drugs. This form of what, in effect, is legalized addiction in the upper social strata has probably increased in prevalence as the legally prescribed penalties have become increasingly severe.

Harry Anslinger, the chief United States advocate of a punitive drug policy, describes unblushingly how he got special treatment for two addicts, one a congressman, the other

> . . . a Washington society woman. I had known her personally for some years. She was a beautiful and gracious lady. She had become so badly addicted to Demerol that no doctor would prescribe for her; her demand was too great.[54]

Millions of people use marijuana, and the police cannot possibly detect and apprehend every violator. Arrest patterns show that five groups bear the brunt of selective enforcement: long-haired hippie types, juveniles, political activists, blacks, and Chicanos. This may be a matter of simple persecution, but a more likely explanation is the natural suspicion the police have for these groups, and the frequency with which they come into contact. Young people, for example, often have brushes with the police over curfew violations, and members of minority groups automatically arouse police suspicions. Typically, arrests occur when a policeman stops a car for a minor traffic offense and legally or illegally searches the occupants. A car full of teen-agers, hippies, or blacks is much more likely to be stopped and searched than a car full of middle-class white people. Usually middle-class whites are arrested for marijuana offenses in freak circumstances—for example, when the babysitter finds marijuana while she's looking for cookies and calls the police.[55] White college students, one of the largest group of marijuana users, generally enjoy the sanctuary of a college campus. It is well known that political activists are arrested for marijuana offenses; the cases of Jerry Rubin and Leslie Fiedler are widely publicized. But less well known is the arrest of Lee Otis

Johnson,[56] a black organizer working in the Houston ghetto, and John Sinclair of Detroit. The circumstances of their arrest and trial, and the 30- and 10-year prison sentences received, suggest political motives.

After arrest, there are the same discrepancies and discrimination. Decisions must be made on whether to grant bail, dismiss or prosecute the charge, which charges to press, whether or not to find the party guilty, and finally on sentence. Prosecutors, judges, and other officials differ greatly in their view of the seriousness of marijuana offenses, their interpretation of the law of search and seizure, and the weight they assign to personal factors. A study[57] of marijuana arrests in Los Angeles found arbitrary and often erratic treatment for the following reasons:

> Since there are many more cases involving marijuana than most other serious crimes, more prosecutors have to handle the cases and tend to apply varying standards in judging whether they are fit for prosecution. Moreover, the usual crime, possession of marijuana, leads to such tenuous concepts as "joint possession," "constructive possession," and "usable amount," which seem to give an especially wide play to prosecutorial standards. Furthermore, since such a large percentage of marijuana offenders have been in no previous trouble with the law, the varying weights this factor is given by different prosecutors introduce an extra element of uncertainty into the entire process. Finally, determinations as to all of the previous issues necessarily reflect what the individual prosecutor happens to think about the propriety of the marijuana laws. Since . . . there is considerable disparity in the views of prosecutors, especially concerning the marijuana possessor, it is hardly surprising that the prosecution of marijuana offenders will depend to a large extent on which prosecutor has received the case.

In Houston, juveniles (under 16) receive special post-arrest treatment. A first arrest, if the juvenile and his parents are cooperative, usually ends there, and no further action is taken. If the juvenile is not cooperative and repentant, the authorities may turn him over to the probation department:[58]

If the probation department gets him it is their practice to turn him back to his parents; it is not a punishment-oriented group. The head of probation does not believe the drug abuse problem is as serious among juveniles as publicity would indicate, and he is fearful of branding young people with a record. He has been quoted as saying "punishing 15 and 16 year olds for selling marijuana doesn't work." Thus, there is a basic difference in philosophy between juvenile enforcement and juvenile probation. The juvenile court seems to agree with probation, for while it can send a juvenile to reform school until age 21, or waive jurisdiction to a criminal court, the stiffest penalty being handed out for marijuana involvement is probation; thus, again the juvenile winds up back home.

So the 16-year-old drug offender may have three chances before being deprived of his freedom, whereas the 17-year-old may go to jail for his first offense. Young drug users have learned to play the system and calculate their chances; their respect for the law is further compromised. The police, for their part, are angered by the different treatment accorded to cases that in their eyes are equally bad.

POLICE-CITIZEN HOSTILITY

The searches, seizures, and other techniques that have been adopted to enforce an almost unenforceable law bring the police into conflict with other segments of the criminal process—in particular, the court. Cases are dismissed or reversed on technicalities where the evidence clearly shows guilt. The police feel obliged to perjure themselves and to justify tactics that are operationally efficient, but technically illegal. Perhaps understandably, the police have often seen the courts and the rules they apply as handcuffing their productivity. In some localities courts have sensed the hostility and only reluctantly applied higher-court rulings to police practices. The police respond by pushing the rules to the extreme in doubtful cases, lobbying for more powers, or disregarding the courts whenever possible. Opposition between the courts and police is a serious matter. For better or worse, the judiciary has been handed the job of protecting constitutional rights.

The police also meet hostility from citizens that intensifies the doubts and uncertainties that they may harbor about their role. In many cases this hostility comes from white, middle-class, educated people, the very groups that police ordinarily respect and aspire to join. Unlike opiate offenders, the new breed of drug user feels justified in his drug use. Often he attacks the policeman for the arbitrariness he perceives in the law. The overt resistance of drug offenders can be troubling to the policeman. His sense of performing a public service in enforcing the law is undermined. If he too doubts the wisdom of the marijuana laws, he is obliged to enforce a law in which he does not believe. In either case he experiences conflict about his role and his usefulness. In the space of a few years his public image has deteriorated from cop to fuzz to pig.

COSTS TO SOCIETY

The costs of the drug laws are seen most clearly with regard to drug policy and the legal process. But there are other costs, reflected in the loss of governmental authority and integrity, increasing social instability, and an erosion of personal freedom.

DRUGS AS A SMOKESCREEN

In the past decade there have been major crises over civil rights, urban affairs, foreign policy, and ecology: crimes of violence have increased alarmingly, and there have been four political assassinations. Yet much public time and energy have been concentrated on the problem of drug use. This not only depletes our limited resources; it also diverts attention from other problems more crucial to the health of the nation and much more dangerous for politicians to handle. Joel Fort[59] calls this the "smokescreening function" of the drug issue, and observes that it is

> . . . particularly utilized by politicians, editors, and publishers, and administrative bureaucrats, who seek, sometimes desperately, for subjects or issues which can easily be oversimplified and distorted, talked about widely, and not antagonize powerful financial blocks. Drugs are ideal for this. The more they are talked about and used to monopolize public attention, the less the candidate or office holder needs to talk about the real criminal or social, and health problems of the society. Reality in effect is obscured by a cloud of smoke or hot air. . . . Many other phenomena in American life are, of course, used in a similar manner as smokescreens, but probably none so consistently or so effectively as a few drugs such as marijuana, heroin, and LSD.

If only drug use were eliminated, goes the current refrain, our cities would be livable, our youth tractable, and crime and poverty would disappear overnight. The logical next step is to pass a law raising penalties for drug use or adding a new drug to the proscribed list. This passes for responsible action, and it does provide temporary respite from having to confront the real difficulties. That this approach frustrates progress, on the drug or any other front, cannot be doubted.

Most recently, drugs have been blamed for two major problems facing the nation. The first is the question of the relation of young people to parental and other authority; the second is the scandal of the My Lai massacre.

Leslie Fiedler[60] has outlined one of the processes by which older generations avoid facing the relevant questions posed by the young:

> But I found an adult community more terrified than myself, more terrified even than I had then guessed, of the gap between themselves and the young; and therefore pitifully eager to find some simple explanation of it all, something with which they could deal, if not by themselves, at least with the aid of the courts and cops. "Dope" was the simple explanation, the simple word they had found (meaning by dope the currently fashionable

psychedelics, especially marijuana); and once that was licked, the gap would be closed, the misunderstandings solved, the mutual offense mitigated. For such a Utopian solution a few arrests on charges of possession and selling, a few not-quite-kosher searches and seizures would be a small enough price to pay.

Something similar occurred in the government's response to the massacre at My Lai. Americans have been shocked and outraged by this example of the brutalizing effects of the Vietnam War, but a few government officials have tried to reduce its impact by blaming the massacre on "dope." Senator Thomas Dodd, chairman of the Senate Subcommittee on Juvenile Delinquency—the committee where much drug legislation originates—told the Senate of information he had heard[61]

> . . . from an outstanding expert that the marijuana toxic psychosis . . . may have played a part in the events at My Lai on March 16, 1968. . . . I plan to conduct hearings to get at the facts, to let our people know if our soldiers in Vietnam have suddenly become brutal stormtroopers or whether, as I consider more likely, some of them have become the victims of a drug problem that has already torn asunder the fabric of domestic American society.

That Senator Dodd can make this unproven and unwarranted statement without fear of contradition from responsible quarters is a glaring example of smokescreening. The harsh realities of the Vietnam War are hidden in the miasma of drug use.

REDUCTION IN PERSONAL FREEDOM

Another cost of the drug laws is the reduction of personal freedom, and the increase in repression that accompanies the denial of individual choice over personal affairs. This effect is the most intangible one we have considered so far, and the one most likely to be disputed as a cost to society. Yet few reasonable men would disagree that in a democratic society an unreasonable or unnecessary reduction of liberty is detrimental. This position has been stated by Judge Charles Wyzanski:[62]

> Every attempt of the law to detect, prosecute, and punish wrong represents an expenditure not merely of time, effort, manpower, and money, but also a concession to the forces of coercion as distinguished from persuasion. . . . In the end liberty tends to be sacrificed for the supposedly greater advantage of health, safety, and morals. To some, including myself, the sacrifice is inconsistent with our ultimate political beliefs.

The social cost of an unwarranted official intrusion, of course, varies with the circumstances of the historical moment and the area of choice concerned. At present, for example, technological and social developments place a premium on personal liberty, particularly on privacy, that was unknown twenty years ago. Today to be alone, somewhere quiet and free from government intrusion, is increasingly in demand—and is increasingly difficult to attain. Electronic surveillance, political dossiers, and computer data banks all circumscribe our freedom to pursue individual goals unhampered by state interference.

Drug use, on the other hand, involves personal choice in the most basic and private area of one's existence—the mind and its contents. A law decreeing that the harboring of certain thoughts is a crime would justifiably arouse indignation. Indeed, if it did not founder on constitutional shoals, it would surely herald a totalitarian police state. Few people realize that criminalizing drug use amounts to a form of thought control. Psychoactive drugs are chemical agents that produce psychic changes. Whether we call these changes "disorientation," "alteration," "modification," "liberation," or "disruption," drugs remain tools for affecting mental states, including the mood and content of consciousness. With these tools, an individual gains temporary control over his consciousness. He is able, within the limits of the drug, to temper, placate, or sharpen a mood, increase or decrease his fatigue, enhance the humdrum, or escape the ugly features of his existence. He can increase concentration and learning ability and open himself to the numinous, or enjoy normally inaccessible esthetic experiences. Undoubtedly, he also can increase his anxiety, develop imagined, unpleasant physiological sensations, and diminish his ability to respond to his external environment. Whether positively or negatively, the drug in each instance produces a change in his mind, within him.

When the state makes drug use criminal, freedom suffers in several ways. First, the control of one's mind, however one may use that choice, is ultimately the prerogative of the individual. In ceding this right to the government, we relinquish control over our most basic privacy. Such a precedent is dangerous. Second, denying an individual certain drug experiences may prevent his full realization of his own freedom. Some individuals cannot adapt effectively to their circumstances, while chronic or sporadic use of a drug may turn them into functioning individuals. Some drugs induce religious or transcendental experiences which lead to a fuller, happier life. However, these chemical substances can direct consciousness from ordinary life to illusory involvements. Drugs can make the user feel that he cares for the welfare of others, while to the observer he appears remote and self-involved. Finally, outlawing drugs brings the apparatus of the criminal law directly into our lives. It may only be a police search, a raid, or questioning, and it may be legal. But the invasion of the law into one's own home is felt deeply and is often resented.

The problem for us throughout this book has been to get the complex double entries in the varieties of ledgers into awareness. Physicians who casually prescribe tranquilizers, energizers, and sedatives remain largely unaware of the cost to their patients in secondary drug reactions and, greater by far, the idea that they can get relief from their ordinary troubles in living with these drugs. These doctors unwittingly promulgate a fundamental alteration in social and group responsiveness to distressed life situations— "solve it with a pill." The youthful user of illegal drugs too thinks that he gets something for nothing. He attends little to the personal and group costs that are exacted by his desire to get "high" and achieve sensory experiences under present social and legal conditions and even less to what those costs will be following any legal changes.

These pressing issues do not minimize the importance of the question we wish to pose here: what is happening *now* in a deteriorating situation? Are the limitations on liberty that present drug laws impose essential to an overriding social purpose? In our view, not only are they not essential, but present laws do not even deal with the harm that undoubtedly flows from drug use. In fact, we suggest that the law itself imposes social as well as legal costs much graver than those of the drug use it seeks to prevent.

8

ALTERNATIVES FOR
DRUG CONTROL

Freud was convinced that "the voice of the intellect will be heard."[1]
But no one understood better than he that if reason is to
triumph, it has to sound above the clamor of conflicting emotions
and the roar of primitive desires. As long as drugs remain primarily a police problem, with the emphasis on condemnation
rather than treatment, they will continue to occupy a position of
exaggerated prominence, and the costs of drug use will be un-
checked. It is the criminal-deviant aura enveloping drugs that
attracts the wrath and anxiety of the public and stirs the rebellious
longings of many drug users. In short, the very fact that drug use is
criminal exacerbates the conflict and serves perhaps more than
anything else to keep drugs a symbolic issue.

Hence, in this chapter we will discuss four essential features of
any drug program: credibility, capacity for change, research and
assessment, and provision of medical care. Then we will postulate
several legal alternatives to the present laws on marijuana. We
suggest a number of programs in the certain knowledge that each
one creates as well as solves problems. Our guiding principle has
been to choose those that offer the greatest degree of informal
social control over drug use.

We shall emphasize changes in the law concerning marijuana rather than any other drug because there are probably over 20,000,000 users[2] in the United States, and it seems likely, and even necessary, that changes will be made in this area first. If our goal of awareness is achieved, changes in the marijuana laws could serve as pilot schemes and perhaps stimulate the development of rational programs for the use and control of all mind-altering drugs.

CREDIBILITY

At the core of a credible drug program must be principles of honesty and justice. This statement would seem like a truism if we did not have a long history of blatantly discriminatory treatment of drug users in the United States. Some of the functions of refraining from making this assessment were discussed in Chapter 2; it is not banal to point out that in connection with drugs, principles that we accept almost without question must be consciously instrumental. Every facet of drug policy must inspire trust—its responsiveness to other related social issues, its methods of collecting and processing data, the facilities it provides, its assessing body, its dedication to justice, the integrity of its administrators. In practical terms this means that we must take into account the program's impact on the black ghettos and political activists and assess the possibility that the program might appear provocative or discriminatory to special-interest groups. Data must be based on accurate sampling; at present most guesses about marijuana use are based on numbers of arrests and quantities of the drug seized by the police. Arrests are a poor gauge because only the flamboyant and the unlucky are arrested on marijuana charges. So data must also be based on those who do not get arrested. Data processing must be performed with strict impartiality, and the statistical methods used in discussing such factors as drug progression and contagion must be free of prejudice.* Conclusions about social good and social harm must have the convincing backing that the medical profession was able to amass about the effects of thalidomide, and must be accepted or rejected on their merits.

If facilities are said to be available, they must be available. Britain shifted to drug-control clinics for heroin users without making adequate preparation; the result was disillusion and a setback in the treatment of addiction.[3] We should profit by this example. If the program includes, say, counseling centers to help youngsters, these centers must be accurately listed and rigorously maintained. Civil commitment programs were introduced in the United States with much fanfare as radical alternatives to criminal processing of addicts. It turned out that few treatment facilities of any kind were provided,[4] let alone any new and ingenious approaches; trust in the credibility of legal and political authority diminished still further. By giving a pseudomedical respectability to what was, in fact, an ill-organized attempt to keep the addict off the street, the authorities acted hypocritically and only worsened the conflict.

Mistrust of government agencies has grown so great that the administration of a program controlling marijuana use would probably have to be carried out by an independent body and funded by a private foundation or professional organization. We doubt that an agency like the Food and Drug Administration could now serve as assessors or administrators of a new drug program. When James Goddard, head of the FDA, testified before a congressional committee in favor of a government bill increasing drug penalties,[5] it was hard not to suspect political coercion. Commissioner Goddard's earlier public statements indicated a different attitude toward marijuana control, as did his statements after resignation.

---

* In *New Society* (April 1968) a statistician with no interest in drugs could not restrain himself from showing the bias in Professor Paton's use of statistics in an article that attempted to show a causal link between marijuana use and heroin addiction. Of course, it is common to use statistics in this way in many other fields besides drug use.

CAPACITY FOR RAPID CHANGE

All proposals for a new drug program must emphasize the need for reliable evaluation and be designed for technological, social, psychological, and historical change. There can be no *permanent "solution"* to the problem of drug use. The program must be able to incorporate into current practice what is learned from the recent past. The organization itself must have a temporary quality and built-in protection against institutionalization.

Any laws concerning drugs would be passed for a period of two or three years, and before they could be renewed evaluation would be mandatory. The organization administering the program would have as its goal the elimination of its present function, so that bureaucratization could be avoided.

ASSESSMENT AND SOCIAL RESEARCH

Any new program must constantly test new ideas, assess current practices, and incorporate its findings into policy. Even to decide what is effective and what is not is a major problem; we must work out which factors to weigh in the scale and how to weigh each one.

These problems must be attacked as soon as possible, and we suggest that the only useful approach is to devise a series of social experiments. This social research would be designed to gain information not just about drugs—we already know a great deal more than we like to admit—but about the impact of different control systems. A few tentative steps are being taken in the United States and abroad to test out alternatives for controversial social issues. The existence of the social clubs Paradisio and Fantasia in Amsterdam amounts to the licensing of specific premises for drug use. There are counties in the United States where such sweeping welfare reforms as the negative income tax are being tried, and

Nevada's relaxation of the law prohibiting prostitution could also be studied as a social experiment.

It is argued that the drug problem is too critical to wait on anything as complex as social experimentation. This line of thinking will prevent us from salvaging a bad situation. If we had accepted that social experiments were necessary and begun to devise them five years ago, we would be far better off now. Late though it is, our best course is to press ahead as quickly as possible.

However, we are under no illusions that it will be easy. Our methodology must provide us with data about the short-term and long-term effects of drug use on both individual and group psychology. We must obtain information about the effect of drugs on personal relations and on trust in social institutions. And, of course, we must investigate further the psychological effects of drugs. Not the least of our difficulties will be the Heisenberg effect (the so-called uncertainty principle whereby the accurate measurement of one of two related quantities produces uncertainties in the measurement of the other). If, for example, the government permits drug use in a certain place as an experiment for research purposes, we will have to take into account the impact that the research has on the pattern and effects of use. This is especially important with a drug as sensitive to set and setting as marijuana. Will the user feel that he is in a laboratory rather than in a social setting, and what effect will this have? How much of the research should be communicated to the public, and when? Should the mass media be permitted to conduct their own formal and informal research, and put out a stream of stories on the experimental area? If their activities are to be limited, how may this be done without infringing the freedom of the press? These and similar questions will have a bearing on research design.

COMPREHENSIVE MEDICAL CARE

In this book we have focused on the millions of new drug users, the second (drug-experimenting) group, who for the most part use marijuana; but we are also keenly aware of the first (dependency-prone) group, whom we regard as a medical problem.

A new program should make provisions for comprehensive medical care for this group, and for whatever incidental medical care is necessary for the other group. In the United States, federal, state, and local government agencies, staggering under the burden of other social problems, have tackled the medical problems of addicts in only the most rudimentary way. Until recently, imprisonment and cold turkey was the usual method for withdrawal. The most popular method at the moment is a system of methadone detoxification and maintenance, by which addicts are given methadone legally at low cost, usually on a daily basis. This synthetic narcotic is reputed to block the desire for heroin. Certainly the methadone program has returned more hard-core addicts to their usual social roles than any other attempt so far,[6] and it is far cheaper than any group-living situation, with or without group or individual psychotherapy.

One can argue with some justification, as its opponents have done, that methadone maintenance is suspiciously like the British system. Dole and Nyswander, who developed the idea, insist that addiction results from a physiological, probably metabolic, deficiency and that methadone operates physiologically, not psychologically. Nevertheless, it is the first breakthrough in medical care that has received sufficient acceptance to enable relatively large numbers of addicts to receive some form of direct attention. The system of methadone prescription is flexible enough to permit useful comparison between samples of addicts who get methadone and therapy, methadone but no therapy, methadone with or without job retraining, and so on.

In the absence of a body of well-documented findings, such as we would hope to gain from extensive research, we depend to a large extent on ex-addicts for information and guidance. In the present legal situation, adequate research is difficult if not impossible, and the emotional atmosphere surrounding drug use makes the ex-addict a natural choice as leader—we want an oracle, and who better than the man who has been there?

Undoubtedly, we can learn a great deal from ex-addicts, but we have lost sight of one of the lessons of Alcoholics Anonymous. Every member of AA recognizes that he has a doppelgänger who will want a drink every day of his life. By projecting that undesirable "twin" onto another afflicted soul, he can wrestle with him more successfully. Members of AA usually refrain from engaging in public controversy about alcohol while they are engrossed in this personal struggle; they know that their vision is limited because of their psychological handicap.

Ex-addicts are denied the outlet of an Addicts Anonymous because of the legal situation and transfer their personal struggle to some of the inadequate treatment and rehabilitation programs that do exist. They bend every effort to stamp out the drug taking that so stirs their inner twin. This has tended to result in repressive programs, and innovations that appear to ease the repression have been resisted.

Although we question the wisdom of relying solely on ex-addicts in treatment programs, we do not wish to limit employment only to doctors and social workers. Many disciplines and skills, some of which may be non-professional, should be enlisted, and the support of the community sought. Successful users, who can offer very little advice under present conditions, could be a valuable source of information about the psychological and physiological hazards that must be overcome if drugs are to be used without damage.

In dealing with the problems of the dependency-prone, there will be casualties, usually minor, among the drug-experimenting group. Under any system in which drugs are more easily available, adverse drug reactions will increase. These reactions may be allergic, idiosyncratic, or psychological, and we must systematically develop procedures for coping with them. Hence, minimum standards of medical care will have to be laid down as part of the basic structure of any new drug program.

ALTERNATIVES FOR MARIJUANA CONTROL

The preceding chapters have shown how neither the known facts about the effects of drug use on user or society nor the results of punitive legislation justify existing drug laws. Public attitudes reflect a distorted and unrealistic picture of drug use which stems partly from the law, and each sustains the other. We have asserted that the law undermines effective regulation of drug use and control of harmful drug effects, and produces important social debits of its own.

While some legal change is necessary, it is not obvious what form or scope the change should take if we are to avoid the mistakes of the past and keep drugs suitably leashed. The need for change is actually greatest in the laws related to heroin. The social costs from keeping heroin illegal are more direct and obvious— addicts die from overdosing and contaminants, they commit crimes, the black market is prosperous—and the problem of dysfunctional effects is crucial. But moral attitudes toward heroin as the devil drug, its potential for causing physiological dependency, and the fact that it is used among groups without political power make reform unlikely. Heroin maintenance, which has worked so well in England, is not being seriously considered by policymakers.

Some drastic change in the marijuana laws, however, appears probable within the foreseeable future. Many minor shifts are already occurring. Dissatisfaction with marijuana policy, its high costs and dubious benefits, has reached a point at which removal of all penalties for personal use and possession is being urged in reputable quarters. We shall consider a number of alternatives for new legislation, without speculating about which is likely to be passed. The problems encountered here, and the premises on which the law is based, apply to the whole range of drug control.

In one form or another the premises underlying the following discussion have been discussed earlier in this book. Essentially, we feel that there are valid goals, consistent with individual liberty and social responsibility, to be achieved through drug regulation. Heavy reliance on criminal sanctions, however, frustrates these goals and creates serious problems. The question then becomes one of finding a legal framework that, on the one hand, does not unduly restrict freedom, subvert legal authority, or lead to unsavory police practices, but, on the other hand, discourages or ameliorates the effects of harmful drug use.

Proposals for marijuana legislation can be divided into two groups: (1) where general possession for personal use is a crime and (2) where possession for personal use carries no penalty. These groups can be further subdivided, each alternative having certain costs and benefits. We offer the following speculations about the strong and weak points of each one. We do not endorse one as the definitive answer, but some are obviously preferable.

A. 1. Status quo: One possibility is to do nothing at all. This alternative seems unlikely. After *Leary v. United States* invalidated the possession sections of the federal Marijuana Tax Act, this alternative for Congress ceased to exist. Now that new federal legislation (Controlled Dangerous Substances Act of 1970) has reduced marijuana penalties, many states are sure to produce changes of their own. There is a growing consensus that the existing regulatory scheme is unjust, unwarranted, and unworkable. The loss of effectiveness incurred in drug programs and the social costs of a law derided and flouted by millions make the status quo a very costly alternative. Its advantages are that it expresses clearly the public condemnation of mood alteration through drugs. It draws a line, albeit blurred and uneven, between the acceptable and nonacceptable, and may be of some service in defining a cultural norm about drug-taking.

2. Misdemeanors: The federal law and several states have recently reduced the penalties for marijuana possession from a

felony to a misdemeanor. A federal offender now may receive up to a year in jail and a fine of up to $1,000. The advantages of this law are fourfold. First, it ensures that no one is punished by severe jail sentences; second, the majority of users will very likely get off without going to jail; third, it maintains the condemnation of marijuana use and possibly discourages those who are deterred by criminal sanctions from experimenting; and fourth, it distinguishes marijuana from dissimilar drugs.

This law also has certain disadvantages, however. First, there is no guarantee that a judge will not send users to jail, and there is still the possibility of suffering the unpleasantness, embarrassment, and expense of being apprehended and labeled a criminal. Second, it may have no appreciable effect on police processes. John Ingersoll, director of the Bureau of Narcotics and Dangerous Drugs, endorsed the pending proposal as a means of encouraging more law enforcement and penalizing marijuana users.[7] We should then expect the police to continue enforcing the law, perhaps more assiduously. All the detrimental effects of the legal system discussed previously will be undiminished. Third, the symbolic overtones of such a change are likely to backfire. Rather than reduce the credibility gap and renew faith in government by showing the state's willingness to recognize and rectify an intolerable situation, it will confirm the features that generate hostility and disrespect throughout the system. The change appears to be a major reform, yet the major premises of drug policy have not been altered one whit. In fact, the *de facto* situation in force, where few users go to jail, will not be improved and, if Ingersoll's prediction is true, might even be worsened.

Fourth, retention of criminal penalties does nothing to deal with those patterns or instances of marijuana use that are rightly of concern to the state. There is no education to help people make an informed decision about whether or not to use marijuana, no instruction on avoiding adverse effects, no facilities to deal with them when they occur. There is nothing to help alleviate the real problems, and yet this should be the basis of legal concern about marijuana use.

3. A final alternative, based on a model of criminal sanctions, would limit penalties to fines.[8] The main advantage appears to be that the imposition of a fine withholds the social endorsement that is implied by removing all penalties from marijuana use. It thus maintains the norm against drug-taking, but lessens the likelihood of the criminal process impinging unjustly—there is considerably less incentive for the police to enforce the law when the penalty is small. However, while this would reduce legal and general social costs, it would still lessen respect for the law.

B. Legislative schemes that do not penalize the possession of marijuana also take several forms. The basic problem here centers around distribution. Should legal possession be coupled with some legal form of distribution? If so, in what circumstances and by what criteria should the distribution take place? This set of alternatives rests on the notion that the dangers of marijuana do not justify the criminalizing of users, and that even if dangers exist, criminal penalties are dysfunctional.

1. One alternative would allow the possession of marijuana for personal use, but maintain the illegality of production and distribution. Whether possession was for personal use would be determined by one of three legal techniques: first, an arbitrary quantity limitation, e.g., two ounces to distinguish the personal user from the one who possesses with intent to sell; second, a presumption in favor of personal use, with the burden on the other party of proving the contrary; third, a separate crime of possession with intent to sell. The suitability of these three devices depends on a consideration of law-enforcement factors, evidentiary questions, and the smooth administration of justice. To a large extent, this is a technical problem, and we will not discuss it further at this point.

When possession for personal use is not subject to criminal penalties, many of the existing defects in the law are cured. The arbitrary and unjust features of enforcement are for the most part eliminated, police resources are freed for other matters, and social tensions are relaxed. In conjunction with reasonable and informed drug education, the aim of the program is to divert from harmful use patterns, to minimize adverse drug effects, and to ameliorate them when they do occur. Strict control over distribution might limit availability sufficiently to avoid a national marijuana habit, pending further investigation of the drug, although given our present situation this seems doubtful. The argument for control over distribution rests on the fear that later knowledge will reveal a potential for serious individual or social harm, which will then be difficult to counter.

The disadvantage of this approach is an apparent inconsistency in legalizing possession but not sale. If marijuana poses no threat to state interests, it seem contradictory to ban sale (this charge was leveled at the Wootton Report).[9] Furthermore, legalized possession will increase demand and, thus, sales. It appears contradictory to say, "You may have x," and then deny access to x. This criticism highlights what is perhaps the most subtle and difficult point to grasp about drug control—its tentative nature. Removal of penalties is not supposed to be a positive endorsement of marijuana use or a bill of good health, merely that criminal sanctions are inappropriate and positively harmful and that other means of control are to be employed.

2. A second control alternative would be identical with the first, except that there would be no distinction between possession for use and possession for sale. One additional point is relevant. The sale provisions would be more difficult to enforce, since no kind of possession could be used to distinguish sellers. While this might prevent certain offensive police practices aimed at procuring evidence and the arrests of those possessing for sale, it would increase pressures on police. The final result would be either no enforcement of sale provision—and hence, no control—or enforcement through the use of such distasteful devices as electronic surveillance, spies, and informers.

3. A third set of alternatives would provide a legal source of marijuana, as well as remove penalties for possession. The virtues of this alternative are consistency between possession and sale, quality and dosage control, elimination of most police activity and

the black market (none of our earlier proposals have tackled the black market). Specific pluses and minuses will be discussed under two of the forms legalized distribution could take:

(*a*) *Alcohol model.* Marijuana could be regulated by permitting certain grades and quantities to be sold under license at specific places and times. If this system were run by private enterprise, profits could be limited by law; or if under state monopoly, profits could be used to support drug research and medical care. Advertising would be forbidden, only a limited quantity of marijuana would be sold to each buyer, and place of use might be regulated—for example, there might be a restriction against marijuana use in public.

We may assume that under this scheme illegal marketing would be minimal and enforcement problems consequently of little concern (a difference from the second alternative, which follows). Such a system will, of course, require the creation of bureaucratic machinery, ranging in complexity from local licensing boards supervised by a state agency—the case with alcohol in most states—to a state licensing authority that grants pharmacists the right to sell marijuana.

(*b*) *Licensing users.* The problem of isolating certain groups or individuals who might use marijuana detrimentally raises the possibility of a system that licenses certain people to use marijuana. Upon attaining a certain age, anyone desiring to use marijuana could apply for a permit or license. The permit would enable him to purchase and possess marijuana legally. One variation would simply make the permit a prerequisite for obtaining marijuana legally, but not penalize one who is in possession without a permit. Similarly, the age requirement does not make it impossible for minors to obtain liquor; however, they are not punished for possession of alcohol, though the seller is. The license might be issued on condition that the applicant could demonstrate his fitness in a number of ways. For example, he would have to show that he was equipped with a minimal level of knowledge concerning marijuana, its effects, mode of use, methods of handling bad moments, activities that cannot be performed well, etc., and that he suffered from no serious psychological problems that the drug would worsen.

The chief difficulty would be in determining the criteria for granting and withholding permits. Further difficulties might be expected from those who were not granted licenses, no matter how sound the reasons for denial. This group might, nevertheless, use marijuana, and several possibilities would arise. First, severe penalties could be attached to selling to unlicensed persons. A second possibility is that no penalties would be imposed on those caught in possession, to avoid problems with law enforcement. Or, third, the harm users might experience could be minimized by the information they have been exposed to and the availability of treatment and other preventive or ameliorative programs. Much will depend on the number of those excluded, the efficacy of education and treatment programs, and changes in attitudes toward drugs.

A licensing system entails a major bureaucratic organization with administrators, examiners, and inspectors. Even if the present law is maintained, we recommend that an agency be created to monitor drug trends, to keep abreast of new knowledge, to sponsor research, and to evaluate the operation of the law. Further functions should include the development of drug education programs and treatment facilities. By "education" is meant, of course, information about what marijuana will actually do, how to use marijuana to avoid known difficulties, and finally, what to do if experiencing difficulty. Adding a licensing function would not necessarily alter the existing orientation significantly but would vastly increase the duties and functions of such an agency.

Three variations on the licensing model are to some extent already in effect. Permitting the use of marijuana on prescription (which happens in England[10]) is actually a licensing system on a small scale. But as it affects only a few people, the major social costs from the law remain, with few of the benefits of diverting harmful use. Licensing research subjects, of sufficient number and for suitable periods, might produce important data about patterns of use and social effects, but will not alleviate existing social problems. Finally, licensing all use in clearly defined places or localities (the Fantasia and Paradisio model) alleviates none of the problems from the drug and the law that arise when used elsewhere.[11] Outside the permitted zone of use, similar problems of law enforcement and control of harmful uses will still exist. Nor is this device likely to yield good data about marijuana and its changing patterns of use. Finally, influx or migration to the permitted zone raises problems.

Each proposal should contain a provision to deal with the following questions: advertising, driving after consumption of marijuana, research, and use in a public place.

PROBLEMS OF LEGALIZATION

If criminal sanctions are removed from the possession of marijuana, what problems will arise? The first, voiced on all sides by the public, is that harm may come to the individual and to society from increased use. Second, there will still be the question of law enforcement for other drug use. Undoubtedly the changed legal position of marijuana will have numerous other social ramifications. When discussing these problems, we must keep in mind the overriding necessity of establishing informal social control over drug use and of developing honest social discourse on the subject.

Most people expect that any relaxation of the law on marijuana will result in a vast increase in use, and that this will inevitably do a great deal of damage. It is not, in fact, clear to what extent a change in law will increase use. Marijuana is already easily available, especially among young people. The legal penalties probably deter only those who are so cautious and law-abiding that they must be considered an extremely low-risk group. Nevertheless, it is indisputable that the removal of penalties will eventually lead to widespread use, ultimately changing the drug habits of the country.

Other drug use—alcohol, for example—shows a fairly consistent percentage of users who suffer deleterious physiological or psychological effects. There is no reason to doubt that the effects of marijuana will show a similar distribution curve. However, following Howard Becker's work,[12] there is evidence that with the social and psychological acceptance of use, some untoward reactions will be prevented. Given the large number of people now using marijuana in an illegal, and thus anxiety-provoking, situation, this is no small consideration. Also, with the removal of criminal sanctions the medical profession could be encouraged to study methods of preventing or alleviating deleterious effects.

No major study has been made of the relation between extent of use and dysfunctional effect, but a certain amount of knowledge has been gathered from both formal and informal investigations. Formal studies have shown that huge doses of marijuana can cause disorientation and psychosis (Harris and Isbell[13]). Some chronic users can still function in society (Zinberg and Weil[14]), but others, such as those we saw at the Fantasia and Paradisio, drop out and appear to be very severely handicapped. It is also well established that people can use the drug in moderation and remain well under control. Thus, we know that marijuana, like so many other drugs, has potential for both damaging and controlled use, although most studies rate it as rather mild.[15]

We must also consider what use may properly be made of the other parts of the cannabis plant (the leaves, stem, and stalk), of the various forms of resin derived from it (hashish, charas), and of synthetic tetrahydrocannabinols. Should they come under the same legal heading as marijuana; or because the synthetics are certainly more potent, should they be regulated under separate legal provisions? It is certainly conceivable that if marijuana alone were legalized, these and other forms of cannabis might be used much more widely, undermining the good effects of the legal change.

In our discussion of social costs we indicate that the safest course is to accept an unavoidable amount of non-medical drug use. The damage done to society under the present system outweighs the damage that will certainly result from increased use. But the latter can be kept within reasonable bounds by the establishment of social controls and realistic discourse.

The second problem arising from the removal of criminal sanctions for marijuana is that of law enforcement. If penalties for possession are excluded but those for sale or distribution remain, the police will still be faced with the need to devise operational techniques for detecting illegal transactions. There will be the same encroachment on privacy, the same tendency to expand police powers beyond constitutional limits (with the real danger of overlapping into other areas). Indeed, for the police, the problem will be worse, since arrest for possession will no longer be a weapon against sellers.

When sale and distribution are legal, as under an alcohol model or a personal licensing system, the police must still enforce laws against control violations, such as selling below the age limit or selling to an unlicensed person. From a purely operational point of view this would be an extremely difficult police problem unless there was mass social acceptance of the control regulations.

Although not condemning an activity is a far cry from condoning it, a legal change in the status of marijuana in the present climate of opinion could well be seen as an endorsement of drug use. One of the curiously ambivalent social problems about marijuana reform is its effect on our thinking about other drugs. It seems unlikely that marijuana could be accepted without some change occurring. Moreover, if the present trend toward increased leeway for each individual to make decisions concerning his own body continues, legalizing marijuana alone will hardly be satisfactory. The comparison with alcohol is always faulty because in Western countries alcohol has never been thought of as a drug (we "take a drink," but we "use a drug"). Also, alcohol use emphasizes the process and ritual of drinking as much as the final effect, while in spite of elaborate rituals with rolling and passing joints and roach holders, the object with marijuana is primarily to get high. You don't share an occasional puff with someone and let it go at that.

A legal change would indicate that the use of a *drug,* nonmedically, in a private social or recreational setting is basically a matter of individual discretion. When the noncriminal status of such drug use is recognized, it will be difficult to distinguish the use of other illegal drugs. The effects of LSD, amphetamines, barbiturates, and opiates do vary greatly from marijuana, but the quality of the individual act in each case is the same. Use of any of these agents is a deliberate attempt to manipulate mental states to arrive at what the user finds more desirable, which may in some cases produce harm. The arbitrary barrier between private social drug use (deviant and antisocial) and medical or socially acceptable use would break down.

Many of the public are anxious to prevent the decriminalization of marijuana use for just that reason. For others, one great advantage of marijuana legalization is that it might be the lever to force us as a society to reconsider the entire question of drug use. We may be sure that drug use, medical and nonmedical, will increase, and we must face the issue and discuss it without pious mouthings.

A LICENSING MODEL

Our recommendations are based on the proposition that a system that permits drug use but does not encourage it, and that accepts restrictions based on age and on psychological or physiological incompatibility with the drug is the best balance of social and individual interests. In short, we propose a system that accords drugs the healthy respect and regulation that we accord that mighty potential weapon, the automobile.

Society must learn to tolerate a reasonable amount of drug use by those members willing and able to make that decision. If marijuana reform did not reduce emotionalism toward other drugs further legal revisions would be in order. Should marijuana be legalized under controls akin to that for alcohol, one might still need a personal licensing system for other drugs. A rational approach would recognize that the controls for one drug may not work well for another. One advantage of the licensing system is that it imposes some selectivity on who gets to use drugs without denying everyone that right. It thus makes the work of the informal control mechanisms easier by discouraging those users who, on the basis of certain criteria, appear most likely to be harmed by drug use or lack the capacity to use drugs wisely.

The second advantage of a licensing system—an advantage that varies with the precise form such a system takes—may be the greater receptivity it meets with the public. The public may be more ready to accept nonmedical drug use under a system that openly recognizes the possibility of harm from drug use, filters out the most obvious instances of harm, and is prepared for harm that does occur, than one in which no attempt is made to prevent susceptible persons from using drugs. This advantage may lie more in the public's perception of differences in the two alternatives than in differences that are actually there, but that is a factor not to be ignored.

All the bureaucratic problems we mentioned earlier in this chapter in connection with marijuana licensing, and more, would arise with this system. The applicant would receive a leaflet detailing the regulations, use, effects, and dangers of any drug that interested him. Before he received his license he would have to be familiar with its conditions. Exclusions would be kept to a minimum, but certain people would be denied licenses: they would probably include anyone convicted of violating licensing statutes, driving under the influence, selling a drug allotment, or giving it to someone below the proper age. Probably people with a demonstrated physiological or psychological sensitivity to certain drugs, or who had recently been in a mental hospital or prison, would be denied licenses, unless they had an appropriate document from a physician or penal authority. As with motor-vehicle operators' licensing, the system would be overseen by civil servants who at best would have little professional expertise. Thus, the system needs to be fairly standardized, requiring its administrators to make as few complex decisions as possible.

There should be no advertising, and profit margins would be fixed for those designated to supply the licensed amounts. This should virtually eliminate crime surrounding drug use. While the intention would be to keep legal restrictions to a minimum, there is no doubt that the drug-dependent group would present problems. Such cases should be detected as soon as possible, and appropriate treatment provided (in some cases this could be a form of drug maintenance).

Resale of licensed supplies would be strictly prohibited. As most people would be able to get reasonable amounts of what they want, there should be little incentive for resale and transfer, as violations would imperil drug access for oneself and, if violations became flagrant, for others. Nevertheless, there will be violators, as there always are. The general philosophy of the program should be to find violators only in order to minimize dangers for themselves and the public. The emphasis is to keep the system heading on a reasonable tack. Troublemakers would be of interest only when they cause trouble, not because they are there. Various interested groups such as police, chemists, doctors, and hospital personnel would be alerted to symptoms of sensitivity or toxicity so that abuse could be detected early.

Another bureaucratic problem that a licensing system must overcome is the creation, financing, and running of a new institution, "The Bureau of Drug Control." Costs, for example, might be paid out of license fees or out of revenues from legal distribution centers, and the excess used to sponsor research and education and provide treatment facilities. Such an institution could serve many diverse purposes, and would certainly cost less than current expenditures on the enforcement of drug laws.

Obviously we have a great deal to learn. That is the basic reason for conceiving any policy temporary. The impact of the program must be studied and the results assessed by an impartial commission. Once credibility is reestablished, we imagine that even far-reaching changes can be made with impunity. After all, if it were discovered today that gin contained cyclamates, it could be withdrawn from sale without too much of a fuss, leaving us to make do with vodka, rum, bourbon, and scotch. After our system had been in operation for two years, we would have conducted a number of studies and could convincingly demonstrate what are now only hypotheses. If it should turn out (as we expect it would) that regu-

lar use of amphetamines by adults causes massive psychic disturbance and offers little redeeming pleasure, either personally or as a
vehicle for improving social interaction, then they would be removed from the market. However, users would still be left with a
cornucopia of other drugs to choose from.

It is not easy for us to advocate making the amphetamines,
besides whatever other terrifyingly powerful drugs technology has
in store for us, available to 18-year-olds who will take them "for a
gas." But it is just because a healthy respect is due these drugs that
we believe that they must be made available. If restrictions are
removed from marijuana, or all cannabis preparations, drug use
would remain a symbolic issue, although now a drug other than
marijuana would be the symbol for other social concerns. We are
aware that unrestricted use of marijuana could produce in a few
years problems similar to those of alcoholism. But this does not
mean that marijuana is bad, any more than alcohol is bad; it
simply means that in the present argument about harm versus
harmlessness we are fighting the wrong battle.

Our final position about drug use, in which we advocate careful
and restrained availability of drugs, depends on our seizing the
initiative. In this muddled area, where things are seldom what they
seem, the psychological significance of change must be carefully
weighed. If concessions about marijuana use are wrung from an
unresponsive majority, we fear resentment and the repeat of the
bitter controversy between generations displaced to another drug.
One could argue that the ease with which stringent legislation
classifying marijuana with narcotics was passed in the early 1930s
resulted from just such a shift of feelings following· the repeal of
Prohibition.[16] Should, however, a bold new plan be introduced,
and both sides agree that innovation and experiment are necessary
before a bad situation becomes an impossible one, we might avoid
repeating history.

Advocating a licensing system for all drugs is not intended to
further the permissive society. Our psychological hunch is that if
concessions occur after vicious and losing battles by the average

voter—middle-class, middle-aged, and extreme only about being in the political center—it will seem part of the decline of respect for authority. Such a view perverts our aim. The establishment of a national licensing system aims for a social consensus that endows the new authority with legitimacy. Permissiveness, like everything else in this field, is in the eye of the beholder, but we intend to establish firm baselines. A minimum age limit, detailed strictures on transfer and resale, rehabilitation facilities, and, above all, a healthy temerity about this new phase of our social life, can be agreed upon by everybody (or almost everybody). Thus, a social standard is established that gives its legal statement validity and accepts authority as a deterrent, not as a symbolic club.

Hence, waiting for more information, for more education, for more understanding, for a better climate of opinion, can subtly defeat the vital aim of legitimizing the proposed program's authority. The United States has a long history of this particular psychological error, evidenced most clearly now in relation to the Indo-China War. At least some of the present policy is based on concerns about retribution from the far right ("Who lost China?"), and all tries for fresh, bold approaches are scorned for fear they will be thought of as giveaways. There are both a psychological and a pragmatic difference between assessing what may benefit most people (though is ideal for none) and throwing up one's hands in despair. Boldness and initiative must change the status quo, and if that is enough to be considered a giveaway, so be it. But when change is offered freely and rationally, it is not permissiveness or defeat of authority but the fulfillment of the highest function of that authority: the common good.

NOTES

CHAPTER 1

1. *Boston Globe*, news item, 1969.
2. The Federal Bureau of Narcotics and Dangerous Drugs official figures for 1970 were only 60,-000 to 70,000 addicts in the United States. These figures were obtained by police and other officials filling out forms whenever they came into contact with an addict. Under present circumstances these figures are considered low, and Mr. Edward Kass, Deputy Director of the Federal Bureau of Narcotics and Dangerous Drugs, felt the 200,-000 figure more accurate.
3. Blum, Richard H., *Students and Drugs*, San Francisco, Jossey-Bass, 1969.
4. Packer, Herbert, *The Limits of the Criminal Sanction*, Stanford, Stanford University Press, 1968.
   Goode, Erich, *The Marihuana Smokers*, New York, Basic Books, 1970.
5. Mesthenes, Emanuel, Director, Center for the Study of Science and Technology, Harvard University, personal communication.
6. Weil, A. T., Zinberg, N. E., and Nelson, J. M., "Clinical and Psychological Effects of Marihuana in Man," *Science*, Vol. 162, Dec. 13, 1968.

7. Merton, Robert, *Social Theory and Social Structure*, New York, The Free Press, 1957.
8. *Ibid.*

CHAPTER 2

1. *Time*, May 16, 1969.
2. *Boston Globe*, June 25, 1969.
3. *International Times*, Vol. 34, June 28–July 11, 1968.
4. Laing, R. D., *The Politics of Experience*, New York, Ballantine, 1968.
   Laing R. D., *Self and Others*, New York, Pantheon, 1970.
5. Geber, B., Pearson, J. F., and Tutton, C. B., "Students, Apprentices and Drugs," London School of Economics, Drug Project, July 1969.
   Geber, B., Tutton, C., and Pearson, J., "Drug Users and Peer Attitudes Amongst University Students and Industrial Apprentices," London School of Economics, Drug Project, July 1969.
6. Delong, James V., *et al.*, Ford Foundation, Drug Abuse Research Project, Aug. 1970.
7. Tauro, G. Joseph, "Marijuana and Relevant Problems—1969," *American Criminal Law Quarterly*.

8. *New York Times*, January 8–12, 1968.
9. *Time*, Sept. 26, 1969.
10. *Newsweek*, Sept. 7, 1970.
11. *Look*, Feb. 1970.
12. *Life*, Oct. 31, 1969.
13. *Boston Globe*, Jan. 4–8, 1971.
14. Pet, Donald D., and Ball, John C., "Marijuana Smoking in the U.S.," *Federal Probation*, Sept. 1968.
15. Blum, Richard H., *Students and Drugs*, San Francisco, Jossey-Bass, 1969.
16. Bloomquist, Edward R., *Marijuana*, Beverly Hills, Glencoe Press, 1968.
17. Paton, W. D. M., "Cannabis: The Unexplored Dangers," *Oxford Mail*, Jan. 14, 1969.
18. Kaplan, John, *Marijuana, The New Prohibition*, New York, The World Publishing Co., 1970.
19. Goodman, Louis S., and Gilman, Alfred, *The Pharmacological Basis of Therapeutics*, New York, Macmillan, 1970.
20. Mass. Dept. of Education, Framingham, Mass., May 14, 1967.
21. Zinberg, N. E., and Lewis, D. C., "Narcotic Usage: I. A Spectrum of a Difficult Medical Problem," *New England Journal of Medicine*, Vol. 270, May 7, 1964.
22. Zinberg, N. E., Preliminary Survey Report, Amsterdam, May 1969.

   Cohen, H., "Psychology, Social-Psychology and Sociology of Illicit Drug Use," University of Amsterdam, Sept. 1969.
23. The Scourge of Narcotics, Spring 3100 at 7 (Dec. 1958), quoted by Richard Kuh, *Dealing with Narcotics Addiction*, Part One, *The New York Law Journal*, June 8, 1960, quoted in Eldridge, W. B., *Narcotics and the Law*, Chicago, University of Chicago Press, 1962.
24. Gerard, D. L., and Kornestsky, C., "Adolescent Opiate Addiction: A Study of Control and Addict Subjects," *Psychiatric Quarterly*, Vol. 29, 1955.

   Hill, H. E., Haertzen, C. A., and Glaser, R., "Personality Characteristics of Narcotic Addicts as Indicated by the MMPI," *Journal of General Psychology*, Vol. 62, 1960.

   Alksne, H., *et al.*, "A Follow-Up Study of Treated Adolescent Narcotic Users," New York: unpublished report of Columbia University School of Public Health and Admin. Med., 1959, quoted in Vaillant, G., "A Twelve-year Follow-Up of New York Narcotic Addicts. III. Some Social and Psychiatric Characteristics," *Archives of General Psychology*, Vol. 15, 1966.

   Crime and Delinquency in California, Bureau of Criminal Statistics, State of California, 1967.
25. *Report of the Indian Hemp Drug Commission*, 1893–94, reprinted, Silver Spring, Md., Thomas Jefferson Publishing Co., 1969.
26. Mayor's Committee on Marijuana, *The Marijuana Problem in the City of New York*, Lancaster, Cattell, 1944.
27. Blum, Richard H., *Students and Drugs*, San Francisco, Jossey-Bass, 1969.
28. Blummer, Herbert, *et al.*, *Add Center Project Final Report: The World of Youthful Drug Use*, Berkeley, Univ. of Cal., 1967.

29. *Crime and Delinquency in California,* Bureau of Criminal Statistics, State of California, 1967.
30. Kaplan, John, *Marijuana, The New Prohibition,* New York, World Publishing Co., 1969.
31. Tauro, *op. cit.*
32. Isbell, H., "What to Know About Drug Addiction 2," Public Health Service Pub. No. 94, 1951.
33. Vaillant, G. E., "Drug Dependence and Alcohol Problems, A Twelve Year Follow-Up of New York Narcotic Addicts," *American Journal of Psychiatry,* Vol. 122, Jan. 1966.

   Vaillant, G. E., "A Twelve Year Follow-Up of New York Narcotic Addicts III, Some Social and Psychiatric Characteristics," *Archives of General Psychiatry,* Vol. 15, 1966.
34. Myerson, D. J., and Mayer, J., "The Drug Addict," *The Practice of Community Mental Health,* Boston, Little, Brown, 1970.
35. Zinberg, N. E., and Weil, Andrew T., "A Comparison of Marijuana Users and Non-Users," *Nature,* Vol. 226, No. 5241, April 11, 1970.
36. Smith, David, ed., "An Analysis of Marijuana Toxicity," *The New Social Drug, Cultural, Medical and Legal Perspectives on Marijuana,* Englewood Cliffs, Prentice-Hall, 1970.
37. Geber, B., Sharpe, S., and Burski, D., "The Drug Squad at New Scotland Yard, A Study of Role and Attitude to Illegal Drug Use," London School of Economics, Drug Project, July 1969.
38. Geber, B., and Turner, S., "The Authoritarian Role of Doctors in Non-Medical Drug Use," London School of Economics, Drug Project, July 1969.
39. Becker, Howard, "History, Culture and Subjective Experience: An Elaboration of the Social Bases of Drug-Induced Experience," *Journal of Health and Social Behavior,* Vol. 8, 1967.

CHAPTER 3

1. Zinberg, N. E., and Weil, A. T., "A Scientific Report—The Effects of Marijuana on Human Beings," *The New York Times Magazine,* May 11, 1969.
2. Andrews, H. L., and Himmelsbach, C. K., *Journal of Pharmacology and Experimental Therapeutics,* Vol. 81, 1944.
3. Zinberg, N. E., and Lewis, D. C., "Narcotic Usage. I. A Spectrum of a Difficult Medical Problem," *New England Journal of Medicine,* Vol. 270, May 7, 1964.

   Lewis, D. C., and Zinberg, N. E., "Narcotic Usage. II. A Historical Perspective on a Difficult Medical Problem," *New England Journal of Medicine,* Vol. 270, May 14, 1964.

   Isbell, H., and Fraser, H. F., "Addiction to analgesics and barbiturates," *Pharmacological Review,* Vol. 2, 1950.

   Kolb, L. "Pleasure and deterioration from narcotic addiction," *Mental Hygiene,* Vol. 9, 1925.

   Lasagna, L., VonFelsinger, J. M., and Bucher, H. K., "Drug-induced mood changes in man," *Journal of the American Medical Association,* Vol. 157, 1955.
4. Eddy, N. B., Halbach, H., Isbell, H., and Seevers, M. H., "Drug

Dependence: Its Significance and Characteristics," *Bulletin of the World Health Organization,* Vol. 32, 1965.

5. Kolb, L. C., ed., *Noyes' Modern Clinical Psychiatry,* Philadelphia, W. B. Saunders, 1968.

Henderson and Gillispie, *A Text-Book of Psychiatry,* New York, Oxford University Press, 1927.

English, O. Spurgeon, and Finch, Stuart M., *Introduction to Psychiatry,* New York, W. W. Norton, 1964.

Gregory, Ian, *Fundamentals of Psychiatry,* Philadelphia, W. B. Saunders, 1968.

Nodine, John H., ed., and Moyer, John H., *Psychosomatic Medicine,* Philadelphia, Lea & Febiger, 1962.

Skottowe, Ian, *Clinical Psychiatry for Practitioners and Students,* London, Eyre & Spolliswoode, 1953.

6. Glover, Edward, "On Drug Addiction," *International Journal of Psychoanalysis,* 3/31, 1932.

Masters, R. E. L., and Houston, J., *The Varieties of Psychedelic Experience,* New York, Holt, Rinehart & Winston, 1966.

Moraes, A. O., "The Criminogenic Action of Cannabis and Narcotics," *Bulletin on Narcotics,* 16/4, 1964.

Limentani, A., "On Drug Dependence: Clinical Appraisal," *International Journal of Psychoanalysis,* 49/4, 1968.

7. Keniston, K., "Tasters, Seekers and Heads," *American Scholar,* Summer, 1968.

8. Geber, Beryl A., "Non-Dependent Drug Use: Some Psychological Aspects," *Scientific Basis of Drug Dependence,* ed. by H. Steinberg, London, J. & H. Churchill, Ltd., 1969.

9. Geber, B., Pearson, J. F., and Tutton, C. B., "Students, Apprentices and Drugs," London School of Economics, Drug Project, July 1969.

Geber, B., Tutton, C., and Pearson, J., "Drug Users and Peer Attitudes Amongst University Students and Industrial Apprentices," London School of Economics, Drug Project, July 1969.

10. Zinberg, N. E., and Weil, A. T., "A Comparison of Marijuana Users and Non-Users," *Nature,* Vol. 226, No. 5241, April 11, 1970.

11. Chein, Isador, *et al., The Road to H,* New York, Basic Books, 1964.

12. *Ibid.*

13. Stearn, Gerald E., *McLuhan: Hot and Cool,* New York, Dial Press, 1967.

14. McLuhan, Marshall, *Understanding Media,* New York, McGraw-Hill, 1964.

15. Zinberg and Weil, *Nature, op. cit.*

16. Erikson, Erik H., *Childhood and Society,* New York, W. W. Norton, 1950; *Insight and Responsibility,* New York, W. W. Norton, 1964; *Identity, Youth and Crisis,* New York, W. W. Norton, 1968.

17. Goffman, E., *Asylums,* Garden City, Doubleday, 1961.

18. Castaneda, *The Teachings of Don Juan,* University of California, 1969.

19. *I Ching,* trans. by Wilhelm, Bollingen Foundation, 1950.

20. Bibring, Grete, L., *Bulletin of the World Federation of Mental Health,* Jan. 1952.

CHAPTER 4

1. *Boston Globe,* editorial, Jan. 17, 1971.
2. *Boston Globe,* Jan. 4–8, 1971.
3. Weil, Andrew T., Zinberg, N. E., and Nelsen, Judith M., "Clinical and Psychological Effects of Marihuana in Man," *Science,* Vol. 162, Dec. 13, 1968.
   Weil, Andrew T., and Zinberg, Norman E., "Acute Effects of Marihuana on Speech," *Nature,* Vol. 222, No. 5192, May 3, 1969.
   Zinberg, Norman E., and Weil, Andrew T., "Cannabis: The First Controlled Experiment," *New Society,* Jan. 16, 1969.
   Zinberg, Norman E., and Weil, Andrew T., "A Comparison of Marijuana Users and Non-Users," *Nature,* Vol. 226, No. 524, April 11, 1970.
   Zinberg, Norman E., and Weil, Andrew T., "The Effects of Marihuana on Human Beings," *The New York Times Magazine,* May 11, 1969.
4. *Science,* Letters to the Editor, Vol. 163, Dec. 28, 1968.
5. *Nature,* Letters, Vol. 222, No. 5194, May 17, 1969. *Nature,* Letters, Vol. 226, No. 526, April 25, 1970.
6. *The New York Times Magazine,* Letters to the Editor, June 8, 1969.
7. Smart, R. G., and Bateman, K., "The Chromosomal and Teratogenic Effects of Lysergic Acid Diethylamide: A Review of the Current Literature," *Canadian Medical Association Journal* Vol. 99, pp. 805–810, Oct. 26, 1968.
8. National Institute of Mental Health, Special Report, "Drug Abuse," issued for in-house consumption and not for general distribution, Nov. 1969.
9. *Ibid.*
10. *Ibid.*
11. *Ibid.*
12. Krantz, J. T., Carr, Jelloff, and LaDu, Burt N., *The Pharmacological Principles of Medical Practice,* 7th ed., Baltimore, Williams & Wilkins, 1969.
13. NIMH, *op. cit.*
14. *Ibid.*
15. *Ibid.*
16. Grinspoon, Lester, *Marijuana Reconsidered,* Cambridge, Mass., Harvard University Press, 1971.
17. Gautier, Théophile, "Le Club des Hachichins," trans. by Gladstone, R. K., in Solomon, D., ed., *The Marihuana Papers,* Indianapolis, Panther, 1966.
18. Ludlow, F. H., *The Hasheesh Eater: Being Passages from the Life of a Pythagorean,* New York, Harper & Row, 1957.
19. Baudelaire, C., "Les Paradis Artificiels," trans. by P. Hedlom in Crepet, M. J., ed., *Oeuvres Complètes de Charles Baudelaire,* Paris, Pouletmilassis, 1928.
20. DeQuincey, T., *Confessions of an English Opium Eater.*
21. Ellis, H., "Mescal, A New Artificial Paradise," *Annual Report of the Smithsonian Institution,* 1898.
22. Leary, T., interview, *Playboy,* Sept. 1966.
23. Weil *et al.,* Science, *op. cit.*
24. Mandell, A. J., and Spooner, C. E., "Psychochemical Research Studies in Man," *Science,* Vol. 162, 1968.
25. Blum, Richard H., *Students and Drugs,* San Francisco, Jossey-Bass, 1969.
26. NIMH, *op. cit.*

27. Gordetzky, Charles W., "Marihuana, LSD, and Amphetamines," *Drug Dependence,* National Institute of Mental Health, Oct. 1970, No. 5.

28. Isbell, H., Gordetzky, C. W., Jasinski, D., Claussen, V., V. Spulak, F., and Korte, F., "Effects of (-) delta^9-transtetrahydrocannabinol in man," *Psychopharmacologia,* Vol. 11, pp. 184–88, 1967.

29. Gordetzky, *op. cit.*

30. NIMH, *op. cit.*

31. *Ibid.*

32. *Ibid.*

33. Gordetzky, *op. cit.*

34. Berger, H., and Krantz, J., Maryland State Psychiatric Research Center in Cantonsville (in press). Harvey Berger, a student, began with the hypothesis that cannabinol, a structural analog of delta-9-THC and believed to be relatively inactive, could block delta-9-THC and that cannabinol alone at 5 and 10 mg/kg had no effect on pentobarbital sleeping time, but that those doses, as well as at 50 mg/kg, were able to block the delta-9-THC potentiation of sleeping time. He also noted that distinct behavioral alterations with all three doses of cannabinol indicated that this marijuana fraction is not inactive.

35. Isbell *et al., op. cit.*

36. Grinspoon, *op. cit.*

37. Walton, R. P., *Marihuana: American's New Drug Problem,* Philadelphia, Lippincott, 1938.

38. Grinspoon, *op. cit.*

39. "Effects of Alcohol and Cannabis During Labor," *J.A.M.A.,* Vol. 94, p. 1165, 1930.

40. Allentuck, S., and Bowman, K. M., "The Psychiatric Aspects of Marijuana Intoxication," *American Journal of Psychiatry,* Vol. 99, 1942.

41. *Life,* "Narcotics," July 19, 1943.

42. Walton, *op. cit.*

43. Winick, C., "The Use of Drugs by Jazz Musicians," *Social Problems,* Vol. 7, 1960.

44. NIMH, *op. cit.*

45. *Boston Globe,* Gallup Poll, Boston, Mass., Jan. 17, 1971.

46. NIMH, *op. cit.*

47. Gordetzky, *op. cit.*

48. *Ibid.*

49. Freud, Sigmund, "On the General Effects of Cocaine," *Medizinische Chirurgie Zentralblatt,* Vol. 20(32), pp. 374–75, Aug. 1885.

50. *Ibid.*

51. *Ibid.*

52. *Ibid.*

53. *Ibid.*

54. NIMH, *op. cit.*

55. Weil, "The Pharmacology of Consciousness-Altering Drugs," *op. cit.*

56. Zinberg, N. E., and Lewis, D., "Amphetamine Use in the Out-Patient Department of a General Hospital," unpublished manuscript.

"AMA Council on Drugs, Abuse of the Amphetamines and Pharmacologically Related Substances," *J.A.M.A.,* Vol. 183, 1963.

Kramer, J. C., Fischman, U. S., and Littlefield, D. C., "Amphetamine Abuse," *J.A.M.A.,* Vol. 201, 1967.

57. Gordetzky, *op. cit.*

58. Schultes, R. E., *Psychedelic Review,* Vol. I, No. 2, Fall 1963.

59. NIMH, *op. cit.*

60. *Ibid.*

61. Krantz *et al., op. cit.*

Report prepared for the President's Commission on Law Enforcement and Administration of Justice by Arthur D. Little. (ADL)

62. Kolb, L., and DuMez, B., "The Prevalence and Trend of Drug Addiction in the U.S. and Factors Influencing It," *Public Health Report,* Mar. 23, 1924.

63. Krantz, *op. cit.*
ADL, *op. cit.*

64. Kolb, *et al., op. cit.*

65. ADL, *op. cit.*

66. Goodman, Louis S., and Gillman, Alfred, New York, Macmillan, 4th ed., 1970.

67. *Ibid.*

68. *Ibid.*

69. Essig, C., "Drug Dependence of the Barbiturate Type," *Drug Dependence,* NIMH, No. 5, Oct. 1970.

70. Isbell, H., *et al.,* "Chronic Barbiturate Intoxication: An Experiment," *A.M.A. Archives of Neurology and Psychology,* Vol. 64, 1950.

71. Essig, *op. cit.*

72. *Ibid.*

73. Committee on Alcoholism and Addiction Report, *J.A.M.A.,* Vol. 197, 1966.

74. *Ibid.*

75. Goodman *et al., op cit.*

76. Essig, *op. cit.*

77. NIMH, *op. cit.*

78. Weil, Andrew T., "Altered States of Consciousness Drugs and Society," report for Ford Foundation.
Cohen, S., *The Beyond Within: The LSD Story,* New York, Atheneum, 1964.
Lake, A., "Drugs, a Student Report," *Seventeen,* Sept., 1966.
Leary, T., interview, *Playboy,* Sept. 1966.

CHAPTER 5

1. *New York Times,* March 30, 1970.

2. Schur, Edwin M., *Narcotic Addiction in Britain and America: The Impact of Public Policy,* London, Tavistock, 1963, pp. 76–77.

3. *Ibid.,* pp. 81–85.

4. "Drug Addiction," Report of the Interdepartmental Committee, London, H.M.S.O., 1961, p. 16.

5. *Ibid.*

6. "Drug Addiction," The Second Report of the Interdepartmental Committee, London, H.M.S.O., 1965, p. 5.

7. *Ibid.,* p. 6.

8. *Ibid.*

9. *Ibid.*

10. *Ibid.,* p. 6.

11. Glatt, Max M., *et al., The Drug Scene in Great Britain,* London, Edward Arnold, Ltd., 1967, pp. 24–25.

12. The Second Report of the Interdepartmental Committee, *op. cit.*

13. *Ibid.,* p. 10.

14. *Ibid.,* p. 13. Dangerous Drugs Act of 1967, Sections 1, 2.

15. *Ibid.*

16. Television interview taped for the BBC by Mr. Richard Kershaw, Summer 1968. The authors are indebted to Mr. Kershaw for a transcript of the interview.

17. *Look,* April 7, 1970, p. 41.

18. *The Rehabilitation of Drug Offenders,* Report of the Advisory Committee on Drug Dependence, London, H.M.S.O., 1968, p. 7.

19. Glatt, *op. cit.,* p. 29.

20. *Sunday Times,* September 23, 1968, p. 1.
21. *The Guardian,* March 10, 1969, p. 14.
22. Jones, Terence, *Drugs and the Police,* London, Butterworths, 1968, p. 12.
23. Silberman, Martin, *Aspects of Drug Addiction,* London, Royal London Prisoners' Aid Society, 1967, p. 103.
24. *The Guardian,* June 27, 1969.
25. Statement of Mr. Alexander Mitchell of the *Sunday Times,* St. Anne's Church, Soho, London, June 1969.
26. Reported in *Hansard,* Jan. 27, 1969, p. 965.
27. The article appeared in *News of the World* in the summer of 1967. Interview with Mr. Stephen Abrams.
28. *Daily Telegraph,* Oct. 18, 1968, p. 1.
29. *The Guardian,* April 27, 1970.
30. *New York Times,* Jan. 5, 1971.
31. Glatt, *op. cit.,* p. 21.
32. *Daily Telegraph,* Feb. 26, 1969.
33. Gusfield, Joseph, "On Legislating Morals: The Symbolic Process of Deviant Designation," 50 *California Law Review,* 61 (1968).
34. Nuttall, Jeff, *Bomb Culture,* New York, Delacorte-Dell, 1969.
35. *Hansard,* July 28, 1967, p. 1155.
36. See for example Glatt, M. M., "A Review of the Second Report of the Interdepartmental Committee on Addiction," *Bulletin on Narcotics,* Vol. 18, No. 2, April–June, 1966.
37. Dangerous Drugs Act of 1965, Section 16.
38. The provisions of the Drugs (Prevention of Misuse) Act of 1964 do not apply in barbiturates.
39. *Cannabis,* Report by the Advisory Committee on Drug Dependence (hereinafter referred to as "Wootton Report"), London, H.M.S.O., 1968, p. 23.
    Powers of Arrest and Search in Relation to Drug Offenses, Report by the Advisory Committee on Drug Dependence, London, H.M.S.O., 1970, p. 16.
40. Wootton Report, p. 20.
41. *Ibid.,* p. 2.
42. *Ibid.,* p. 7.
43. *Ibid.,* pp. 12–13.
44. *Ibid.,* pp. 16–17.
45. *Ibid.,* p. 28.
46. *Ibid.*
47. *Ibid.,* p. 20.
48. *Daily Express,* Jan. 8, 1969, p. 1.
49. *Daily Mail,* Jan. 8, 1969, p. 1.
50. *Daily Sketch,* Jan. 8, 1969, p. 1
51. *Evening News,* Jan. 8, 1969, p. 1.
52. *Daily Sketch, op. cit.*
53. *Daily Telegraph,* Jan. 12, 1969, p. 6.
54. *Hansard,* Jan. 27, 1969, p. 955.
55. *Ibid.,* p. 965.
56. *Ibid.,* p. 967.
57. *The Times,* Jan. 28, 1969.
58. *Hansard, op. cit.,* p. 962.
59. *Ibid.,* p. 59.
60. Hawks, D. V., "The Dimensions of Drug Dependence in the United Kingdom," 6 Int. Journal of Addictions (1971), p. 140.
61. See references in note 39, *supra.*
    London Times, Sept. 19, 1970, p. 1.
62. *Daily Telegraph,* Aug. 10, 1968, p. 1.
63. *The Times,* Aug. 15, 1968, p. 8.
64. Skolnick, Jerome, *Justice Without Trial,* New York, John Wiley, 1966, p. 18.
65. Fiedler, Leslie, *Being Busted,* New York, Stein & Day, 1970.

66. *Powers of Arrest and Search in Relation to Drug Offenses,* pp. 73–74.
67. Wootton Report, p. 33.
68. Statement by the National Council on Civil Liberties before the Deedes Sub-Committee of the Advisory Committee on Drug Dependence.
69. *Powers of Arrest and Search in Relation to Drug Offenses,* pp. 24–28.
70. *Ibid.,* p. 30.
71. *Ibid.,* p. 57.
72. *Ibid.,* pp. 41–42.
73. *Ibid.*
74. *Ibid.,* p. 77.
75. *Hansard, op. cit.,* p. 965.
76. *The Times,* March 27, 1969, p. 1.
77. *The Observer,* March 15, 1970, p. 9.
78. *The Times,* July 27, 1970, p. 1.
79. *New Statesman,* Nov. 30, 1968, p. 18.

CHAPTER 6

1. 9B Uniform Laws Annotated 409–10 (Table of States).
2. Massachusetts General Laws 94 § 187 is typical of states' "harmful"-drug statutes. See the Drug Abuse Control Amendments of 1965, Public Law 87-74, 79 Stat. 226, 87th Cong. (1965) for the comparable federal provisions.
3. *Commonwealth v. Leis,* unreported opinion of the Superior Court of Massachusetts.
4. The Comprehensive Drug Abuse Prevention and Control Act of 1970 alters these penalties in several respects. 8 *Criminal Law Reporter* 3015, Oct. 28, 1970.
5. Controlled Substances Act, Sections 408, 409.
6. *People v. Shannon,* 15 Ill. 2d 494. *People v. Aldridge* 19 Ill. 2d 176.
7. Eldridge, William, *Narcotics and the Law,* Chicago, University of Chicago Press, 1962.
8. Report by the Advisory Committee on Drug Dependence, (the "Wootton Report"), London, H.M.S.O., 1968.
9. Narcotics Control Act of 1956.
10. Eldridge, *Ibid.*
11. Kaplan, John, *Marijuana: The New Prohibition,* New York and Cleveland, The World Publishing Co., 1970, p. 324.
12. *Ibid.*
13. Rotenberg, Daniel L., and Sayer, John W., "Marijuana in the Houston High Schools—"A First Report," 6 *Houston Law Review,* 1969.
14. Report of Committee on Criminal Law of the Massachusetts Bar Association on Proposed Amendment of Criminal Drug Penalties, 1970.
15. Skolnick, Jerome, "Coercion to Virtue," 41 *University of Southern California Law Review,* 624 (1968).
16. Jackson, Bruce, "The Next Best Thing: New York's Concentration Camps" (unpublished paper).
17. Kramer, Stanley, "Uncivil Commitment," 50 *Boston University Law Journal,* pp. 10, 16 (1970).
18. Lindesmith, Alfred, *The Addict and the Law,* Bloomington, University of Indiana Press, 1965, p. 3.
19. Becker, Howard, *The Outsiders,* New York, Free Press, 1963, p. 135.
20. Hearings before the Subcommittee on Taxation, U.S. Senate, 1937.

21. Taxation of Marijuana (Hearings before the Committee on Ways and Means of the House of Representatives, 75th Congress, 1st Session).
22. *Ibid.*
23. *Ibid.*
24. Mandel, J., "Who Says Marijuana Use Leads to Heroin Addiction," 43 *Journal of Secondary Education,* 1968.
25. Wootton Report, p. 12.
26. *Commonwealth v. Leis,* 355 Mass. 189, 1969.
27. *Ibid.*
28. *Ibid.*
29. *Ibid.*
30. Crancer, Alfred, *et al.,* "A Comparison of the Effects of Marijuana and Alcohol on Simulated Driving Performance," *Science,* Vol. 164, 1969.
31. William McGlothin, "Toward a Rational View of Hallucinogenic Drugs," presented at the National Association of Student Personnel Administrators Drug Education Conference, Washington, D.C., Nov. 7–8, 1966.
32. Wilner, Daniel, and Kassebaum, Gene, eds., *Narcotics,* New York, McGraw-Hill, 1965, p. 33.
33. Eldridge, *op. cit.*
34. Lindesmith, *op. cit.*
35. *Ibid.*
36. *Ibid.*
37. *Ibid.*
38. Mandel, J., "Problems with Official Drug Statistics," 22 *Stanford Law Review,* 991, May 1969.
39. Dangerous Drug Act of 1967, 82 Elizabeth II 4.
40. Eldridge, *op. cit.*
41. *New York Times,* May 16, 1970.
42. Skolnick, Jerome, *Justice Without Trial,* New York, John Wiley, 1966, p. 161.
43. Kaplan, *op. cit.,*

44. Tauro, *op. cit.*
45. Fuller, Lon, *The Morality of Law,* New Haven, Yale University Press, 1964, pp. 5–6.
46. Packer, Herbert, *The Limits of the Criminal Sanction,* Stanford, Stanford University Press, 1969, p. 265.
47. Gusfield, Joseph, *Symbolic Crusade,* Urbana, University of Illinois, 1963.
48. Lawrence Grauman, "The Pot Dilemma," *The New Leader,* February 26, 1968.
49. Blum, Richard, *et al., The Utopiates,* New York, Atheneum, 1964, p. 241.

CHAPTER 7

1. Lowes, Peter D., *The Genesis of International Narcotics Control,* Geneva, Libraire Droz, 1966.
2. *New York Times,* June 21, 1970.
3. *Ibid.*
4. *New York Times,* Sept. 23, 1969.
5. Cleaver, Eldridge, *Soul on Ice,* New York, McGraw-Hill, 1968, p. 4.
6. *New York Times,* March 24, 1969.
7. *Village Voice,* July 23, 1970, p. 5.
8. Smith, David, ed., "An Analysis of Marijuana Toxicity," in *Marijuana: The New Social Drug, Cultural, Medical and Legal Perspectives on Marijuana,* Englewood Cliffs, Prentice-Hall, 1970, p. 8.
9. *Ibid.,* p. 71.
10. Massachusetts General Laws, C.94 §212B.
11. *New York Times,* Feb. 27, 1970.
12. Kaplan, John, *Marijuana, The New Prohibition,* New York and Cleveland, The World Publishing Co., 1970, pp. 37–38.

13. Zinberg, Norman, "Rehabilitation of Heroin Users in Vietnam," p. 34 (unpublished).
14. Goode, Erich, "Multiple Drug Use Among Marijuana Smokers," *Social Problems,* Summer 1969, p. 54.
15. *Ibid.*
16. *Boston Globe,* July 1, 1970.
17. *New York Times,* Feb. 11, 1970.
18. *Ibid.*
19. *New York Times,* Jan. 20, 1970.
20. U.S. Bureau of the Budget, *The Budget of the United States Government,* Washington, D.C., Government Printing Office, 1965–70.
21. Miller, Donald (chief counsel to Bureau of Narcotics and Dangerous Drugs), letter to the *Yale Law Journal,* Jan. 6, 1969. Reported in 78 *Yale Law Journal,* 1969, pp. 1180–81.
22. *New York Times,* Oct. 11, 1970.
23. Kaplan, *op. cit.*
24. "Marijuana Laws, An Empirical Study of Enforcement and Administration in Los Angeles County," 15 *UCLA Law Review,* 1968.
25. *New York Times,* Feb. 27, 1970.
26. *New York Times,* July 1, 1970.
27. Kaplan, *op. cit.*
28. Rotenberg, Daniel L., and Sayer, John W., "Marijuana in the Houston High School—A First Report," 6 *Houston Law Review,* 759, 775 (1969).
29. *UCLA Law Review, op. cit.*
30. *New York Times,* Aug. 6, 1970.
31. Packer, Herbert, *The Limits of the Criminal Sanction,* Stanford, Stanford University Press, 1968, pp. 151–52.
32. Skolnick, Jerome, *Justice Without Trial,* New York, John Wiley, 1966, p. 144.
33. Chevigny, Paul, *Police Power: Police Abuses in New York City,* New York, Pantheon, 1969, p. 187.
34. Defendant's brief, pp. 7–8.
35. Barlow, Sarah, "Patterns of Arrests for Misdemeanor Narcotics Possession: Manhattan Police Practices, 1960–62," 4 *Criminal Law Bulletin,* Dec. 1968.
36. Younger, J., in *People v. McMurty,* Vol. 64 Misc. 2d. 63 at 64–5. See also *People v. Clothilda Berrios et al.,* 28 N.Y. 2d—1971.
37. Smith, G. R. W., "Possession of Marijuana in San Mateo County: Some Social Costs of Criminalization," 22 *Stanford Law Review,* 1970, pp. 100–101.
38. *New York Times,* Dec. 22, 1970.
39. *Harvard v. Commonwealth,* 356 Mass. Adv. Sh. 1341, 1970.
40. Rotenberg and Sayer, *op. cit.,* pp. 759, 765, 766–67, 782–83.
41. *Ibid.,* pp. 759, 765.
42. *New Yorker,* June 27, 1970.
43. *New York Times,* June 7, July 24, 1970.
44. *Boston Globe,* July 9, 1970; *Village Voice,* July 23, 1970.
45. *The Nation,* Sept. 23, 1969, pp. 271–72.
46. *New York Times,* Sept. 25, 1969.
47. *Ibid.,* p. 30.
48. *New York Times,* July 2, 1971, p. 1.
49. *Ibid.,* Sept. 25, 1969.
50. Lindesmith, Alfred R., *The Addict and The Law,* Bloomington, Indiana University Press, 1966, pp. 37–38.
51. Ginsberg, Allen, "First Manifesto to End the Bringdown," *The Marihuana Papers,* New York, Signet, 1968.
52. Fiedler, Leslie, *Being Busted,* New York, Stein & Day, 1970.

53. Lindesmith, *op. cit.,* pp. 88–89.
54. *Ibid.*
55. Kaplan, *op. cit.*
56. *Village Voice,* Feb. 26, 1970.
57. 15 *UCLA Law Review,* 1505, (Foreword by John Kaplan).
58. Rotenberg and Sayer, *op. cit.,* pp. 759, 768.
59. Fort, Joel, *The Pleasure-Seekers,* Indianapolis, Bobbs-Merrill, 1969, p. 220.
60. Fiedler, *op. cit.*
61. *Boston Herald Traveler,* Dec. 5, 1969.
62. *Harvard Crimson,* Oct. 5, 1967.

CHAPTER 8

1. Jones, Ernest, *The Life and Work of Sigmund Freud,* Vol. III, New York, Basic Books, 1957.
2. *Newsweek,* Sept. 7, 1970.
   Kaplan, John, *Marijuana, The New Prohibition,* New York and Cleveland, The World Publishing Co., 1970.
3. *New Society,* April 11, 1968.
4. Kramer, John, "Uncivil Commitment," 50 *Boston University Law Journal,* 1970.
5. *Medical World News,* March 22, 1968.
6. Dole, Vincent, "Research on Methadone Maintenance Treatment," *The International Journal of the Addictions,* Vol. 5(3), 1970.
7. *Washington Post,* Oct. 21, 1969.

8. Included in this alternative are all fines, whether labeled "civil" or "criminal."
9. *Daily Sketch,* Jan. 8, 1969: *The Guardian,* Jan. 10, 1969; *Daily Telegraph,* Jan. 9, 1969.
10. Dunbar, Ian, "Cannabis and Society," paper given at St. Anne's House, Soho, London, Aug. 31, 1968.
11. The equal-protection clause of the Fourteenth Amendment, needless to say, would make most social experiments involving locality difficult to initiate.
12. Becker, Howard, "History, Culture, and Subjective Experience: An Exploration of the Social Bases of Drug-Induced Experience," *Journal of Health and Social Behavior,* Vol. 8, 1967.
13. Isbell, H., Gordetzky, C. W., Jasinsky, D., *et al.,* "Effects of (−) delta-9-Transtetrahydrocannabinol in Man," *Psychopharmacologia (Berlin),* Vol. 11, 1967.
14. Zinberg, N. E., and Weil, A. T., "A Comparison of Marijuana Users and Non-Users," *Nature,* Vol. 226, No. 5241, April 11, 1970.
15. Grinspoon, Lester, "Marijuana," *Scientific American,* Vol. 221, Dec. 1969.
16. *New York Times,* editorial, Aug. 30, 1970.
17. National Institute of Mental Health Report on Marihuana, Government Printing Office, Washington, D.C., July 1970.

INDEX

277